METHODS OF METAPHYSICS

Methods of Metaphysics

Alan R. White
Ferens Professor of Philosophy in the University of Hull

CROOM HELM
London • New York • Sydney

© 1987 Alan R. White
Croom Helm Ltd, Provident House,
Burrell Row, Beckenham, Kent BR3 1AT

Croom Helm Australia, 44–50 Waterloo Road,
North Ryde, 2113, New South Wales

Published in the USA by
Croom Helm
in association with Methuen, Inc.
29 West 35th Street
New York, NY 10001

British Library Cataloguing in Publication Data

White, Alan R.
    Methods of metaphysics
    1. Title
    110   BD131
    ISBN 0-7099-5234-1
    ISBN 0-7099-5233-3 pbk

Library of Congress Cataloguing-in-Publication Data
    ISBN 0-7099-5234-1
    ISBN 0-7099-5233-3

Photocomposition in Baskerville by
Pat and Anne Murphy, Dorset
Printed and bound in Great Britain by Mackays of Chatham Ltd, Kent

Contents

Contents

To Nicholas, Helen and Hilary

Preface

This book is intended primarily for students since the main material consists of critical expositions of the thoughts on metaphysics of well-known philosophers, ancient and modern, which will, therefore, be familiar stuff to my expert colleagues. I would hope, however, that the central thesis running through the book, as well as the conception of the whole, is original enough to provide something of interest even for professional philosophers.

I am grateful to my colleagues, David Walker for reading the chapters on Plato and Aristotle, and Paul Gilbert for reading the whole book in draft. Mrs Audrey Solly's excellent typing has again put me in her debt.

Introduction

Metaphysics is often thought both by the layman or the new student and by the professional philosopher as the essential core of philosophy. Many of the great classical philosophers, Plato, Aristotle, Berkeley, Leibniz, Spinoza and Hegel did, amongst other things, build metaphysical systems. Furthermore, it is considered to deal with questions which are, in some sense, as one translation of its name implies, 'beyond' physics or science in general. Indeed, though the name 'metaphysics' derives from the historical fact that Aristotle's writings on the subject were placed in an early edition 'after' his writings on physics, it is true that these writings do portray metaphysics as being 'beyond' physics. This feature is undoubtedly present in the systems of all the classical metaphysicians. It is a feature which writers on the nature of metaphysics try to capture in describing it as dealing with problems which the sciences do not or cannot answer, as attempting to be more general, more comprehensive or more fundamental than science, as searching for a reality which underlies the mere appearance of things, for the nature of things not merely as we experience them but as they are in themselves, as dealing systematically with the whole of reality rather than, as do the sciences, piecemeal with its parts, or with kinds of things rather than particular instances of them. It is in this spirit that metaphysics has been called the queen of the sciences and in which metaphysics would applaud Hamlet's remark that there are more things in heaven and earth than are dreamt of in our philosophies.

But such characterisations give rise to difficulties. Critics of metaphysics ask in what sense it is more comprehensive or fundamental than the individual sciences. Surely not in the sense that an encyclopaedia is comprehensive. Are the problems of metaphysics unanswerable by science because they are of a different kind from those of science and, if so, of what kind, or are they unanswerable by science because, as a critic suggests, they are insoluble or even meaningless questions? Is this why there are not the agreed solutions among metaphysicians that there are among chemists, physicists, geologists, etc.? Indeed, though there are well-established and agreed ways of testing the truth or falsehood of what scientists say, how does one confirm or refute what a metaphysician says? Are critics correct in thinking that the metaphysicians' assertions are neither true nor false? Finally, what is this contrast drawn by the metaphysician between appearance, which science is alleged to be restricted to, and reality, which metaphysics is supposed to be able to lay bare, or between things as they are experienced by us and things as they are in themselves?

I have set myself a three-fold task. First, to see, by an examination of the methods of a representative sample of those who would universally be acknowledged to be metaphysicians — such as Plato, Aristotle, Berkeley, Leibniz and Bradley — how far metaphysics has been usually an attempt to go beyond and below science, to reveal 'more things in heaven and earth'. And, further, how successful or unsuccessful it has been in this endeavour. I shall maintain that there is a typical common pattern of methods and results present in all these metaphysicians which in many ways parallels the methods of science, but which is also crucially different. It has, as we shall see, three stages analogous to three stages of procedure in science, the last of which will carry it 'beyond' science, and make it quintessentially metaphysics.

Second, though in the first part I shall argue that each of these actual metaphysical systems is based on particular fallacious arguments which prevent us from accepting their conclusions, and hence, their picture of reality, I want to consider the general objection of some critics that what is wrong with metaphysics is not just the particular arguments of particular metaphysicians, but the nature of the whole enterprise. The two most substantial criticisms of this kind are those of Kant in the eighteenth century and of the Logical Positivists in the twentieth, whose inspiration dates back to Hume in the eighteenth. Both Kant and the Logical Positivists, we shall see, deny the metaphysicians' claim that there can be knowledge of what is beyond our experience, but the Logical Positivists in addition even deny the intelligibility of talking about what is unexperienceable. I shall also look at Wittgenstein's attitude to metaphysics, which in a way combines the objections of both Kant and the Logical Positivists.

Thirdly, I shall describe and examine a selection of post-Positivist accounts of metaphysics which are declared attempts to bypass the objections of the Logical Positivists and, presumably, of Kant. We shall see that the proponents of these accounts, namely Collingwood, Wisdom and Lazerowitz, are ambivalent on the question whether they provide a correct interpretation of what the classical metaphysicians were doing, or whether they offer a substitute task for metaphysics.

I shall, therefore, divide my essay into three parts corresponding to these three tasks, namely systems of metaphysics, rejections of metaphysics and rehabilitations of metaphysics.

Part I
Systems of Metaphysics

In investigating and describing the methods, objectives and results of the classical metaphysicians whom I discuss in this part, I shall try to show that each exhibits, in quite different forms and with quite different results, a pattern which is analogous to, though in crucial respects importantly different from, that of science.

First, a metaphysician, like any other philosopher and like a scientist, begins with a particular problem which interests him or which he thinks important. The scientist's problem will be empirical. For example, how are we to account for the path of the planet Uranus, which differs from that which our Newtonian calculations would lead us to expect; how can we explain the distribution of parental characteristics among their offspring, whether in plants, animals or humans; or how can we explain various optical phenomena, such as the length of shadows, the blocking or the penetration of light? The philosopher's problem will be logical, that is, how to explain the nature and behaviour of certain concepts which occur in the areas of ethics, science, religion or psychology; e.g. the acquisition and use of knowledge, whether moral judgements are objective or subjective, how the mind is related to the body, whether free will is compatible with determinism, how knowledge is different from true belief, etc. The metaphysician differs from other philosophers in that the concepts which set him his problems are of the most general kind, that is, concepts which are not confined to a specific area of thinking, such as in ethics, religion, science or the acquisition of knowledge, but permeate all our thinking. These are concepts such as existence, reality, truth, necessity, causality, similarity, identity, and contradiction. The most fundamental, and historically both the earliest and the most commonly treated, of these concepts is that of existence. Thus, Parmenides, who may perhaps be regarded as the first metaphysician in Western philosophy but of whose work not enough survives to enable us to appreciate his system, sought to discover the difference between existing or being and not existing or not being. Aristotle, the Thomists and modern Existentialists asked 'What is it to be something?' and, as we shall see in Aristotle, considered the nature of *Being* as the central metaphysical question. What intrigued Plato was the relation between a particular item, whether a man, a bed or a bee, or a just, a courageous or a holy act, and that of which this item was an instance, that is humanity, a bed or a bee as such, or justice, courage and holiness. This is a relation commonly expressed by saying of a particular, 'This *is* a man, a bed, a bee' or 'This *is* just, courageous, holy'. What, wondered Plato, is humanity, a bee as such, justice or courage? We shall see that Berkeley set himself the task of discovering what it means to say either of a material object, such as a tree or a book, or of a spiritual object, such as our minds or God, that it *exists*. Leibniz wondered what it is about a statement of the form 'S *is* P', for example Socrates is wise, David is the father of Solomon, two and two is four, which makes it true. The English metaphysician Bradley's main work *Appearance and Reality* was devoted to the question how what appears to be is related to what really is.

Secondly, in reflecting on his particular problem, both the scientist and, I shall try to show, the metaphysician, apply to it a certain principle or principles of whose power and efficacy they have been convinced for other reasons. For instance, the astronomer approaches the aberration in the path of the planet Uranus with a commitment to Newton's law of gravity which will base any explanation on data about the position and mass of bodies; the geneticist's explanations of characteristics in offspring will be dictated by, for example, Mendelian theories; and the physicist may try to solve his problems about shadows, interference, etc. in accordance with the hypothesis of the rectilinear propagation of light. Similarly, we shall see that Plato undertakes his enquiry into the nature of humanity, courage, holiness, justice, etc. in the conviction that there can only be particular items, for example a man, a courageous or just act, if these are instances or examples of something, for example humanity, courage or justice, which is common to the instances, but at the same time different from and existing apart from them. Berkeley's enquiry into the nature and existence of material and non-material objects is dominated by the belief that existence is logically related to perception, so that a material object can exist only if it is perceived, and a spiritual or mental object only if it perceives. Leibniz's explanation of the truth of statements of the form 'S is P' depends on the idea, of which he was convinced by certain features of logical, mathematical and biological enquiries, that all the characteristics and consequences of anything are in some way contained in the thing of which they are the characteristics and consequences. Bradley likewise carries on his search for the difference between appearance and reality under the guidance of a principle which he calls an 'absolute criterion', namely that 'ultimate reality is such that it does not contradict itself'.

The third and last stage in both the scientist's and metaphysician's enquiries — and the stage which, I maintain, most characteristically marks out Plato, Aristotle, Berkeley, Leibniz, Bradley, etc. as metaphysicians — is the hypothesising or postulating of the existence of unobserved items additional to or underlying those observed items with which the enquiry started. These are entities which seem, either to the scientist or to the metaphysician, to be demanded by the joint existence of the initial phenomena to be explained and the guiding principle to which the scientist or metaphysician feels bound to adhere. For the scientist these additional items may be entities which are at the time only in practice unobservable, as when the astronomers were led by the aberration in the path of Uranus and Newton's law of gravity to postulate the existence of another planet, Neptune, with a certain mass and position, whose presence contemporary instruments were not able to detect. Or they may be entities which, at least at the time, and, perhaps, — as I shall discuss later — in principle, are theoretically unobservable, as when the geneticists postulated new chemical substances, such as genes, or physicists new physical particles, such as light waves or corpuscles. For the metaphysician, on the other hand, these additional items which he is led to postulate as, he thinks, the logically inevitable consequences of the first two stages of his enquiry, are unobservable in principle, at least by any empirical or experienceable means. They are non-empirical and transcendent entities beyond what exists in our familiar world, though, perhaps for religious reasons, most of the classical metaphysicians would allow that they could be observed, after death, by the eye of the mind. Thus, as we shall see in detail, Plato's metaphysical system contains another world of Forms, such as humanity, justice, courage, a bed as such, etc.; Aristotle's has a supreme substance or Being; Berkeley's has an infinite mind or God; Leibniz's has an infinite number of spiritual atoms or Monads; and Bradley's something which he calls the Absolute. Even Kant, the critic of metaphysics, was led to postulate the existence of some unknowable entities called Noumena.

Though, I shall maintain, these three stages of enquiry are common both to scientists and to metaphysicians, there are, as we shall see, fundamental differences between these practitioners within each stage which will lead us to examine closely the exactness of this analogy. An important part of this examination will be, first, of the particular right of each metaphysician, such as Plato or Berkeley, to the postulation, at the third stage, of his world of unobservable, transcendent entities, and, secondly, of the general right of metaphysicians, as compared to scientists, to any hypothesis of unobservables.

1

Plato

Plato, the first metaphysician in western philosophy of whose works we have enough extant to be able to appreciate and evaluate, provides a good example of the three stages which I suggest are typical of a metaphysician's work.

We all ask questions such as 'What is democracy, freedom, beauty, infinity?' and scientists ask questions such as 'What is space, time, heat, force, matter?' So Plato in his early dialogues asked 'What is holiness, courage, justice?' and later 'What is knowledge, time, identity, contradiction?' He always insisted that it was not particular instances or examples of, for example, courage or justice, equality or humanity, which he sought, but that of which these are instances or examples. What puzzled him was partly the relation between an instance or example of something, for example a man or a just act, and that of which this is an instance or example, for example humanity or justice — that is, the relation expressed in, for example, 'This *is* just' or 'This *is* an example of justice' — and partly the nature of that, for example justice, of which these particulars, for example just acts, are merely instances. At this stage the problem is set.

In embarking on an answer to this problem, Plato enters the second stage of the metaphysical method, namely his assumption of several principles which guide and colour his answer and lead him on to a metaphysical system.

From his earliest writings[1] he assumed a principle which in the *Parmenides* he suggests was advocated also by Socrates in his youth.[2] In the *Republic* he makes Socrates refer to it both as something 'which we have said before and have often stated elsewhere' and as 'our ordinary method'[3] and in the *Philebus* as an 'assumption we should always make'.[4] This is the principle — usually called since Aristotle 'the one over many' — that whenever we have two or more Xs, two or more examples of Xness or two or more things both of which we call 'X', there must be something the same in all of them in virtue of which they are all Xs, examples of Xness or called 'Xs' by us.[5] For example, two or more good or beautiful things, two or more examples of swiftness, courage, health or virtue, two or more figures or bees. This something which is the same in all examples of it or in all things of the same name is called by Plato 'the thing itself', for example justice itself, equality or beauty itself, the circle itself.[6] It is also often simply called Xness, i.e. justice, equality, beauty, the circle — which in Greek is usually expressed as 'the just, the equal, etc.'.[7] Plato often states his main principle as, for example, 'Beautiful things are [or are made] beautiful by beauty'.[8] In the *Phaedo* he says this is 'something he has always been saying'.[9]

At first sight it seems a reasonable, even an obviously correct, assumption that all Xs have something in common which makes them Xs. And it is certainly an assumption that has been made by most philosophers and by non-philosophers.[10] It was, however, questioned long ago by Aristotle, whose counter-examples were 'healthy' and 'medical', and more recently by Wittgenstein, who said of *games*: 'Don't say: "There *must* be something common, or they would not be called *'games'*"' — but *look and see.*'[12] Whether this assumption is correct or not, I shall examine later. At this stage what we should note is the conclusion it led Plato to.

The next step which he took seemed an equally reasonable and obviously correct one. He moved from the view that all examples of Xness must have something in common, in virtue of which they are examples of Xness, to the view that one can distinguish between the examples of Xness and that which they have in common, what he called 'the X itself'.[13] Now certainly one can distinguish between, for example, beautiful things and beauty, triangles and triangularity, instances of injustice and injustice itself. We can indeed insist that there could not be an example of Xness unless there were Xness for this to be an example of it. But here he made a crucial move. He took this distinction to be a distinction between two *things*. That is, he moved from the supposition that there must be *something* common to two examples of Xness, namely the X itself, to the supposition that there must be some *thing* in common between them and, therefore, that the X itself or Xness is a sort of *thing* other than those things which are examples of Xness.[14] This move was strengthened by the assumption that that in virtue of which all Xs are examples of Xness, namely the X itself, is a *Form* or *Idea*, by which Xs are X.[15] Even when, as in the *Parmenides*, Plato shows the young Socrates as uncomfortable with the assumption that there will be a Form of such things as mud and hair — as well as baffled by the kind of relation there could be between examples of Xness and the Form of X — he also reports Socrates' antagonist, Parmenides himself, as insisting that despite these difficulties, there must be one Form for all the examples of Xness, whether Xness is beauty or mud or whatever.[16]

Even if Plato had not subscribed to the view that there must be something common to all examples of Xness, he would — and could correctly — still have argued that there is a distinction between an example of Xness and the X itself of which this example is an example, for example between an instance of justice and justice itself. He would then have made a similar move from this position to the same conclusion that that, namely the X itself, of which the item before us is an example, must be a different thing from this or any other item which is an example of it. He has assumed that the relation between an example of Xness and X itself is a relation between two things. Such a problem gave rise to difficulties — formulated in the *Parmenides*, but into which we need not enter here — of the nature of this relation. Do instances of X 'partake' in Xness, 'copy it', 'share' part or all of it, or what? Is the X itself *in* the instances or *apart* from the instances? Plato's views on this question may have differed at different times.

This move from the correct premises that X and Y are distinct and that X is one thing, whose characteristics are unproblematical, to the conclusion that Y is another, even though problematical, thing, is a common one in many central problems in philosophy. For example, the many attempts in the history of philosophy to discover the relations between the mind and the body — or, more recently, between the mind and the brain — which have resulted in such theories as parallelism, interactionism, epiphenomenalism — all rest on the assumption that, since the mind is clearly distinct from the body and distinctly characterised — for example the mind can be feeble while the body is strong; the mind can be thoughtful, but not grey, while the brain can be cut open, but not dismayed — it is a distinct entity, perhaps a non-physical entity. Such theories of meaning as the theory that the meaning of a word is the object referred to by the word, the mental image aroused by the word or the relation between the word and what it refers to, all assume that the difference between a word and its meaning entails that its meaning is as much a separate entity as the word itself. Similarly, the postulation of propositions either as psychological entities, or as things which subsist in a world neither physical nor psychological, stems from the recognition that a proposition is different from the sentence which expresses it. Finally, the difference between an act, such as murder or assault, and the act, such as shooting or setting one's dogs off, by which the first act is committed, is commonly alleged to entail that the murder or the assault is an act additional to the shooting or the setting off of one's dogs.

In all these major philosophical problems a common assumption is that Y cannot be distinct from X without being additional to X. Contrariwise, those who, rightly, deny that Y is additional to X, for example that minds or propositions or meanings or the act which results from committing another act are entities for whom a home has to be found additional to the home in which bodies, words, sentences, or acts like shooting and setting off one's dogs, live, are so much in the grip of the same assumption as their opponents that they feel that the denial of an additional item entails the denial that, for example, minds are different from bodies, meanings from words, propositions from sentences or murder from shooting. It is not surprising that Plato was in the grip of an assumption which has seized so many philosophers on so many other problems.

He is thus led to his third stage, that is a belief in a Form, supposedly present in all things which are called by that name or are instances of that entity. An enquiry into this, he says, is the chief aim of philosophy. It is an enquiry into the X itself, the nature of Xness, what X itself is,[17] or, sometimes, 'What X happens to be',[18] whether it be justice, beauty, love, desire, equality, a sophist, unity, etc.[19]

A second principle whose assumption led Plato to posit the existence of Xness as something over and above its instances arose from his thoughts on the nature of *recognition*. It took two forms.

First, he argued that we can only recognise something to be what it is, for example to be equal, beautiful, good or just, because we can see that it is an example of something, for example of equality, beauty, goodness or justice, and we can only see this by comparing the item before us with that of which it is an example.[20]

This too is, at first sight, quite a plausible assumption, which leads many to suppose, in an analogous way, that we recognise, for example, a fork, a bed or a triangle, an instance of justice or courage, by comparing the item before us with an image, in a sort of mental dictionary or picture catalogue, of the archetypal fork, bed, triangle, justice or courage. Hence, Plato concluded, we must have acquired our knowledge of the archetype somewhere previously and be reminded of it by the example or copy of it presented to us.[21] Such a conclusion led him to his doctrine that all acquisition of knowledge is really a species of 'recollection' or being reminded of what we once knew.[22] More importantly, it seemed to support the third-stage hypothesis that, for example, goodness, justice, courage, triangularity and the archetypal fork or bed are items over and above the particular instances of goodness, etc., which we daily encounter.

The second way in which this hypothesis arose out of his views on recognition was this. In the *Phaedo* he pointed out that no instance of Xness ever seems to be a perfect or complete instance of it.[23] We can see that no beautiful thing is flawless, no circle is perfectly round, no man is absolutely happy, no two equal things are exactly equal. Plato expressed this point by saying that, for example, equal things are seen 'to fall short of' equality itself, though they strive towards it.[24] From this he concludes that we could only have recognised that an instance of Xness is less than perfect, entire or absolute by comparing it with the X itself and seeing that it 'falls short of it'. The philosophically important point here is the conceptual assumption on which Plato's argument rests; namely that to recognise that A is not quite or absolutely or entirely X implies that we know or have an idea of what it is for something to be absolutely or entirely X, and that it is by comparing A with this that we see that it falls short. That this is a very plausible assumption is clear from the fact that it occurs in later thinkers and in other contexts. It is the assumption made in one of Descartes' arguments in the third *Meditation* for the existence of God, and it is shared as well by some theological writers. 'How could I know,' says Descartes, 'that something is wanting to me and that I am not wholly perfect, if I possessed no idea of a being more perfect than myself, by comparison with which I knew the deficiencies of my nature?' The same assumption underlies a commonly accepted theory about thought; namely that, when we are looking for the right word for an idea that we have, what enables us to reject various suggestions as inadequate and accept one as being right, is that during our search we have before our mind the thought we are trying to express, and that it is against this that the alternatives are sized up. This assumption led Plato not only to differentiate between examples of Xness and Xness itself, but to stress the imperfection and changeableness of such examples by contrast with the perfection and unchanging nature of Xness itself.

A third set of reasons for Plato's belief in the existence of Xness or the X itself in addition to particular X things stems from his view of the nature of knowledge. Three features of this view were, first, that to know is to be in some direct relation to what is known;[25] secondly, that what can be known must be different from what can be believed;[26] and most importantly, that what is known must be something which cannot change.[27]

The first feature may have been partly due to the frequency with which in Greek the verb 'to know' is followed by a direct object, in the way that in English we talk of 'knowing Mr Jones' or 'knowing the height of the Arts Building', and partly due to an assimilation of 'knowing' to non-visual 'seeing'.[28] This idea of knowing as a direct relation between the knower and what is known appears frequently in the history of philosophy, for example in Descartes and in Bertrand Russell's so-called 'knowledge by acquaintance'.

The second feature, that what can be known must be different from what can be believed, rested partly on an analogy which Plato drew with seeing and hearing. He argued that just as colours (or sights), which he said are what can be seen, cannot be heard, and sounds, which are what can be heard, cannot be seen, so what can be known cannot be believed, and what can be believed cannot be known.

The third feature, that is, the idea that what is known must be unchanging, may have been due to a point, later emphasised by Aristotle, that if what is known could change — as, for instance, the truth of 'The kettle is boiling' could change to falsity or what is now beautiful could become ugly — it would apparently follow that one could know something other than what is so.[29] Hence, Plato held that knowledge must be of what is, ignorance of what is not, and belief of a mixture of the two. This supposition about the unchanging and unchangeable nature of any object of knowledge has also proved popular in much subsequent philosophy. It occurs in Descartes' argument in the second *Meditation* that what we know when we know that a piece of wax, all of whose perceptible qualities of colour, shape, smell, etc. have changed, is nevertheless the same piece of wax, is some unchanging characteristic of the wax detected by our intellect. It occurs also in the thesis of Hume and the Logical Positivists that knowledge is confined to necessary and, therefore, unchangeable truths, such as occur in mathematics and logic, while contingent truths, such as occur in science, can only be believed.

All this led Plato to argue that knowledge is only possible on the assumption that there exist unchanging objects with which one could have a quasi-visual relation. Since, in his view, whatever is equal or just or courageous or beautiful, etc., could change and become otherwise, whereas equality, justice, courage, beauty, etc. themselves could not change and become other than they are, then only the latter could be known.

Having reached from these various second-stage assumptions about the meaning, recognition and knowledge of, for example, 'This is an instance of justice' or 'This is just' the third stage conclusion that in addition to the instances of justice there must also exist justice itself, Plato was led by various other conceptual assumptions to suppose that this justice — and the corresponding Form of each thing — must exist somewhere other than in the everyday world in which the instances of justice exist and that, therefore, there must be a world other than this everyday world. He may, as a matter of fact, have moved from a less to a more transcendent view of the Forms as his philosophy progressed.

First, he claimed that our world contains only such things as just men and just states, beautiful and good people and objects, equal sticks and distances, courageous deeds. It does not contain justice, beauty, goodness, equality or courage themselves. These must, therefore, be elsewhere.[30]

Secondly, he supposed — what is plausible about abstractions — that, unlike beautiful houses and equal sticks, beauty and equality are not perceivable by any of the senses, but can only be grasped by thought. From which he concluded that only that part of us, the mind or soul, which he supposed thinks, could grasp them. For various reasons, he held that what the soul 'sees' are the denizens of another world.[31]

Thirdly, he argued that whereas any examples of justice or goodness, beauty or equality, could change and become examples of injustice or badness, ugliness or inequality — as when one's beauty fades, one's goodness vanishes or one thing loses its equality with another — justice, goodness, beauty or equality themselves could not be different from what they are. That is, the

Forms are unchanging.[32] Plato believed that to be unchanging was a mark not only of that which alone could be discernible by thought and be known, as contrasted with being believed,[33] but of that which was divine and existed elsewhere.[34] Hence, he was led to the conclusion that, as he expressed it at different times, the things which really exist, the essence of things, or the things themselves, as contrasted with examples of them, can only be known by the mind, or soul, and can only be found somewhere other than in the physical world around us.[35]

Fourthly, he argued that if — as his analysis of our recognition both of the identity and of the imperfection of particular things implied — we must have previously seen the perfect exemplars of which these particulars are the imperfect copies, then such exemplars must exist somewhere. Since it is the examples and not the exemplars — just things and not justice — which we encounter in this world, the examplars must exist somewhere else.

What I want to emphasise about all these assumptions and arguments which led Plato to a belief in a supersensible world and made him, therefore, a metaphysician of the grand kind, is that they are purely logical in nature. They are attempts to solve purely conceptual problems, whether they be lesser ones, such as how is it possible to recognise imperfection or to know that a particular item is an example of so and so, or whether they be the major problem, what exactly is it for something to be an instance of Xness and how does one distinguish between an example of something and that of which it is an example. Plato is led to posit the existence of Forms, that is, goodness, justice, beauty, courage, the archetypal bed, etc. because his attempt to solve the conceptual problem led him to suppose that as well as the examples of goodness, etc., there must exist that of which these are examples, that is, goodness itself, etc. And since he could not find them in this world, he was led to posit the existence of another world in which they could dwell.

Additional purely conceptual reasons and arguments for the existence of such a world arose from other assumptions and conclusions Plato made in his thoughts about the human mind or soul (psyche).

First, he argued that 'It is necessary that everything that has an opposite comes to be from its opposite', that is, if A becomes Y it must have become Y from being not-Y.[36] For instance, what becomes smaller (weaker, just, awake, hot, disgraceful) becomes so from being bigger (stronger, unjust, asleep, cold, noble). Hence, since 'living' and 'non-living' (dead) are the names of opposites, the living, that is, that which is imbued with life (soul), must have become living from being non-living (dead). From which he concludes that there must be another world, the world of the non-living (dead) from which the principle of life (soul) comes into our physical bodies at birth.

Secondly, he reaches the conclusion that there must be another world to which the principle of life (soul) goes after our death, that is, after it has left our bodies, on the unargued ground that the soul is not made of parts and, therefore, cannot suffer any change or dissolution, but must, unlike the body, continue to exist somewhere.[37]

Thirdly, having in his previous arguments, as we saw, supposed that justice, beauty, etc. are both unperceivable by the senses and unchanging, he concludes that knowledge of them is only possible by something, the mind or soul, which is different from our senses. Furthermore, since justice, beauty, etc. exist in another world, they can only come to be known by something which can go to that other world and meet them face to face.

Fourthly, we saw that his doctrine of knowledge makes it the mind's power to recollect the exemplars of particular things; which it must, therefore, have first encountered before it encounters the particulars in this world. It must have encountered the exemplars in that other world where they exist.

It must be admitted that Plato probably believed, quite independently of any of his logical arguments, in the existence in men of a separate mind or soul, which was immortal and both came from and went to another world before and after its sojourn in this world — indeed, he may have partly believed in the Pythagorean doctrine of the transmigration of souls — just as Bishop Berkeley who, we shall later see, was led to argue from conceptual premises to the existence of God, undoubtedly had independent grounds for such a belief. Plato often speaks of stories and myths which he had heard and believed about such things.[38]

Nevertheless, it seems quite clear that his actual arguments for such a conclusion are of the purely conceptual nature which I have suggested. And it is, I submit, this characteristic that is typical of the method of metaphysics and the classical metaphysicians, namely the reaching of conclusions about the existence of a world beyond this by arguments designed to explain a logical point.

Such methods would account for Plato's belief in a supersensible world irrespective of whether his arguments were good or bad and of whether his conclusions were true or false. But it is worth examining some of his actual logical arguments to show that the assumptions he makes in them and the conclusions he reaches are in fact false, and, more importantly, that the conceptual facts which he tried to explain — and which undoubtedly do need explanation — do not entail the supersensible hypotheses which he felt forced to offer.

Consider, first, the basic assumption which definitely set him off on his metaphysical road, namely, that since there is a difference between an example of Xness and the Xness of which this is an example, for example between a particular triangle and triangularity or between an example of justice and justice itself, then Xness itself — or, as he put it, 'the X itself' — of which these are only instances, must be a separable and separately existing entity from its instances.

One reason for this assumption may have been — as it has often been in the history of philosophy — the idea that all words are the names of things and, therefore, that general words, whether nouns, adjectives, verbs, etc., are the names of anything of which there can be many instances. Furthermore, it is easy to move from the plausible-sounding view that any such word is the name of *something* of which there are or may be many instances to the view that it is the name of some *thing* of which there are such instances (or copies, imitations, examples, etc.). It is arguable that this naming theory of meaning was made more plausible for the Greeks by the fact that the same word '*onoma*' was used for 'name' and 'word'.

What makes this assumption seem so plausible is that there are many cases in which a difference between Z and the Q of Z is undoubtedly a difference between two separate items, for example the difference between a box and the lid of a box, between a car and the owner of a car, between a cake and the consumer of the cake, between a band and the leader of the band. More significantly, this is also the difference between a picture and a copy of the picture, one of the analogies according to which Plato thought of the relation between, for example, justice and an example or instance of justice.[39] It is also the difference between something and its parts, another analogy which Plato had in mind.[40]

But there are lots of cases where the difference between a Z and the Q of Z is not a difference between two separate entities. Thus, even the very familiar cases of something and a characteristic of that thing, for example a flower and its smell, a car and its colour, a rock and its weight, do not exemplify the difference between two entities, since the smell, colour or weight of things is not something that can exist separately from things which smell, have colour or weight. Still less is the difference between, for example, a house and its southerly aspect, a line and its slant, a man and his build, an official and his influence or a tool and its use, a difference between two entities, the latter of which could exist separately. Though one could put one's tools into a box, there could not be another box into which one put the uses of one's tools.

What the existence of cases of a Z and a Q of Z, where the Q of Z is clearly not an entity separable from the Z, shows is that it is not logically necessary that the difference between Xness and an example of Xness be explained — on, for example, the analogy of a picture and its copy[41] — as the difference between two entities, one visible before us and the other only able to be encountered somewhere else, for example in a supersensible world.

Furthermore, there are good reasons for thinking that the relation between, for example, examples of justice and justice is in this respect more analogous to the relationship between, for example, a man and his build or a tool and its use than that between, for example, a picture and its copy or a car and its owner. Thus, it is as difficult, as indeed Plato discovered, to characterise the alleged separately existing justice or triangularity as it would be to characterise the build of a man or the use of a tool independently of the man or the tool. Though Plato realised it could not be a physical or perceivable entity, he gave no hint as to what positively it could be. Just as to talk about the build of a man or the use of a tool is to talk not of some related entity but of how the man is built or how the tool is used, so to talk about a particular deed as being an example of justice or a particular figure as being an instance of a triangle is to say what kind of deed or figure it is. It is to classify the particular deed or figure. The next question is whether the only way to classify two things as of the same kind is by supposing that there is a separable something which they have in common. Plato, we might say, thinks that the *kind* of thing (for example a bed or bee, justice or beauty) which something (for example a particular bed or bee, a particular instance of justice or beauty) is, is a kind of *thing*. Indeed, it may be, as some scholars think, that he moved from the view in his middle dialogues that the Forms are separate paradigmatic entities to a view in his later dialogues that they are kinds (*genē*).

As I mentioned earlier, Plato's second basic assumption, that two or more examples of the same thing or two or more things called by the same name must have something in common — which he, of course, thought was that of which they were examples, their Form — though very commonly held throughout the history of philosophy, has been questioned, partly by Aristotle and wholly by Wittgenstein and others.

Wittgenstein claimed, sometimes with specific reference to Plato, that in many cases at least our reason for applying the same word to many things, for example games, languages, numbers, beautiful or good things, is not that they share some common property but that the various instances have a host of overlapping similarities and relationships, somewhat in the way that the various members of one family may share one or other of a set of family characteristics, such as the family chin, nose, gait, etc.[42] Because the various instances, for example of games or numbers, form a single family of resemblances, there is the concept of a game or a number. The difference between something, such, perhaps, as triangularity or mass, all of whose instances have an element in common and something, such as a game or a number, whose instances have only family resemblances, is, suggested Wittgenstein, like the difference between a rope through which there runs a single strand and a chain in which any two links are directly joined to each other but not to the remainder. He suggested, at various times, that such words as 'game', 'number', 'colour', 'red', 'language', such psychological words as 'thinking', 'meaning', 'intending', 'believing', 'expecting' and such formal words as 'property', 'proof', 'proposition' are 'family-resemblance' words.

Aristotle had earlier claimed that some words, such as 'healthy' or 'medical', apply to various things, not because of some common property, but because each of the particular things was related in some, perhaps different, way to a central characteristic.[43] Thus, exercise is healthy because it gives health, a complexion is healthy because it is a sign of health, and a body is healthy because it has health.

In order to throw doubt on Plato's assumption that it is because of a common element that every word is used of many things, it is not necessary to agree that all words are used because of family resemblances among those things to which they are applied or because all these things are related to one central item, but only that at least some are. And it is clear, I think, in the light of the examples given that this more modest thesis is correct. It is significant that a chief characteristic of Plato's early dialogues in which he looked for the common elements for the instances of, for example, holiness, courage, swiftness, equality, beauty, etc., is that he always found objections to all the preferred candidates except holiness, courage, etc. themselves. That is, he always ended up with the tautology that what is common to all Xs is that they are X. We have seen how he interpreted 'They are all X' to mean 'They all participate in (copy etc.) Xness.'

A third assumption which, we saw, led Plato to posit the existence of Forms in another world was that our ability to recognise something as an example of, for example, justice, presupposes a prior knowledge of justice itself by reference to which we can see that this item before us is, indeed, an example of justice analogously to the way in which we can see that what we have before us is a copy of a certain picture, because we already know what the picture itself looks like. Hence, concludes Plato, we must have previously encountered justice itself, just as the spotter of the copy must have had a previous glimpse of the original, in the area where such exemplars exist.

This assumption too has been very common in the history of philosophy, often in the form that we can only recognise something to be an example of X if we have a mental idea or picture of X with which we compare and hence recognise the item before us. Locke's theory of the meaning of a word as a mental image is an illustration of this assumption. The analogy that this assumption has in mind is that of someone who checks up, for example, particular colours, such as indigo, azure blue, aquamarine or emerald green, by comparing the samples with the British Standard Colour Chart, or of someone who makes or draws something by reference to an original which he is copying. Plato himself took it very much in this way in his theory that what a furniture maker does is to construct, for example, a bed with his mental eye on the Form of the bed as a pattern for his work.[44] The artist, Plato critically insisted, is merely an imitator at secondhand, for what he takes as his exemplar is not the Form of the bed, but an actual bed from which he paints his picture of a bed.

To this assumption, it may be objected, first, that no entity could play the role of exemplar here. For what would be its characteristics? Justice itself or the paradigm Bed which particular examples of justice or particular beds are supposed to copy or resemble cannot be like any particular example of justice or any particular bed — indeed, for Plato, the Form of a bed cannot even have perceptible characteristics such as colour, shape, etc. It would have to be, as Berkeley scornfully said of Locke's abstract triangle, 'neither oblique nor rectangle, neither equilateral, equicrural, nor scalenon, but *all and none* of these at once . . . something imperfect that cannot exist . . .'[45] Further, what kind of features would an abstract thing, like justice or infinity — or a relative thing, like size, weight, proximity, or a negative thing, like injustice or inequality — as contrasted with triangularity or the Form of a bed, have?

Secondly, as Plato himself makes Parmenides point out to the young Socrates[46] and as Aristotle later emphasised,[47] to suppose, as we must, that a particular example of justice or triangularity must copy or resemble justice or triangularity itself would entail something common to both, namely their resemblance, and, therefore, a third Form in virtue of which this common property exists. Because Aristotle used the example of a man and manhood here, this is often called 'The Third Man Argument'. If, on the other hand, we are allowed to get away unproblematically with a resemblance between an example of justice or triangularity and justice or triangularity itself, why should we not rest content with the resemblance between two examples of justice or triangularity as sufficient reason for their both being examples of justice or triangularity, and do without the need for the separate existence of justice and triangularity themselves to explain the resemblance.

An interesting variant on this assumption was criticised by Wittgenstein.[48] It is assumed that to cry, for example, 'This crash was not as loud as I expected' implies that I must have had, perhaps in my imagination, an idea of the particular loudness of crash compared with which I can now see that this actual crash falls short. But, as Wittgenstein points out, nothing of the sort need be, nor usually is, so.

A fourth and similar assumption, mentioned earlier, was that the ability to recognise imperfection in this world — and, according to Plato, all examples of justice, beauty, triangularity, etc. are imperfect — presupposes our possession of knowledge of the perfect, that is, of justice, etc. themselves, which we could see the instances before us to fall short of. This also, we saw, has been in various forms a popular assumption in the history of philosophy. What gives it its plausibility — rather like what gave the first assumption its plausibility — is that in many cases we do seem to argue like this. We do in fact often say that A is not X or not absolutely X on the strength of our knowing what X is, to the extent of having a sample or an idea of X with which to compare

A. For instance, we compare the liquid in the not quite full glass with the whole glass; we compare the alleged indigo blue with the colour chart; we accept a pattern because it fits the template and we reject a glove because it does not fit the hand.

It is, however, a conceptual mistake to suppose that recognition of imperfection in A implies a knowledge of what perfection would be. First, this is not always true in fact. A candidate's examination paper is given less than the top grade, not necessarily because the examiner has a specimen of the perfect paper, but because he can see how the candidate's paper could have been better. If I can see how A could be rounder or more beautiful, how B could be more charitable or more just, or how A and B could be more equal than they are, then that enables me to see that A is not absolutely round or beautiful, that B does not show perfect charity or justice, and that A and B are not exactly equal. I do not have to know what absolute circularity or beauty or charity or justice or equality is. Secondly, and more importantly, I could not see that, for example, a particular number is not quite as great as it could be by comparing it with the greatest number, for there neither is nor could be a greatest number with which to compare a given number. Therefore, I do not have to know and sometimes cannot know the perfect in order to recognise the existence of imperfections.

Furthermore, though it is not implausible to talk of something's 'falling short' of the equal, the just or the perfect, what would it mean to say that it fell sort of the unequal, the unjust or the imperfect, or even of the large, the distant or the old? Yet we can as easily distinguish between instances of injustice or inequality and injustice or inequality themselves, or between instances of largeness and largeness itself, as we can between instances of justice or equality and justice or equality themselves. It is significant also that though something can be completely, absolutely or perfectly certain, well, content, or equal, nothing can be completely, absolutely, or perfectly dubious, ill, discontented or unequal.

Running parallel to Plato's assumption and arguments about the existence of Forms, that is, justice, beauty, triangularity, etc., and about a supersensible world in which they dwell, were assumptions and theories about the existence of a separable mind (or soul) as one of the two elements that make up a human being. Sometimes belief in the existence of the soul was used to support belief in the existence of the Forms and of another world; sometimes *vice versa*. It would take us too far afield to consider all Plato's arguments for the existence of a soul which continues to exist before it enters into a human body in the world and after it leaves it and which must, therefore, have another world in which to exist. It is sufficient to point out, first, that his arguments for its existence, of which I shall mention just two, are purely conceptual in nature and, secondly, that, as is clear in Aristotle's writings as well as those of such modern philosophers as Ryle and Wittgenstein, it is equally possible to explain the characteristics of the concept of mind (or soul) without supposing, as dualist philosophers from Plato to Descartes have done, that the mind (or soul) is an entity separable from the body.

One of Plato's arguments for the existence of a mind (or soul) prior to its occupation of a body is really a variation on his view that, for reasons we have seen, our knowledge of things in this world must be analysed as recollection of things we learned before we were born, things which exist only in another world. If knowledge is recollection, then some part of us must have had the previous experience necessary for recollection. Incidentally, Plato's other view about knowledge, for example that it can only be of what is unchanging, unperceivable and, perhaps, divine, go with his view that it can, therefore, only be had by something, for example a mind (or soul), capable of grasping the unchanging, the invisible and the divine.

A second purely conceptual argument for the existence of a soul prior to the existence of the body and for a region where it can dwell before it enters the body was, as we saw, based on the assumption 'It is necessary that everything that has an opposite comes to be from its opposite' — that is, that if A becomes X it must have become X from being not-X. For instance, what becomes smaller (weaker, worse or just) becomes so from being bigger (strong, better or unjust) and *vice versa*. Hence, since 'living' and 'non-living' are the names of opposites, the living must have become living from being non-living. So far the argument is impeccable, for it is a logical truth that, if A becomes X, it must have been other than X before. But this does not prove what Plato wants — namely, that what is alive must have come from what is not-alive and that there must be something in the land of the not-alive from which things in the land of the living can come. He thinks that he has proved this only because he confuses a logical principle — that what becomes X could only become so from having previously been the opposite of X — with a similar-sounding but causal principle — that what becomes X must have come from, that is must have been produced out of, the opposite of X. To say that A becomes X from being not-X is not to say, as Plato does, that A becomes X from not-an X. If I become rich, I must, to be sure, have previously been poor; but my riches did not 'come from' my poverty. Becoming rich from being poor is not like becoming rich from being thrifty. To say that what becomes alive becomes so from being not-alive is not to say that what becomes alive becomes so from the not-alive. Similarly, the logical truth that what comes into existence must previously not have existed does not contradict the old causal law that nothing can come from what does not exist (*ex nihilo nihil fit*). Plato has given no good reason to suppose, therefore, that there must be another region or world from which life (or the soul) comes into our bodies.

Not only do Plato's arguments not prove the existence of a separable mind (or soul) and, therefore, a region for it to dwell in apart from the body, there are equally or more plausible arguments for analysing the concept of mind (or soul) as signifying a set of functions (for example thinking and feeling), dispositions (for example patience and irritability) and abilities (for example to solve problems or to remember facts) which are manifested in human and, perhaps, animal behaviour. Such an analysis, originally offered by Aristotle, has been resurrected by twentieth-century psychologists and philosophers.[49]

Finally, it could be shown, though it would take us too far afield here, that none of the arguments advanced by Plato, nor those of Descartes, Hume or the Logical Positivists, succeeds in proving that knowledge requires as its objects something unchanging or necessary, much less a set of separate eternal entities and, therefore, another region in which they abide.[50]

Plato provides a paradigm example of the way in which conclusions about the existence and nature of a world beyond or different from this one are based on purely logical arguments and assumptions made in an attempt to unravel important, but purely conceptual, problems. Indeed, this is characteristic of his predecessor, Parmenides, who can probably be called the very first metaphysician in the history of European thought, but whose works do not survive in great enough bulk to allow a clear illustration of his methods.

Notes

1. I have disregarded controversies about the consistency of Plato's views and whether he changed or even abandoned in his later writings his Theory of Forms.
2. *Parmenides*, 132a.
3. *Republic*, 507, 596.
4. *Philebus*, 16d.
5. *Philebus*, 13b, 34e; *Laches*, 191e, 192a–b; *Meno*, 72c–e, 75a; *Parmenides*, 132a, 135b; *Greater Hippias*, 287c, 292d, 294b.
6. *Phaedo*, 65d, 74a, 100b; *Epistles*, 342b. In Greek *'auto to dikaion'* or *'to dikaion auto kath hauto'*, etc.
7. *'to dikaion'*, etc.
8. *Greater Hippias*, 289d; *Phaedo*, 100c; *Gorgias*, 497e.
9. *Phaedo*, 100b.
10. B. Russell (1912), *The Problems of Philosophy*, Thornton Butterworth Ltd, London, Chapter 9, called Plato's theory of meaning 'one of the most successful attempts hitherto made'.
11. *Metaphysics*, 1003a 30–1003b 5.
12. L. Wittgenstein (1953), *Philosophical Investigations*, Basil Blackwell, Oxford, sects. 65–77.
13. *Greater Hippias*, 287d–e.
14. *Greater Hippias*, 287c–d; *Phaedo*, 74.
15. *Euthyphro*, 5d, 6d; *Meno*, 72c–d; *Phaedo*, 101c, 102a; *Sophist*, 253d; *Greater Hippias*, 289d; *Parmenides*, 132a, 135b; *Philebus*, 16d; *Republic*, 476, 596a.
16. *Parmenides*, 130d, 135b.
17. *'to ho esti, ho ti pot esti'*.
18. *'ho tunchanei on'*, *Meno*, 72c.
19. *Euthyphro*, 6d, 11a; *Phaedo*, 74b–76a; *Phaedrus*, 273c; *Sophist*, 217b; *Philebus*, 34d; *Laches*, 190b; *Meno*, 71a, 72c; *Greater Hippias*, 286e–287d; *Theaetetus*, 145e, 146e; *Republic*, 524.
20. *Euthyphro*, 6d–e; *Meno*, 72c; *Cratylus*, 389a–c.
21. *Phaedo*, 72e, 91e; *Phaedrus*, 249b, 254b; *Meno*, 81b, 86a.
22. anamnesis.
23. *Phaedo*, 74d–76a.
24. *endei*.
25. *Republic*, 476–8, 533a.
26. *Republic*, 476.
27. *Republic*, 485b; *Cratylus*, 439b–440c; *Parmenides*, 135b–c; *Theaetetus*, 182d–e; *Sophist*, 245b–c, 249b; *Philebus*, 59a–c, 88c; *Timaeus*, 27d–29d, 38a.
28. *Phaedo*, 76c–d.
29. *Metaphysics*, 1039b 27–1040a 7.
30. *Parmenides*, 130b.
31. *Phaedo*, 65c–e; *Timaeus*, 52a; *Cratylus*, 423e, 440c; *Phaedrus*, 247e; *Theaetetus*, 185e; *Sophist*, 248b; *Republic*, 585.
32. *Phaedo*, 78d; *Sophist*, 248; *Republic*, 485, 538; *Cratylus*, 493d.
33. *Timaeus*, 29b.
34. *Timaeus*, 28a; *Politicus*, 269d; *Symposium*, 211b.

35. '*ta onta, ousia, auto to* ———'; *Timaeus*, 52a; *Phaedo*, 65c; *Theaetetus*, 185e; *Sophist*, 248b; *Republic*, 585.

36. *Phaedo*, 70c–72b.

37. *Phaedo*, 78c–80d.

38. *Apology*, 40d; *Phaedrus*, 247c; *Meno*, 81b; *Gorgias*, 532a; *Epistles*, 335a.

39. *Phaedrus*, 250b; *Parmenides*, 142d; *Timaeus*, 52a.

40. *Parmenides*, 131; *Protagoras*, 329b; cf. 'partaking', *Symposium*, 211b; *Phaedo*, 100c; *Parmenides*, 130b.

41. *Phaedrus*, 250b.

42. Wittgenstein, *Philosophical Investigations*, sects. 65–71; (1958) *The Blue and Brown Books*, Basil Blackwell, Oxford, 20; (1974) *Philosophical Grammar*, Basil Blackwell, Oxford, 120ff.

43. *Metaphysics*, 1003a 30–1003b 5.

44. *Republic*, 596; *Cratylus*, 389a–c.

45. *Principles of Human Knowledge*, Introduction, sect. 13.

46. *Parmenides*, 132a–b.

47. *Metaphysics*, 990b, 1079a.

48. *Blue and Brown Books*, 40–1.

49. cf. A. R. White (1967) *The Philosophy of Mind*, Random House, pp. 46–55.

50. cf. A. R. White (1982) *The Nature of Knowledge*, Rowman and Littlefield, Chapter 3.

2

Aristotle

The name 'metaphysics' comes, as I mentioned earlier, from a later title given to a particular collection of lecture notes composed at various times and, perhaps, reflecting changing opinions by Aristotle and collected subsequently by various ancient scholars. This collection illustrates two different views of metaphysics. One regards metaphysics as a logical study of the most basic concepts, the other as an ontological study of the most basic entity or entities. The former is a view much favoured by contemporary analytic philosophers, the latter a view which has become common throughout history and often expressed in introductory text books nowadays. It is summarised by the nineteenth-century English metaphysician Bradley, whose system we shall look at later, as 'an attempt to know reality as against mere appearance, or the study of first principles or ultimate truths, or again the effort to comprehend the universe not only piecemeal or by fragments, but somehow as a whole'. Most of the work which Aristotle actually does in these lectures is of the former conceptual, logical, often linguistic, kind, but it is because of his acceptance of the latter view that he fits into the usual picture of a metaphysician as one who postulates the existence of things beyond our experience. Though many scholars deny that he ever satisfactorily reconciles these two sides of his work, I shall suggest an explanation of the logic of this move from the conceptual to the ontological in terms of the influence on his thinking of several philosophical principles. I leave aside the much debated question about the chronology of any such move.

What we shall see to be Aristotle's main theme and almost his very wording recur in the twentieth-century German metaphysician Heidegger, who begins his *Introduction to Metaphysics*, written as recently as 1953, with the claim that the question 'Why are there things ("beings"; German "Seiend") rather than nothing?' is the first, most fundamental, most general, widest and deepest of all questions. He contends that this is a question which we all ask ourselves at some time or other, whether in moments of despair, joy or boredom. It is a question whose answer, he says, will give us the basic explanation of all else. Like Aristotle, he too begins with a logical examination — what he even calls the 'grammar' — of the concept of being and ends with an ontological enquiry into being itself.

We also saw earlier that a common view of metaphysics is that it investigates questions which science cannot answer. We asked whether this was because the questions are different or because they are unanswerable. It is a main thesis of Aristotle that metaphysical questions are different from, more fundamental than and primary to, those of science. But we shall see in this thesis an ambiguity in the idea of 'fundamental' or 'primary' which also accounts for the shift in Aristotle's philosophising from a logical examination of basic or general concepts to an ontological introduction of a supersensible entity or entities.

In his lectures Aristotle called his subject by as many as ten different names which, I think, can be shown to be connected. In addition to such non-committal titles as 'the knowledge we seek',[1] 'wisdom',[2] 'knowledge of truth',[3] and 'philosophy',[4] he referred to it as 'first philosophy',[5] 'knowledge of cause',[6] 'the study of Being as Being',[7] 'the study of *ousia*',[8] 'the study of the eternal and immovable',[9] and 'Theology'.[10] The common thread running through all these titles is one of his main themes, namely that the objective of knowledge is to discover the explanation, cause, origin or first principle, of any and everything.[11] Such a cause or explanation is, he thinks, to be found in what he calls the Being or the *ousia*, particularly in the sense of the essence or, in his words, the 'what it was to be', of anything. But the first cause or origin of the Being of each and every thing is, he argues, a separate supreme Being, which he claimed was generally accepted to be God. Hence, the link from 'knowledge of causes', through 'study of Being or *ousia*' to 'Theology'. As contrasted with the study of mathematical things (*ousiai*), which exist unchangingly but not separately, and of physical things, which exist separately but not unchangingly, first philosophy, or metaphysics, will study a separate and unchanging thing. Being as Being exists separately,[12] but only the divine is a separate unchanging *ousia*, and its study is Theology.[13]

Aristotle explains the primary nature and the special subject matter of metaphysics or first philosophy by drawing a three-fold distinction between it and the various sciences. First, the sciences seek knowledge of the essential nature of the various particular kinds of things there are, whether these be perceivable objects, such as plants, animals and stars, or abstract objects, such as numbers and figures. Metaphysics, by contrast, asks what essentially is it to say of any of these things that they 'are'. Aristotle calls this a contrast between enquiring about the 'being' or the 'What is' of each kind of thing, that is, what is it to be a thing of this or that kind, for example a plant or a number, motion or goodness, and enquiring about the 'being' or the 'what is' of being or what is itself, that is, what is it simply to be. Hence, we can say, that whereas science studies the being of this or that, metaphysics studies being *as* being, the what is *as* what is (*to on hē on*). For example, physics studies the first principles of the things that are *as* moving things, while metaphysics studies them *as* things that are.

In metaphysics, that is, the study of Being as Being, we are studying a characteristic, namely Being, which everything has, while in the sciences we are studying those things — that is, of course, all things — which have this characteristic. So metaphysics is at once more comprehensive than any science and more fundamental than them all. Aristotle emphasises, as Heidegger does later, the ubiquity of Being by arguing that even to say that so and so 'is not' such and such or that so and so simply 'is not' or that 'not-being is not being' is to characterise so and so as 'being' such and such.[15]

The second contrast with science which shows the primary nature of metaphysics and its subject matter is this. Metaphysics studies not only being, but various other primary principles which are common to and presupposed in the sciences. These include such logical principles as the law of contradiction that nothing can be so and so and not so and so at the same time,[16] and such mathematical principles as the rule that when equals are added to equals, the results are equal.[17] It also studies various primary notions, common to all thinking, such as contradiction, sameness, unity, etc. These principles and these notions are not scientific and, therefore, not explicable by science. Being prior to and presupposed by science, they must be investigated by a study logically prior to science.

Thirdly, metaphysics is primary in that Being, which it studies, is prior in existence to and accounts for all the things which the various sciences study.

Aristotle also contrasted metaphysics or 'first philosophy' with other branches of philosophy, such as ethics or philosophy of science, partly because, whereas they study what it is to be, for example, justice, beauty, number, space, motion, etc., metaphysics studies Being as such and partly because, whereas these concepts are confined to special areas, the concepts which metaphysics studies, including not only Being, but also contradiction, identity, unity, plurality, genus, whole, etc., are common to all areas of thought.[18]

In this characterisation of metaphysics as a study of Being as Being, or as the study of certain primary and common notions such as contradiction, identity, unity, etc., Aristotle is presenting it as a purely analytical, conceptual study of the most basic and general of our concepts. How can we account for his move from this view to his other view of it as the study of something supersensible?[19]

One reason for the move is that, like Plato and most philosophers up to the twentieth century, Aristotle did not distinguish clearly between enquiries about the concept of something, for example the concept of a man, justice or triangularity, and enquiries about that of which it is a concept, for example a man, a triangle, or an act of justice, between asking 'What is it to be an X?' and 'What is an X?' He identified the meaning of a word with that for which the word stands, so that he talked indifferently of defining words and defining things, and held that both words and the corresponding things could be ambiguous or unambiguous.[20] 'What do we mean by "Being"?' became 'What is this thing called "Being"?' Hence, though he can distinguish between metaphysics as a study of Being as Being and the particular sciences as studies of parts of Being,[21] he is usually thinking of Being as in both cases a sort of thing, despite his attempts to distinguish between Being as a category and as a thing.[22] Aristotle would regard himself as primarily interested in the thing X rather than either the word X or the concept X. In Greek basically the same words — *to on* and *ta onta* — are used to signify either 'Being' or 'the things which are'. Thus, metaphysics will search as much as any science for the first causes and elements of that which it studies, namely Being.[23] The Being as Being, which it studies, will be something separate; an *ousia*.[24] Indeed, it will, in Aristotle's view, be a divine *ousia*.[25]

This common assumption that the concept of X is as much an entity as, though quite different in character from, X — which Plato held in the form that X itself is as much a thing as any example of X — is a form of what is sometimes called the Object Theory of Meaning. It confuses the use of a word to refer to an X with the X to which the word is used to refer to or, in Wittgenstein's analogy, the use of money to buy a cow with the cow which the money is used to buy.

It is significant that much of the misunderstanding of the nature of philosophy throughout history has been due to philosophers' assimilation of questions about concepts and questions about the things to which these concepts apply. Thus, early philosophy was not always distinguished from physics because questions such as 'What is motion, space, time, matter?' can be interpreted as questions either of the former or of the latter kind. Similarly, until recently, no clear division was made between philosophy and psychology because of a failure to distinguish logical enquiries about the concepts of mind, thought, perception, etc. from empirical enquiries about the nature of minds, thoughts, and perception themselves. Thus questions about the logical relations of the concepts of mind and body became entangled with questions about the empirical relations between one's mind and one's body.

A second, related but perhaps more powerful, reason for Aristotle's shift from a conceptual to an ontological object of study, is the part which the notion of *ousia* played in his metaphysics. This Greek word, which is a noun formed from Being (*on*), is commonly, but misleadingly, translated as 'substance' after the Latin 'substantia' which mediaeval translators of his works used. I shall stick to '*ousia*' and its plural '*ousiai*' as transliterations of the Greek. Aristotle held that 'Being' has various senses. One sense corresponds to each of what he elsewhere called 'categories', or 'predicates', such as qualities, relations, locations, activities, etc. For example, something might *be* red (quality) or *be* walking (activity). But these senses are all related in that they all refer to one central sense. They are, says Aristotle, all 'towards one' (*pros hen*). Hence, this principle is sometimes called the 'many towards one'. This one central sense of 'being' is *ousia*. It is central because primarily 'to be' means, he thought, 'to be some thing (or entity)', for example a man, a table, that is, something which could exist separately and as an individual.[26] Thus, he held that some things are said 'to be' because they are *ousiai*, others because they are modifications, qualities, locations, etc. of *ousiai*, in the same way that one thing, for example a man, is, in the central sense, healthy, because he has health, another thing, for example exercise, is healthy because it promotes health, and another thing, for example a complexion, is healthy because it is a sign of health.[27] Metaphysics, which is the first philosophy, should mainly be regarded as the study of being in the sense of *ousia*, because it is this primary sense of 'being' on which all other ideas of being depend.[28] So he says 'The question "What is being (*to on*)?" becomes the question "What is *ousia*?"'[29] and he often seems to use being (*to on*) and *ousia* interchangeably. Further, as we shall see, he considered a particular thing to be nothing other than its *ousia*,[30] so that a study of *ousiai* is a study of things or entities.

While Plato's metaphysics basically arose from his conceptual thesis that the question 'What is X (justice, equality, courage, etc.)?' implied that there is some one thing X which is common to all examples of X, Aristotle's metaphysics basically arose from his conceptual thesis that everything is to be explained in terms of its Being, and that this in its turn is to be explained by the primary sense of 'being', namely *ousia*, just as something like the healthiness of exercise or a complexion is to be explained in terms of the primary healthiness, that is, the healthiness of a body. As Plato found the explanation of everything in his idea of 'one over many', so Aristotle found it in his idea of 'many towards one'.

The study of *ousia*, which conceptually would be a study of what it is to be an *ousia*, often became a study of a thing called '*ousia*', and even the question 'In what things is *ousia* present?' and, hence, 'What things are *ousiai*?' So he asks whether *ousiai* include animals, plants, material objects, the sun and moon, mathematical objects, individuals such as Socrates, Platonic Forms, etc.[31] Aristotle's original pursuit of Being as Being (*to on hē on*) became an investigation of the whole of existence (*pasa hē ousia*),[32] and his classification of senses of 'being', that is, his categories, became a classification of the things that are. His question 'What is it to exist?' became 'What things exist?' in somewhat the way in which a modern philosopher's question 'What is it to be a number (or mind, etc.)?' sometimes becomes 'In what sense are there numbers (minds, etc.)?' or even 'Do numbers (minds, etc.) exist?' Moreover, Aristotle explicitly uses *ousia* both to indicate a kind of thing, for example a man or a circle, and a particular thing, for example this man Socrates or this circle. And, whereas in the former sense *ousia* is a category, a sense of 'being', in the latter it is an entity. Yet it is the latter *ousia* which Aristotle regards as primary, as the subject of predication, as one of the fundamental constituents of the world,[33] and, therefore, something for metaphysics to investigate. *Ousia* is said by him to be 'first in definition, in order of knowledge, in time'.[34]

A third reason for Aristotle's assimilation of the conceptual and the ontological, and of his move from an examination of concepts to an examination of entities, lies in his puzzlement whether each thing is the same as what he calls its '*to ti ēn einai*', literally its 'the what it was to be ', a phrase commonly translated as 'essence'.[35] He held that this is a question which can really only arise when we are considering the meaning of 'Being' which is *ousia*,[36] because, as we saw, he held that a thing and its *ousia* are the same.[37] Since he also often identified essence with *ousia*,[38] it follows that the thing and its essence must be the same.[39] On the other hand, he tried to differentiate a thing from its essence. He thought of the essence of something not as an element in it, and *a fortiori* not an entity in it or identical with it, but as the principle of the structure of its material, which changed it from a mere collection of materials into a structured whole. So the essence of a man is the principle according to which his flesh and bones, and perhaps his abilities and dispositions, are organised towards a suitable end. This comes out clearly in his suggestion that the *ousia* or the 'What it was to be' of a lintel is its position, and of a dinner its time.[40]

Aristotle's exact position on this question is very debatable. Generally he seems to have thought that a kind of thing could be equated with its essence,[41] but to have been less certain whether an individual thing can be. Thus, a Platonic Form, such as goodness, is the same as its essence. Indeed, Aristotle sometimes defined the Platonic Form as essence,[42] while Plato had sometimes called his Form the *ousia* of its instances.[43] Similarly, Being and its essence are the same. Again, whereas 'circle' and the essence of circle are the same,[44] and 'a right angle', 'being a right angle' and 'the *ousia* of a right angle' are the same,[45] a particular example of the kind, for example this circle, is said not to be the same as its essence because the particular must also have some matter as well as its essence.[46] Yet a particular man, for example Socrates, is allowed to be the same as his essence,[47] though man, who is composed of soul and body, is not the same as his essence, which is soul alone, despite the fact that soul and its essence are the same.[48]

What Aristotle is trying to express here is a belief in essence as something separable from individual things, but yet, unlike Plato's view, not in fact existing separately, but only in individual things which, by uniting with their matter, it makes to be what they are, for example a particular man or statue. It is that thing which, in another sense, makes each of them a thing. It is their explanation.[49] Because the essence of something is its explanation or cause, knowledge of it will be a knowledge of causes. But a knowledge of causes, as we saw, is wisdom or first philosophy, that is, metaphysics. Hence an enquiry about essence is metaphysics.

Quite apart from these reasons for moving from an examination of concepts to an examination of supposed entities, even if these entities exist only in particular things which arise from his difficulties in distinguishing between questions about so and so and questions about the concept of so and so, or between something and its essence, there were several reasons why Aristotle viewed metaphysics as a study of supersensible entities, though he rejected Plato's separate world of Forms.

One reason for his belief in the existence of the supersensible was his assumption that in addition to perceivable *ousiai*, there must exist unperceivable, unchanging and separable *ousiai*.[50] He held, like Plato, that if there was any study of the immovable and separable — which he could not help supposing — this study was something separate from either physics or mathematics, the great speculative sciences.[51] It was in fact metaphysics. But, since what is separable and immovable is divine, it could also be called 'Theology'. His adherence to this assumption, strongest in his earlier writings but to some extent abandoned later, was partly due to the influence of Plato's teaching about the Forms.[52] But it was also due to his worry that, however great the difficulties in the idea, there must be something separate and eternal to explain the existence and the order of this world.[53]

A second particular reason for this belief in the existence of a supersensible, separately existing, immovable and eternal entity, which he had discussed in his *Physics*, is that since entities are primary, the absence of an eternal entity would mean the eventual cessation of everything including motion.[54] But motion, he argued, is eternal, since it cannot ever be started or stopped. Time too is infinite, because logically there could not be anything *before* or *after* time, since these presuppose time. Yet, there must, he thought, be something which moves this eternal movement and which does not itself need a further mover. Hence, he posited an eternal unmoved mover which moves everything else. His explanation of how it can move if it is not itself moved is that it moves in the way that an object of desire, though itself unmoved, can move those which desire it.[55] Indeed, Aristotle also supposed that in addition to this first mover, there was an unmoved mover inspiring each planet, whose number would be a question for astronomy.[56]

We need not go into the difficulties of this object of desire which ultimately moves everything, but simply note that Aristotle's reason for positing the existence of an unmoved mover was that, though he could see the possibility of both infinite motion and infinite time, he nevertheless felt the logical need of something to begin this infinite series. Likewise, though he allowed motion and time to be infinite, he felt unable to admit an infinite series of causes, but insisted that there must be an origin of the series.[57] In a fragment of a missing work he subscribed to a logical assumption analogous to that which we saw used by Plato and Descartes: 'Where there is a better, there is a best; among existing things one is better than another; therefore, there is a best, which must be the divine'.[58] This is the kind of need which has prevented many metaphysicians from resting content with a world without a beginning and has led them to posit something beyond it to explain it.

The third and most general reason for Aristotle's belief in the supersensible lies in a slide from the position that metaphysics (or 'first philosophy') is a study of those ideas, and ultimately of that one idea, Being, which are logically prior to the ideas of the special sciences, to the position that metaphysics (or 'Theology') is the study of those entities, or ultimately of that entity, which is ontologically prior to and causes the entities studied in those sciences.[59] Furthermore, as we saw, he thought that the Being which metaphysics should primarily study is not a Being which is common to all instances of Being, for example to relations, accidents, etc., but the central Being in regard to which these are said to be. Most of his early classical commentators certainly thought that Aristotle argued that because Being was primary to everything else it was the primary Entity. In line with his view that to understand Being, or anything else, is to discover its origins and causes, which will be its *ousia*,[60] he concludes that any instance of Being is ultimately explained by the existence of this first separate Being, just as any instance of health, whether in exercise or complexion, is explained by the health of the body, which is the primary instance of health. His view might possibly have seemed more plausible to him if he had unconsciously slipped from 'Every Being has its *ousia*' to 'There is a Being which is the *ousia* of everything.'

In summary, Aristotle seems to have moved from metaphysics as the study of Being to metaphysics as the study of the primary instance of being, that is, *ousia*; thence, to the primary instance of *ousia*, that is, separate *ousia*; and, finally, to the primary instance of separate *ousia*, that is, separable and immovable and, therefore, divine *ousia*. Such a study is Theology. Just as the various senses or categories of Being are to be explained by reference to a central Being, so the various instances of *ousia*, whether matter, form or the composite of the two, are to be explained by reference to a central *ousia*.

Notes

Unless otherwise specified, all references are to the *Metaphysics*.

1. 983a 22, 995a 24, 1059a 35, 1059b 13, 22, 1060a 4.
2. 981b 28, 996b 14.
3. 993b 20.
4. 1003b 18.
5. 1004a 5, 1061b 20.
6. 982a 1–3, 982b 9.
7. 1003a 21, 1003b 16, 1004b 15, 1005a 3, 1005a 20.
8. 996b 31, 1003b 18, 1004a 33, 1026a 32, 1028b 4, 1060b 30, 1061b 5, 1069a 18.
9. 1026a 30, 1091a 20.
10. 1026a 20, 1064b 2.
11. 98lb – 983a.
12. 1064a 28 – 30.
13. 1026a 10 – 33.
14. 1003a 31 – 2, 1003b 16, 1059a 19, 1061b 34, 1064a.
15. 1003b 10.
16. 996b 27 – 997b 15, 1005a 19 – 1011b 25, 1062a – 1063b 18.
17. 1005a 19, 1061b 19.
18. 1004a 15, 1005a 18.
19. 997a 34, 1059a 39 – 1060a 7 – 13.
20. *Categories*, la 1 – 6.
21. 1003a 21 – 5.
22. 1053b 17 – 20.
23. 1003a 32.
24. 1064a 29, 1069a 24.
25. 1064a 35.
26. 1029a 27 – 8.
27. 1017b 20 – 30, 1029a 10 – 30, 1036b 6 – 10, 1045b 28, 1060b 32, 1089a 8.
28. 1003b 18.
29. 1028b 3.

30. 1031a 17.
31. 997a 34 – 998a 20, 1001b 27 – 1002a 30, 1017b 10, 1028b 3 – 33,
1042a 3, 1069a 30.
32. 1005b 7.
33. 1017b 10 – 25, 1039b 20.
34. 1028a 30.
35. 1031a 15.
36. 1031a 10.
37. 1031a 17.
38. 983a 28, 987a 19 – 24, 988a 35, 988b 29.
39. 1007a 26, 1017b 23, 1028a 15, 1028b 33, 1029b 13, 1041a 11 – 33.
40. 1042b 10.
41. 1031a 15.
42. 1022a 26.
43. *Cratylus*, 386a – c; *Phaedo*, 65e, 76d.
44. 1036a, 1037b 3.
45. 1036a 18.
46. 1036a 2, 1037b 5.
47. 1022a 26.
48. 1043b 3.
49. 1041a – b.
50. 1071b – 1074b 15.
51. 1026a 10 – 22, 1059a 20, 1060a 8, 1064a 33 – 1064b 6, 1071b 5.
52. 997b; contrast 1039a 24 – 1041a 5.
53. 1060a 25 – 1071b 5.
54. 1071b 3.
55. 1012b 3, 1072a 25.
56. 1073a 30.
57. 994a.
58. *Fragment* 1476b 22 – 4.
59. 1064a 33 – 8.
60. 1041b 20 – 5.

3
Berkeley

The writings of the eighteenth-century Irish philosopher Bishop Berkeley furnish another good example of our general thesis that metaphysics is an enquiry which begins from an examination of the nature of general concepts and ends with a theory about the nature of this world and a belief in a world beyond it. His work provides also a clear illustration of the view that a link between the initial conceptual examination and the subsequent metaphysical system is some principle which the metaphysician sees as being both the key to the original problem and an irresistible commitment to the metaphysical system.

At the first stage we find him confronted with a problem which might occur to any of us, and one which we saw is the basic problem of all metaphysics, namely 'What is it for something, for example a tree or a person, to exist?' or even 'What is it to be something, such as a tree or a person?'. At the second stage he expresses his conviction that the key to this problem is a necessary connection of the ideas of existence and perception expressed by the principles that for a material object, such as a tree, to exist is for it to be perceived, and for a spirit, whether embodied in a person or disembodied in an angel or God, is for it to perceive. But the acceptance of the former principle, that to be is to be perceived, immediately gave rise to two further problems. First, if the existence of the books and trees we perceive around us depends on their being perceived, what causes this perception of ours on which their existence appears to depend? Why, for example, do we have the visual, auditory and tangible experiences we do have when we turn the pages of a book? Secondly, if we believe, as we all do, that those same books and trees exist when not perceived by any of us,

41

how can this be? Why, for example, do the books in my study not vanish when I leave it?

Berkeley felt that the only way to answer these two questions was to enter on the third, the essentially metaphysical, stage of his philosophical journey, that is, to postulate the existence of something additional to and beyond what we ordinarily experience. For Berkeley, as we shall see, this additional supersensible entity was an infinite spirit which both causes us to have the perceptions we do have when we perceive anything and preserves what we can perceive when we do not perceive it. This spirit he identified with God. One might cynically suppose that Berkeley, as a bishop, who therefore already believed in God, was simply looking for arguments to support this belief. And it is true that he expressly says that he was concerned to refute atheism and materialism. But an important part of understanding his metaphysics is to see how such a hypothesis is not a premiss but, as he himself stressed,[1] what seemed to him the inevitable conclusion of his purely logical arguments.

As a philosopher, Berkeley constantly called on his readers, on the one hand, to look closely at the exact everyday use of such key concepts as *existence*,[2] *see*,[3] *at a distance*,[4] *material object*, *cause* and *abstraction*, and, on the other, to subject to criticism such philosophical jargon as 'abstract ideas',[5] 'substance',[6] and 'matter'.[7] Such a practice, he claimed, would help to banish bad metaphysics and recall us to common sense.[8]

But his prime aim was to become clear about the concept of *existence*, that is, the meaning of the word 'exist', whether it is used of material or non-material objects, of time, number, motion or any relation between things.[9] In this enquiry, however, his first assumption was that the meaning of 'X exists' or 'There is an X' depends on the meaning of 'X', so that what he in fact always tried to explain was not simply the meaning of 'exists', but of 'A person exists', 'The tree exists', 'Time exists' or 'There exists a relation between A and B.' This he explained wholly in terms of the meaning of, for example, 'person',[10] 'tree',[11] 'time',[12] or 'relation'. He, in fact, runs together two different, though related, questions, namely 'What is it for something to be an X?' and 'What is it for an X to be (i.e. exist)?' Because his ostensible, and often his real, interest is in the second question, he expresses what I called his guiding principle by saying that the *esse*, that is, the *existence*, of a physical object, such as a tree, is to be perceived and the *esse* or existence of a non-physical object is to perceive. But this is different from answering the first question by showing that *to be* (which, of course, in Latin would also be '*esse*') a physical object is to be something which is perceived and *to be* a non-physical object is to be something which perceives. He has given no reason — nor could he — why what it means for something to exist depends on what kind of thing it is. What we mean by saying that trees and people, numbers and time 'exist' — or that 'there are' trees and people, numbers and time — is the same whatever we mean by 'trees', 'people', 'number', 'time'. More importantly, by assimilating what we mean by 'tree' or 'person' and what we mean by 'exists' when used of a tree or person, Berkeley is already part of the way to a corollary of his principle, namely that material objects, such as trees, cannot exist unless they are perceived and non-material objects, such as people, cannot exist unless they perceive. Thus, he says, 'the various sensations or ideas imprinted on the senses . . . cannot exist other than in a mind perceiving them . . . an intuitive knowledge may be obtained of this, by anyone that shall attend to what is meant by the term *exist* when applied to sensible things'.[13] The assimilation of the meaning of 'X' and the meaning of 'X exists' is made from the opposite direction when Berkeley argues, as he occasionally does, from the premiss that X's being perceived is sufficient evidence for its existence to the conclusion that what is meant by 'X' is something that is perceived.[14]

Berkeley, following the traditional thinking of his time, supposed that all the things we can know fall basically into two groups, those that can both know and be known and those which can only be known. The former group, which includes human beings, spiritual things, such as angels, and God, he calls 'spirits'. The latter group was more miscellaneous, including relations, time and motion, thoughts, dreams, bodily feelings of pain and pleasure, but especially and largely physical objects, such as trees and houses, desks and apples. His problem was to analyse the notion of *existence* as it applied to the various kinds of members of each of the two groups. This he attempted to do, as we have just seen, by considering what it meant for any of them to exist.

It is here that he advances his guiding principle. By a 'spirit' we mean, he suggested, something which perceives various objects, which wills to bring about certain ends, and which performs certain acts. 'Perceives' was used in a wide sense, to cover not only sense-perception, but also having bodily feelings of pain and pleasure, imagining, dreaming, and understanding and knowing things, such as other spirits, which are not perceivable by the senses. It would not be altogether fair to Berkeley to examine too closely his views about spirits, especially how we obtain any knowledge of them, since he never published his final views on the subject, having lost his original manuscript while travelling in Italy.

Though he wavered between holding that 'to be a spirit' means to be *something* which perceives, wills and acts,[15] and holding that it simply means to perceive, will and act,[16] he considered that on either alternative a spirit must always perceive, will or act and would not exist unless it did; that is, that for a spirit to exist is to perceive.[17] This view was expressed in the Latin slogan, *esse est percipere*. Support for this view that a spirit always perceives was provided by his theory that the passing of time is a subjective succession of ideas in one's mind.[18] Though the second alternative would have fitted in better with his general approach, since it would not leave, as the first alternative does,[19] any awkward and never answered questions about the nature of this alleged *something* which perceives, wills and acts, he could never quite bring himself to accept it. The general tenor of his remarks, and sometimes his explicit argument, favours the view that a spirit is an entity, albeit one whose existence depends on its perceiving.[20]

In his extant works, however, Berkeley's chief interest is not in analysing the meaning of the term 'existence' as applied to spirit, that is, to what can know various things, but in analysing its meaning as applied to those things which can only be known, especially those which can be perceived. Just as he had suggested that for a spirit to exist is for it to perceive, so he now claims that for these objects of knowledge other than spirits to exist is for them to be perceived — in Latin, *esse est percipi* — or, as we shall see he sometimes allows, to be perceivable.

To appreciate Berkeley's analysis of the concept of existence as applied to such objects, we must note both the wide sense in which he uses the notion of *perceive* and the wide sense which he gives to his technical term 'idea', which he is going to use for *what is perceived*.

Berkeley uses 'perceive' in such a way that it covers not only perception by the five senses, that is, seeing, hearing, tasting, smelling and touching, but also bodily sensations, such as feeling a pain or a pleasurable sensation,[21] thinking about something,[22] imagining something,[23] dreaming,[24] and also being aware of various sorts of things, such as relations,[25] numbers,[26] time,[27] etc.

The result of this wide use is that perceiving something by one of the five senses gets assimilated to feeling, thinking of, dreaming of, or imagining something. Since the latter can with some plausibility be analysed as having something, for example a pain,[28] thought, dream,[29] or image,[30] which does not exist independently of the having of it, Berkeley is led to suppose that perceiving something by the senses can be analysed as the having of something, for example a sensation, which does not exist independently of the having of it.[31] Furthermore just as what is felt, what is thought of or dreamt of, and what is imagined, need not exist when it is not felt, thought of or dreamt of, or imagined, so what is perceived by the senses need not exist when not perceived.[32] But though we might accept the former thesis as a correct account of our ordinary idea of *feeling*, *thinking*, *dreaming*, we would not accept the latter as a correct account of our ordinary idea of *perceiving*.

The same result, namely that what is perceived cannot exist when it is not perceived, also comes about from a similar assimilation of *what* is perceived with *what* is felt, thought of or dreamt of, or imagined. Berkeley, like his immediate predecessors, uses the word 'idea' to cover both what is perceived by the senses and what is felt, thought of or dreamt of, or imagined. Moreover, though he does distinguish between what is perceived, as when we see a tree or hear a train, and what is 'immediately' perceived, as when we see the colour of the tree or hear the sound of the train, he uses 'idea' to cover not only what we should call a sensible quality of the tree or train, for example its colour or sound, but indirectly also what we should call the physical object itself, i.e. the tree or train. For he argues that the tree or train is just a collection of its sensible qualities, i.e. its colour, smell, taste, sound and texture, and therefore, a collection of ideas.[33] Indeed, he goes even further, for he expressly holds that there is no difference between a sensible quality — or the physical object which is a collection of sensible qualities — and the perception of that sensible quality. As he puts it, the idea and the perception of the idea are the same. Further still, he allows no difference between the sensation which he thinks we receive when we perceive, for example, a loud noise or a bright colour and the perception of that noise or colour. Both sensation and perception are called 'ideas'. Because the same concept, that of *idea*, is deliberately used to cover such a wide range,[34] particularly that between perception or sensation[35] — even a sensation of pain[36] — on the one hand, and the sensible quality,[37] for example the colour or sound, or even the sensible thing,[38] for example the collection of ideas which he thinks constitutes the tree or train, on the other hand, Berkeley is again led to the view that what is perceived, whether it is the train or the sound of the train, the tree or the colour of the tree, cannot exist when it is not being perceived. Since an 'unperceived perception' is a contradiction, he thinks an 'unperceived object of perception' is also a contradiction.[39] In his language, an idea, such as a colour or sound, cannot exist when no-one is having an idea, for example a sensation of colour or sound, any more than a pain, a thought, a dream, or an image can exist when no-one is having one of these. Hence, though he does distinguish between what we feel, think, dream and imagine on the one hand, and what we perceive by the senses on the other, by pointing out the differences not only in the order, liveliness and independence of the will of the perceiver between the latter and the former, but also the differences in their causes, they are nevertheless all ideas, and, therefore, all treated as existing only when perceived.[40] Moreover, not only does Berkeley's analysis of perception in terms of the having of sensations lead him to suppose that perceiving a tree or train is a necessary condition of the existence of the tree or train, it also leads him to suppose that having certain sensations of colour, sound etc. is a sufficient condition for the existence of the tree or train.

The prime objection to this argument is that the ordinary use of our concepts of perception, sensation, physical object, etc. allows that trees and trains can exist without being perceived and that one can have the sensations associated with perceiving a tree or train without the tree or train existing. A further objection is that Berkeley's theory commits one to supposing that the collection of ideas which constitute a particular object, for example an apple, must be those existing at a particular time and for a particular person; a conclusion which contradicts the common beliefs that one person can see the same object twice and that two people can see it. When Berkeley thinks of an idea as an object perceived by someone he emphasises that the idea can be perceived by another;[41] but when he thinks of the idea as a sensation had by someone he emphasises its peculiarity to that person.[42]

Berkley's supposition that trains and trees cannot exist unless they are being perceived was buttressed also by his tendency to waver between the metaphorical and the literal use of a phrase which he originally introduced as a figurative synonym for 'to be perceived'. This was the phrase 'in the mind'.[43] Berkeley clearly intended 'in the mind' in his metaphysics to mean 'perceived'[44] and 'without the mind' to mean 'unperceived',[45] and did not intend either in any 'gross literal sense',[46] that is in any spatial sense, or in the sense of 'imaginary'. And it is true that everyday language is familiar with many idiomatic uses of 'in the mind' which also are not gross literal senses, for example, 'I'll bear you in mind for the post', 'I can't get it out of my mind.'

But his repeated warnings did not prevent his contemporaries or his commentators from interpreting the phrases in a non-Berkeleian way. More importantly, he himself was misled by these phrases, especially the phrase 'without the mind', into thinking that material objects only exist, like sensations, as objects of and in the mind. This can be seen most clearly in his views on vision; but it is also evident from (a) his comparison of the objects of imagination, dreaming, and feeling, with those of perception, (b) his lack of a distinction between sensation, perception, and the object of perception, and (c) several remarks that are only appropriate if the phrases in dispute are misinterpreted.

(a) Berkeley believed 'That neither our thoughts nor passions, nor ideas formed by the imagination exist without the mind, is what everybody will allow.'[47] He then uses the arguments from *imagination*[48] — 'are not things imagined as truly in the mind as things perceived'; from *dreams*[49] — 'you do not thence conclude the apparitions in a dream to be without the mind'; and from *feelings*[50] — 'intense heat is nothing else but a particular kind of painful sensation; and pain cannot exist but in a perceiving thing; it follows that no intense heat can really exist in an unperceiving corporeal substance'; to support his view that the objects of sense-perception are not 'without the mind'. Referring to the blind man, he says, 'The objects intromitted by sight would seem to him (as in truth they are) no other than a new set of thoughts or sensations each whereof is as near to him as the perceptions of pain or pleasure, or the most inward passions of his soul.'[51] These sentiments exist side by side with his clear distinction between ideas of imagination, etc., and ideas of sense[52] and his rejection of the accusation that he made things of sense 'purely notional'.[53]

(b) Berkeley, as we have seen, used the word 'idea' synonymously with 'object of perception', 'perception', and 'sensation', and explicitly refused to allow the usual distinctions between them.[54] He used 'sensation' as ambiguously as 'idea'. So he thought that to show that sensations are in the eye,[55] or in the finger-tips,[56] or in the mind,[57] was to show that the objects perceived are in the mind too.[58] So he confused himself because he talked of 'perceiving' sensations in the same way as 'perceiving' objects.[59] But objects are not sensations (bodily or mental) and sensations are not seen or heard or touched (though they may be felt or had). Sensations and objects are 'in the mind' in different senses of that phrase. To call both 'ideas' inevitably leads us into thinking that they must be in the mind in the same way and that arguments about one are valid also about the other.[60]

(c) By using phrases with a physical connotation about objects 'without the mind' Berkeley seems to be using the spatial sense of 'without', for example 'without the mind in the ambient space'.[61] He contrasts existence in the mind with existence in external space, and thinks that objects must be 'supported' in one or other of these places.[62] Objects are said to be 'as near to us as our own thoughts'.[63] The spatial use is indeed the predominant one in his *Theory of Vision*.

Berkeley admittedly says, 'All these things that are intangible and of a spiritual nature, his thoughts and desires, his passions, and in general all the modifications of the soul, to these he would never apply the terms upper and lower except only in a metaphorical sense . . . in their proper signification [these words] would never be applied to anything that was not conceived to exist without the mind.'[64] But the objections to this are that if the argument is to be used to show that *ideas* are not 'without' the mind then (1) we have a clear example of mistake (a) above; and (2) we do properly and non-metaphorically apply spatial words to the objects of sight, which ought therefore on the reasoning of this passage to be declared to be 'without' the mind.

I think that in general the ambiguity of the preposition 'without' is more insidious and, in his views on vision, more operative than that of 'in'. 'Without' has a privative meaning, i.e., Latin *sine*, and a spatial, i.e., Latin *extra*, which are not always easily distinguished in a given context. 'Who is without?' is obviously *extra* and 'No cause without an effect' *sine*; while 'There is a green hill far away without a city wall', though *extra*, is near enough to *sine* to make a pun plausible.

Throughout Berkeley's philosophy there are many cases where 'without the mind' either explicitly or obviously is used privatively in the special sense of 'unperceived by';[65] cases where its sense is perhaps debatable;[66] and cases where the spatial use is most plausible,[67] especially those where 'at a distance' is given as an alternative.[68] There is also the privative use where 'without' means 'apart from' but not 'unperceived by', and this is common in phrases like 'length without breadth'.[69] A confusing and perhaps confused case is in the *Three Dialogues*, p. 199, where 'without the mind' is followed immediately by 'color without extension'. There is a similar ambiguity in Berkeley's use of 'external', 'exterior', 'outward', etc. Although their primary sense is spatial rather than privative, and they are sometimes so used by him,[70] yet the privative use occurs more frequently.[71] Here, too, there are some debatable cases.[72]

Berkeley admits that the view 'that we should in truth see external space, and bodies actually existing in it, some nearer, others farther off, seems to carry with it some opposition to what hath been said of their existing nowhere without the mind'.[73] Now if 'without' has the sense *sine*, there need be no problem here. But Berkeley seemed to think there was; hence his *Theory of Vision* was written to show that 'distance or outness is neither immediately of itself perceived by sight . . .',[74] and he suggests in the *Principles* that the same is true of the objects of touch.[75] Similarly, Berkeley argues that 'you ought not to conclude that sensible objects are without the mind, from their appearance or manner wherein they are perceived'.[76] Now no-one would conclude from the fact that an object is perceived in a certain way that it is 'without' *sine*, i.e. 'unperceived', though he might conclude that it is 'without' *extra*; indeed this latter is just what the blind man does about touch.[77] Therefore, I argue that Berkeley is using 'without' (*extra*) here. Indeed he goes on to say quite explicitly that 'sight therefore does not suggest or in any way inform you that the visible object you immediately perceive exists at a distance', and he refers the reader to the two works on vision. But if Berkeley did, as I argue, think like this, he was wrong. We can assert that nothing is 'without' (*sine*) and yet not have to prove that nothing is 'without' $\overline{(extra)}$. Objects may exist at a distance and yet not exist unperceived. The questions whether they do exist in these ways are two, and their answers are logically independent; whereas Berkeley, by considering each as the question whether things exist 'without' the mind, felt compelled to give the same answer in each case.[78] Furthermore, having denied externality to the objects of sight in the *TV*, there seemed every reason to deny it to the objects of touch in the *Principles*.[79]

The passage in *Principles*, sect. 43, shows how the question arose for Berkeley, and I have argued that in this sense it was wrongly answered because it was misunderstood. But it might be said that he gave independent evidence against existence at a distance. Even if this were so — which I doubt — he could only be said to have done so in the *TV* for sight, but not for touch. In the *TV* he still considered that tangible objects exist at a distance.[80] In the *Principles* he gives no fresh evidence to deny this, but argues — as he does also of course with vision — that since they are ideas and therefore not 'without' the mind (*sine*) they are not 'without' the mind (*extra*). And this is the old ambiguity.

In the *TV*, when Berkeley speaks of tangible objects as 'without the mind' and contrasts them with the visible which are 'in the mind',[81] he does not and cannot mean that the tangible are unperceived, since he always calls them ideas.[82] He must mean that they are at a distance.[83] In his *Theory of Vision*, sect. 55, he quite explicitly speaks of 'the object which exists without the mind, and is at a distance'; and in the previous section (54) equally clearly, in distinguishing two sorts of objects, speaks of 'the one properly tangible, i.e., to be perceived and measured by touch'.[84] The only sense in which the tangible is 'without the mind' is 'at a distance', and the only sense in which it could be called 'unperceived' is 'unseen', i.e., 'not immediately falling under the sense of seeing' (ibid.). 'That vulgar error' of *Principles*, sect. 44, is not that the tangible are 'without' (*sine*), but that they are 'without' (*extra*). Far from it being assumed in the *TV* that the tangible are unperceived, this is explicitly denied in the remarks on abstract ideas.[85] Therefore, he is using 'without' in the *TV* in sense *extra*. In sense *sine* the tangible are as far from being 'without' in the *TV* as they are in the *Principles*, and there is nothing 'interim' about Berkeley's metaphysics here. The sense in which it can be said that the tangible are 'brought into the mind' in the *Principles* is the spatial sense.

It was the whole object of the *TV* to deny distance of sight.[86] And since in the *TV* it is in this sense that the tangible and visible are contrasted, it must be in this sense that the contrast is denied in the *Principles* and the tangible 'brought into the mind'.[87] The *TV* was designed to show how 'the mind by mediation of visible ideas doth perceive or apprehend the distance . . . of tangible objects'.[88] The *Principles* took the step — which was really already taken in *TV*, sect. 45, — of asserting that 'the ideas of sight . . . do not suggest or mark out to us things actually existing at a distance, but only admonish us what ideas of touch will be imprinted on our minds at such and such distances of time'.[89]

The confusion with the spatial is seen also in his writings where an alternative phrase to 'in the mind' is 'in the eye'.[90] The use of the blind man example shows quite clearly that Berkeley was thinking in spatial terms.[91] Long after the *Principles* were published Berkeley welcomed the support of the Chesselden case, where the blind man 'thought all objects whatever touched his eyes'.[92]

Just as Berkeley wavered on the question whether a spirit is something over and above its perceiving and, therefore, could exist, if it was capable of perceiving, when it was not actually perceiving, so he was sometimes undecided whether a material object's existence depended wholly on its being perceived or whether it would exist when it was perceivable, but not actually perceived. He did sometimes toy with the latter possibility, which was later taken up by Mill in the nineteenth century and by the Logical Positivists and others in the twentieth.[93] Thus, to say categorically that a flower blushes unseen would, on this view, be to say hypothetically that it would be seen to blush if anyone were there to look at it. In other words, 'The rose is red' is analysed as 'The rose has the ability to look red, for example in normal conditions' analogously to the way in which 'He is patient, irascible, intelligent' is analysed as 'He has the ability or tendency to behave patiently, irascibly, intelligently.' The difference between a red rose before us in good light and a red rose in the dark is that the former is manifesting, while the latter is not, its ability to look red.

Berkeley never seems, however, to have felt this conditional existence of the unperceived material object to be sufficient. For him the *esse* of a physical object was to be perceived, not merely to be able to be perceived, just as the *esse* of a spiritual object was to perceive, not merely to be able to perceive. Indeed, at times he argued that the perceivable must be perceived because each is an idea.[94]

Berkeley realised that his analysis of a material object in terms of its actually being perceived raised two problems. First, when we do perceive a tree, how do we account for those ideas or sensations we get whose collection constitutes the tree? Might these not be ideas purely of our imagination? Secondly, how can we defend the belief which we all have that the tree continues to exist when it is not perceived by any of us? It is the attempt to answer these two questions which leads Berkeley to the third stage of his metaphysical journey, namely the postulation of something supersensible whose existence he thinks is necessary to explain the existence of the objects in the world around us both when they are perceived by us and when they are not perceived by us.

He rejected various possible answers to the first question.

Clearly other people are not the cause of our perceiving what we do, that is, of our having the ideas or sensations we do have. Nor, thinks Berkeley, can one idea cause another idea;[95] it can only be a sign of it.[96] He also argued at length against the view, which most people would hold, and which was held by his predecessor Locke and by such seventeenth-century scientists as Newton and Boyle, that those ideas are caused by some physical constituents of the material objects, such as atoms or molecules. Such a cause was scornfully rejected by him, for reasons we need not examine here, as 'inert', 'passive', 'unknown', 'incapable of causing anything'.[97] Nor can these ideas which we have in seeing, hearing, touching, etc. be the products of our imagination, which for Berkeley was admittedly a faculty of forming ideas, since we have considerable powers over our imagination and to some extent over our thoughts and dreams, but we cannot help, for example, seeing what we see when we open our eyes and turn them in a certain direction.[98]

The formation of ideas by our imagination, however, gives us the vital clue, namely that ideas are caused and created by and only by spirits.[99] Any cause of an idea is a power and only spirits have powers.[100] Since it is not our own spirit or any other human spirit that imprints on us the ideas we get through our senses, that 'excites sensations in our mind', it must be an infinite, divine spirit, that is, God.[101]

This argument for the existence of God as the cause of our ideas explains also why Berkeley explicitly argued that his analysis of what it is to see something at a distance logically necessitates a theological metaphysics.[102] For the result of his analysis was that 'the ideas of sight do not suggest or mark out to us things actually existing at a distance, but only admonish us what ideas of touch will be imprinted on our minds at such a distance of time'.[103] God is the cause of that regular sequence of sights and touches that we wrongly think of as first seeing an object in the distance and then coming up to and touching it.

Since Berkeley agreed, in conformity both with common sense and with the Mosaic account of the creation of the world, that the objects around us continue to exist when none of us perceives them, that, as he said, 'the trees are in the Park whether I think about them or not',[104] and since, as we saw, he rejected any explanation of their continued existence in terms of the bare possibility of their being perceived, he is faced with his second problem, that is, of accounting for this continued existence. This he solves in a way similar to his solution to his first problem. He postulates the existence of an eternal spirit, that is, God, to hold in existence those things which we all believe to exist when they are not ordinarily being perceived.[105] Such a spirit, Berkeley usually argued, gives continuity to the humanly unperceived by eternally perceiving it.[106]

As an adaptation of the old limerick puts it, 'the tree which we see continues to be since seen by Almighty God'. Unfortunately, he never tried to work out the details of this hypothesis nor faced up to its problems. Thus, how could God, a spirit which he also held has no physical senses and is incapable of having sensations, perceive anything?[107] Secondly, how could God, a spirit which he also held was purely active, perceive anything, since perception, as contrasted with imagination, was, in his view, the passive acceptance of ideas?[108] Thirdly, what exactly is God supposed to perceive when we are not perceiving anything? Berkeley always insisted that no two people can perceive the same thing, since to perceive is to have one's own set of sensations. Does God, therefore, perceive something other than any human participant? If so, what particular aspect of anything does he perceive? Does he see the colour of the tree as one who is situated a hundred yards from it in the twilight does or as one standing in front of it in broad daylight? Does he hear the sound of the train as the engine driver or a station-master does? Or does he somehow perceive all the possible aspects of it all at once?

Sometimes Berkeley gave a half-hearted acquiescence to the view that perhaps the different ideas which you and I have when we look at the tree or hear the train are copies of another set of ideas, called archetypes, which God has.[109] But how can your ideas and mine, which are different, both be copies of his archetypes? Sometimes he avoided any reference to perception by speaking of God's knowledge or comprehension of ideas.[110] Similarly, he suggested that God could cause and know pain, though he could not perceive it, since he could not be a recipient of pain.[111] But any such views would make the existence of humanly unperceived ideas very different from the existence of humanly perceived ideas and even make the idea of 'idea' different in both cases.

Berkeley's first argument for the existence of God as a spirit which causes those ideas which constitute the objects perceived by us — apart from any of its own difficulties, into which we need not enquire here, about how a spirit could cause sensations — is inconsistent with his second argument for his existence as a spirit which perceives those objects when unperceived by us. We cannot say that the reason why the tree which we see continues to be when no-one is about in the quad is that God sees it. For the tree which we see is a collection of ideas in our mind caused by God, whereas the tree which exists when no-one is about is at most a collection of ideas in God's mind. Furthermore, when I see and smell, but do not hear or touch or taste, an apple in front of me, God would, on Berkeley's twin hypotheses, be causing the ideas of sight and smell in me, but perceiving the ideas of sound, touch and taste, which go to make up the apple. The ideas which God causes and the ideas which he perceives cannot be the same ideas. In his notebooks, Berkeley considered, but abandoned, the possibility that the existence of what is unperceived might be explained not as an idea, but only as a power in God, presumably the same power which would cause the existence of what is perceived.[112] In addition to its inconsistency with the thesis that God perceives ideas, the thesis that he causes those same ideas has similar difficulties to the former thesis in explaining how a spirit without sensible or physical properties can cause others to perceive by the senses. A further similarity between the two theses, which may sometimes have confused Berkeley, comes out in his double use of the doctrine that ideas are 'dependent on' minds as meaning, on the one hand, that they must be perceived or had by a mind and, on the other, that they must be caused by a mind.[113]

Berkeley's metaphysics consists of a world with God but without matter.[114] It is reached by analysing the idea of the existence of a physical object in terms of the perception of its perceivable qualities, and analysing the perception of these qualities in terms of the having of sensations of these qualities. God is introduced, on the one hand, to provide a causal explanation of our having such sensations and, hence, to account for the existence of that which is presently perceived by us; and, on the other, to provide a spirit who can himself hold ideas in his mind and, hence, account for the existence of that which is not presently perceived by us.

Notes

The references are to A. A. Luce and T. E. Jessop (eds.) (1948–57) *The Works of George Berkeley*, Nelson and Sons, Edinburgh.
D — *Three Dialogues*; *P* — *Principles*; *PC* — *Philosophical Commentaries*; *TV* — *Theory of Vision*; *TVV* — *Theory of Vision Vindicated*.

1. *D* 212.

2. *PC* 408, 491, 593, 604; *P* 3, 89.
3. *TVV* 43.
4. *TV* 44.
5. *TVV* 123–5; *P* Introduction.
6. *D* 172.
7. *D* 198.
8. *PC* 751.
9. *PC* 408, 491, 593, 604; *P* 3.
10. *P* 138, 139.
11. *P* 3.
12. *PC* 4, 13.
13. *P* 3.
14. *D* 224, 234.
15. *PC* 848; *P* 2, 7, 27, 36, 39, 138; *D* 231, 233.
16. *PC* 580, 614, 615, 637.
17. *PC* 561, 562; *P* 98.
18. *PC* 48, 590; *P* 38.
19. *PC* 581.
20. *D* 233–4.
21. *TV* 41; *D* 176.
22. *TV* 41, 51, 94; *D* 178, 180, 188.
23. *P* 23, 33; contrast *PC* 582.
24. *P* 18, 42; *D* 201.
25. *P* 11; *D* 192; contrast *P* 89.
26. *P* 12.
27. *PC* 4, 13.
28. *D* 176–8.
29. *P* 18, 25.
30. *PC* 972.
31. *PC* 301, 378, 756; *P* 3, 7; *D* 197.
32. *PC* 280, 792; *P* 3.
33. *P* 1; *D* 249.
34. *PC* 609, 656, 792; *P* 90; *D* 196. cf. J. S. Mill (1843) *A System of Logic*, I. iii, 9, 'the distinction which we verbally make between the properties of things and the sensations we receive from them, must originate in the convenience of discourse rather than in the nature of what is signified by the terms'.
35. *P* 10, 54, 56; *D* 195.
36. *D* 176.
37. *P* 5, 78, 87, 90.
38. *D* 174, 180; *PC* 427, 437, 775; *P* 90.
39. *PC* 249, 280; *D* 195.
40. *P* 29, 30, 34, 36.
41. *D* 153, 156, 175.
42. *P* 11, 14; *D* 124–5, 147.
43. What follows is a shortened version of A. R. White (1954) 'The Ambiguity of Berkeley's "without the mind"', *Hermathena*, 83, pp. 55–65.
44. *P* 2, 33, 49; *D* 249.
45. *PC* 342, 874; *P* 23, 38, 67, 91; *D* 211, 246, 251, 260, etc.

46. *D* 250; cf. *P* 49 'not by way of mode or attribute but only by way of idea'; *D* 237.

47. *P* 3; *TV* 94.

48. *D* 209; *P* 3; *PC* 472, 792, 886.

49. *D* 201; *P* 42.

50. *D* 177, 176–81; 191, 197; *PC* 692; *TV* 41; *P* 14–15.

51. *TV* 41.

52. *P* 33; *D* 235.

53. *P* 34; contrast *P* 5, 'the things we see and feel, what are they but so many sensations, notions, ideas or impressions on the sense'.

54. *D* 194–7.

55. *TV* 16–17, 27, 41; *TVV* 66; *D* 187, 230.

56. *D* 176–81.

57. *D* 192, 197; *PC* 18.

58. *D* 201, 214, 230; *P* 4, 19–20; *TV* 41.

59. *TV* 16–18; *TVV* 66.

60. *TV* 41; *P* 5, etc.

61. *TV* 94; cf. *TV* 43, 96, 98, 106; *P* 10, 11, 67, 68; *D* 194, etc.

62. *P* 67; *TV* 14, 43, 111, etc.

63. *P* 42; *TV* 41.

64. *TV* 94.

65. *PC* 33, 270, 280, 289, 342, 363a, 874, 878; *TV* 81; *TVV* 19, 23; *P* 3, 6, 12, 18, 22, 23, 33, 38, 56, 67, 86, 87, 90, 91, 116; *D* 175, 200, 205, 206, 211, 230, 251, 260, etc.

66. *PC* 55, 74, 121, 222, 359, 362a, 363, 376, 656, 689, 692; *TV* 117; *P* 10, 11, 53, 54, 73, 110; *D* 183, etc.

67. *PC* 58, 95, 97, 318, 378, 603, 656; *TV* 94, 96, 111; *P* 44, 56, 67; *D* 186–7, where 'distant', 'external', 'without' have the same reference; *D* 222, etc.

68. *PC* 603; *TV* 41, 43, 50, 55, 95, 96; *P* 42, 43; *D* 201–2.

69. *PC* 365, 460, 476, 483, 572, 646, 704, 722, 841; *P* 7, 10, 11, 14, 19, 20, 45, 46, etc.

70. *TV* 64, 77, 78, 99, 111, 117.

71. *TVV* 12, 20; *P* 8, 15, 83, 90, 91, 97; *D* 175, 179, 181, 188, 191, 195, 203, 205, 206, 220, 230, 235, 246, etc.

72. *D* 186–7, 203.

73. *P* 43.

74. *P* 43.

75. *P* 44.

76. *D* 201.

77. *PC* 95.

78. *P* 44, and the whole of *TV*.

79. *P* 44.

80. *TV* 55, 59, 62, 94, 96, 99, 111; *TVV* 53, 64.

81. *TV* 50, 55, 96, 111; *TVV* 48, etc; *PC* 95.

82. *TV* 1, 45, 46, 96, 99, 103, etc; *TVV* 9–11; *P* 1; *D* 174.

83. 'distance of things from the eye', *TVV* 64.

84. cf. *TV* 94–6, 135.

85. *TV* 122 ff.

86. *TV* 45, 50, 52, 77, 112, 117, 119, 126; etc; *P* 116; *D* 201; *PC* 58,

62, 74, 121, 215, 603.
  87. *P* 44; *TVV* 35, 38.
  88. *TV* 121, 147.
  89. *P* 44; *D* 202.
  90. *PC* 58; *TV* 36, 41, 77; *TVV* 64, 67, 68, 71, etc.
  91. *PC* 95; *TV* 41, 94, 95; *P* 43; *D* 202, etc.
  92. *TVV* 71.
  93. *PC* 185a, 282, 293a; *P* 3, 58; *D* 251.
  94. *D* 209, 234.
  95. *PC* 433; *TVV* 11, 13; *P* 25.
  96. *P* 65.
  97. *P* 61; *D* 214–6.
  98. *P* 26–9, 56.
  99. *P* 18, 28.
  100. *PC* 41; *D* 214–5, 240.
  101. *P* 26, 29, 57, 72, 146; *PC* 489; *D* 215.
  102. *TVV* 1, 38; *P* 44.
  103. *P* 44.
  104. *PC* 98, 185, 312, 408, 472, 802; *P* 45, 48, 90; *D* 195, 230–2, 235.
  105. *PC* 52, 675; *P* 6, 30, 46, 48, 90; *D* 195, 212, 214, 230–2, 235, 250–6.
  106. *P* 6, 7; *D* 212, 213, 234–6. J. Bennett (1971) *Locke, Berkeley, Hume*, Clarendon Press, Oxford, sects. 37–41, disagrees with the orthodox view in doubting whether Berkeley used this argument.
  107. *D* 241; Berkeley to Johnson 282.
  108. *D* 231.
  109. *D* 214, 248; Berkeley to Johnson 292.
  110. *D* 215, 230, 235, 251, 254. G. Pitcher (1977) *Berkeley*, Routledge and Kegan Paul, London, Chapter 10, after giving passages from Berkeley's writings which hint at various views, argues for the view that God only thinks of, but does not perceive, ideas. cf. G. H. Thomas, 'Berkeley's God does not perceive', *Journal of History of Philosophy*, 14 (1976), pp. 163–8.
  111. *D* 240.
  112. *PC* 52, 282.
  113. Bennett (1971), sect. 36 collects Berkeley's uses of 'dependent'.
  114. *PC* 19.

4

Leibniz

The seventeenth-century philosopher Leibniz is famous, on the one hand, as a formal logician and a mathematician who invented the differential calculus independently of Newton and, on the other, as the author of a system of metaphysics so grand and abstract that Kant called it 'a kind of enchanted world', Hegel 'a metaphysical romance' and Bertrand Russell 'a fantastic fairy tale'. It portrays a universe consisting of an infinite number of mutually independent spiritual atoms created to be from the beginning and for all time in constantly changing harmony with each other by a creator whose principle of operation was to choose always the best of all possible alternatives.

I shall try to show how this vast system, whose main details I will sketch later, arose from Leibniz's application to a basic logical problem of certain guiding conceptual principles of whose validity he had, for reasons we shall see, become completely convinced.

Asking himself why it is that some propositions are true and some are not, Leibniz wondered whether there was any general reason because of which any true proposition is true. He thought he had discovered the clue to the answer in a principle which seemed to him to underlie both the disciplines of mathematics and logic, with which he was thoroughly familiar, and also the theories currently gaining ground in the physics and, especially, the biology of the day.

He said in his correspondence with the French philosopher and divine, Arnauld, 'Regarding the subject of metaphysics, I claim to advance by geometrical demonstrations, positing only two primary truths; to wit, in the first place, the "principle of contradiction" . . . and, secondly, the "principle that nothing is without a reason'', or that every truth has its proof *a priori*, drawn from the meaning of the terms, although we have not always the power to attain this analysis.'[2] Underlying these two 'primary truths' was the general idea, familiar to him from his knowledge of logic and mathematics, that all the conclusions in these disciplines flow inexorably from and can, in a sense, be said to be 'contained in' their first premisses or axioms. Thus, Euclid's thirteen books of theorems can be deduced from his small set of five common notions, or axioms, and five postulates, together with a few principles of logic. By analysing out the results implicit in the axioms and postulates one never arrives at anything logically new, that is, anything not implied by them. No appeal is made to outside or empirical experience. The better a geometer one is the more clearly and easily one can see the theorems in the axioms; the less able the more one has to work them out. It was common in those days to make the distinction, in Galileo's words, between 'those inferences which our intellect apprehendeth with time' and those which 'the divine wisdom, like light, penetrateth in an instant'.[3] Later, in the nineteenth century, the mathematician Peano similarly showed how to derive the whole of the arithmetic of natural numbers from three primitive ideas and five primitive propositions. As a mathematician, Leibniz held that a formula could always be found to describe, explain and give a pattern for any set of points, however randomly they had been set down.[4]

Equally in logic, the conclusion of any particular argument is 'contained in' its premisses in the way that 'Socrates is mortal' is contained in the two premisses 'Socrates is a man' and 'All men are mortal.' This is clear in the Euler and Venn diagrams which illustrate the first premiss as a point (Socrates) within a circle (men) and the second premiss as that circle (men) within a second circle (mortals), from which it is clear that we thereby have the orginal point (Socrates) also within the second circle (mortals), that is, the illustration of the conclusion 'Socrates is mortal.' Similarly, Wittgenstein argued in the *Tractatus* that 'If p follows from q, the sense of "p" is contained in the sense of "q" '.[5] Further, the various particular principles of logic itself can be exhibited as derived from certain basic axioms, such as 'p implies p' and 'a is either b or not-b'.

Leibniz felt that his general principle that 'every truth has its proof *a priori*, drawn from the meaning of its terms' — a doctrine illustrated by mathematics and logic — had an anology in the recent investigations of the microscopists, Leuwenhoek and

Malpighi. These investigations seemed to support the doctrine of 'pre-formation', that is, the theory that a germ contains in miniature the whole of the adult plant or animal and that the 'form' or life principle of the full-grown plant or animal exists in the spermatozoon in a contracted state.[6]

Hence, he felt certain that, as he says, 'The present is big with the future, the future might be read in the past, the distant is expressed in the near. We might get to know the beauty of the universe in each soul, if we could unfold all that is enfolded in it and that is perceptibly developed only through time.'[7] Leibniz was delighted to be able to assert of the scientists' theories that 'these reasonings made *ā posteriori* and drawn from experience, are in perfect agreement with my principles deduced *a priori*'.[8]

Naturally, therefore, Leibniz accepts Plato's doctrine of reminiscence that we already know, at least potentially, all those things which are drawn out of us in the process of education and supposed learning.[9] We do not acquire them externally as Aristotle and Locke thought.[10]

Support for his general principles came mainly through Leibniz's acceptance of the current traditional Aristotelian formal logic which assumed that all propositions are of the subject – predicate form, that is, attribute some predicate or other to a subject, as in 'Socrates is mortal' or 'Plato is wise.' This traditional logic also held that what might at first sight seem not to be the attribution of a predicate to a subject, but the expression of a relation between two or more subjects, as in 'David is the father of Solomon' or 'A is near B', could be reduced to the subject – predicate form. Leibniz followed the tradition here too.[11] To admit relations in addition to subjects and their predicates would, he held, be to admit something extra and external; but 'There is', he insisted, 'no denomination so extrinsic as not to have an intrinsic one for its foundation.'[12] Taking the example 'David is the father of Solomon', he argues, 'I hold as regards relations, that paternity in David is one thing and filiation in Solomon is another but the relation to both is a merely mental thing, of which the modifications of singulars are the foundations.'[13]

Assuming, therefore, that all truths are expressible in the subject – predicate form, Leibniz argues that 'always, in every true proposition, necessary or contingent, universal or particular, the concept of the predicate is in a sense included in that of the subject; the predicate' [and he adds from elsewhere 'past, present and future'][14] 'is present in the subject'.[15] If the proposition is 'identical', the predicate is 'expressly comprised' in the subject, otherwise it must be compromised in it 'virtually'.[16] On the ground that there must be some basis for the connection between the terms of a true proposition, Leibniz arrives at what he calls 'my great principle', namely that such a basis must be found in the concepts of the subject and the predicate and, therefore, by the rule that the predicate is contained in the subject, such a basis lies in the subject.[17] From this follows the important consequence that, in the way that someone who knows the axioms of a system thereby, potentially at least, knows its theorems, so 'whoever understood perfectly the notion of the subject would also judge that the predicate belongs to it'.

Leibniz then relates this principle to the logical distinction between a species or kind of thing and what he calls an 'individual substance'. First, he claims that 'everything (whether genus, species or individual) has a complete concept . . . which contains or includes everything that can be said of that thing'.[18] But, whereas the concept — often called the idea, essence or nature — of a species, such as a sphere, contains only eternal or necessary truths, for example that all the points in its circumference are equidistant from the centre, the concept of an 'individual substance', such as the particular sphere on Archimedes' tomb, contains 'what is related to the existence of things and to time',[19] and its nature is 'to have a notion so complete that it is sufficient to comprise and to allow the deduction from it of all the predicates of the subject to which this notion is attributed'.[20] Similarly, we can distinguish between *an* Adam, i.e. a first man in a garden of pleasure from whose rib God makes a woman, of whom there can be an infinite number, and *the* individual Adam who lived in the Garden of Eden from whose rib Eve was made and to whom a host of particular things happened.[21] We can distinguish between what would and must be so in all possible worlds and what is and must be so in the actual world. X would, says Leibniz, only have been our Adam if he had had these particular attributes. Leibniz, therefore, following Aristotle, takes the individual substance as the most important kind of subject. It is a subject which can have many predicates but which cannot itself be the predicate of any other subject.[22] For example, whereas we can either predicate 'a sphere' of a particular object or predicate 'the perfect shape' of a sphere, we can only predicate 'wisdom' of Socrates but not 'Socrates' of anything.

Secondly, Leibniz applies his doctrine of the predicate being in the subject to individual substances. Thus, though 'the quality of King which belongs to Alexander the Great in abstraction from the subject is not sufficiently determined for an individual and does not include the other qualities of the same subject, nor all that the notion of this Prince comprises', for this is only the concept of a species; when we have the concept of an individual substance, 'God seeing the individual notion or *haecceity* of Alexander sees in it at the same time the foundation and reason of all the predicates that can be truly said of him, as for example that he would conquer Darius and Porus, even to the point of knowing from it *a priori* (and not by experience) whether he died a natural death or by poison, which we can only know by history. Also, when we consider well the connection of things, we can say that there are at all times in the soul of Alexander vestiges of all that has happened to him and the mark of all that will happen to him, and even traces of all that happens in the Universe . . .'[23] Leibniz is at pains to point out that, though this consequence is a paradox, nevertheless 'when I say that the individual concept of Adam contains everything that ever happened to him, I mean nothing other than what all philosophers mean when they say that the predicate is present in the subject of a true proposition'.[24] He emphasises that though what would happen to an individual substance necessarily follows from the nature of its concept — this is what explains why it has the particular attributes it has or ever will have — he is not saying that the having of each of these attributes, for example that Julius Caesar will cross the Rubicon, is itself necessary and its contrary contradictory, but only that it is certain and hypothetically necessary, given the nature of the subject, and the assumption that God has decreed that its course and that of the rest of the world will always be dictated by the principle of the best.[25] The concept of a particular man, for example Judas, will contain his future free acts.[26]

Often the doctrine that the predicate of a true proposition is contained in the subject is strengthened by an appeal to another doctrine about truth itself, namely that once true always true. So Leibniz says that if at any time anything can be truly said of a subject, for example that I graduated in Classics and Philosophy, then 'since the beginning of my existence it could truly be said of me that this . . . would happen to me'.[27]

It is from this idea of an individual substance, and the principle that it, like any subject, contains in it all its true predicates, that Leibniz arrives at the metaphysician's third stage, the development of a metaphysical system of supersensible entities. In one of his final letters to Arnauld he claims that 'in conceding me these beginnings [i.e. his idea of the concept of an individual substance] one is subsequently obliged to grant me all the rest'.[28] Such a development consists in finding something to play the role of individual substance and explaining the universe in terms of it. Leibniz takes his clues for this partly from what he thinks we are all most familiar with, namely ourselves — or our spirit (soul, mind) as he sometimes refers to it — partly from mathematics and partly from some conclusions he reached after an examination of the current Cartesian doctrines on physics.

As regards physics, the current Cartesian and atomistic doctrines, commonly called the 'mechanistic philosophy', maintained that matter was essentially extension, that is, had the so-called geometrical qualities of shape, weight, etc. and that all the changes in it were reducible to motion. As Descartes said 'in corporeal things, there is no other matter than that which can be divided, shaped and moved in all kinds of ways . . .'[29] The quantity of motion in the world, he held, is constant and is external to every body, which remains at rest until externally moved. Leibniz, who may have himself subscribed to these views in his youth, came to disagree on several counts.

First, '. . . the ideas of size, figure and motion are not so distinctive as is imagined, and they stand for something imaginary relative to our perceptions as do, although to a greater extent, the ideas of colour, heat, and the other similar qualities in regard to which we may doubt whether they are actually to be found in the nature of things outside of us . . .'. To which he added '. . . if there is no other principle of identity in bodies (they) would not subsist more than for a moment'.[30] Secondly, motion is not in a body, but is relative to bodies. Thus, he says, 'motion, if we regard only its exact and formal meaning, that is change of place, is not something entirely real, and when several bodies change their place reciprocally, it is not possible to determine by considering the bodies alone to which among them movement or repose is to be attributed . . .'[31] Thirdly, 'We cannot', argues Leibniz, 'draw from [Descartes' Extension] any activity or change. It expresses only a present state, and not at all the future and the past, which the notion of a substance ought to express.'[32] Nor, of course, will motion, which in Leibniz's view is relative, explain activity in a substance. All this leads him to his fourth objection, which is that Descartes had not properly distinguished between motion (in modern terms 'momentum') and force (in modern terms 'energy'). It is, holds Leibniz, force which is constant, which is presupposed by motion, and which is non-relative and is present in substance.[33] According to him, no body is ever in a state of absolute rest; there is always an infinitesimal movement. It is force, as in a taut bow, which gives substances the activity to enable them to pass from one state to another and thus to unfold the predicates present in them.[34] Force is, insists Leibniz, metaphysically necessary.[35]

But though, when concentrating on physics, Leibniz pictured individual substances as centres of force, unextended and indivisible, without spatial properties, he often treated them more ideally on the analogy of mathematical points. So he said, 'It is as in the case of a centre or point, in which, although it is perfectly simple, there is an infinite number of angles formed by the lines which meet it.'[36]

Finally, he advanced to a picture of substances as entities on the analogy of the human self. 'I am', he said, 'of opinion that reflection suffices for finding the idea of substance in ourselves, who are substances'[37] and, 'Since I conceive that other beings have also the right to say I or that it may be said for them, it is by this means that I conceive what is called substance in general.'[38] He pictured, as we shall see, the qualities of his basic metaphysical individual substances on the analogy of perception and their power of change on the analogy of desire.[39] As regards one's self, he argues that the only explanation of the feeling that, despite all the changes in my physical and psychological parts over the years, *I* have remained the same, is that all these past and present attributes are predicates of the same subject, the I.[40] A connection between Leibniz's mathematical idea of substance as a point and his psychological idea of substance as a mind is made in his view that a mind is itself a point.[41]

Nor did he confine this analogy of substance and self (or 'soul', as he often referred to it) to what are normally called living creatures. Just as he had argued earlier that there is a force and, hence, movement in what is apparently at rest, so he held that there is life in what is apparently inanimate. This was a view which seemed to him to be made more plausible by the researches of the microscopists of the day. Their discoveries convinced him that 'there is almost an infinite number of little animals in the smallest drop of water' and that 'matter is everywhere full of animate substances'.[42]

The centre-piece of Leibniz's system of metaphysics is, therefore, the individual substance or, as he also calls it, 'the substantial form'. In later writings he calls it the *monad* and entitles his book about it the *Monadology*. To this he applies the logical principles which I have already mentioned as well as several others which I shall discuss later.

He calls the monads the 'real atoms of matter . . . the elements of things'. They are simple and without parts.[43] Since they have no parts, they cannot arise or perish gradually, but only by instantaneous creation or annihilation.[44] For the same reason, 'there is no way of explaining how a monad can be altered in quality or internally changed by any other creative thing . . . the Monads have no windows through which anything could come in or go out'.[45] Yet they 'must have some qualities, otherwise they would not even be existing things . . . and we could not explain how things in the world are distinguishable from each other'.[46]

To explain this, Leibniz first has recourse to the two logical principles mentioned in the quotation given in my opening paragraphs, each of which he thinks follows from his main idea that the reason why the predicate is true of the subject is to be found in the nature of the substances. The two principles are that of *Contradiction* 'in virtue of which we judge *false* that which involves a contradiction, and *true* that which is opposed or contradictory to the false' and that of *Sufficient Reason* 'in virtue of which we hold that there can be no fact real or existing, no statement true, unless there be a sufficient reason, why it should be so and not otherwise', although, he adds, 'these reasons usually cannot be known to us'.[47] The former principle applies to everything possible, the latter to what is not merely possible, but actual. Thus, the principle of contradiction will explain why any triangle has its exterior angle equal to the sum of its interior opposites, but the principle of sufficient reason why this particular triangle is, for example, an equilateral triangle with seven-inch sides. If we seek the reason for something actual, we trace it back, perhaps through an infinite series of causes, to various concepts.[48] When we seek the reason for the existence of these concepts, for example why the notion of the historical Adam rather than another possible Adam, the answer must be that they are chosen from all those possible on the principle that the actual is determined by the idea of the best. Equally, though the concept of a particular subject explains its predicates, that concept must be explained by reference to something beyond it, namely by the whole set of composite concepts of which what exists are the best.

In either case, we ultimately come to the final cause or explanation of what is actual, which, thinks Leibniz, must be the goodness of God. God, being all good and all wise, necessarily chooses the best.[49] The only reason why this world, rather than any of the infinitely many alternatively possible worlds, exists, is that this is the best of all possible worlds. Although Leibniz seems occasionally to have used the name 'principle of sufficient reason' as equivalent to the name 'principle of the best',[50] his main view is that ultimately the sufficient reason for anything contingent is that it is in conformity with the principle of the best.[51] The former principle is logical, the latter theistic.

Since, as we have seen, the monads have no parts and can, therefore, suffer no external change, the quality which each monad has in order to differentiate it from others, must, Leibniz insists, be internal. This is the force which, we saw, substance has to have to enable it to unfold its predicates over time. The activity of making a passage from one change to another Leibniz calls 'Appetition' (from 'appetite' or desire) and the changes themselves he calls 'Perceptions' because he thinks that each consists in a representation of the whole universe from its point of view analogous to the way in which, for example, our mind changes as it perceives different things. 'Each monad', he says, 'is a living mirror, or a mirror endowed with inner activity, representative of the universe according to its point of view.'[52] Though Leibniz often uses a pictorial metaphor for his idea of each monad 'representing' or 'expressing' every other, he holds that strictly it is analogous to the logical or mathematical idea of 'a constant rational law by which particulars in the one can be referred to corresponding particulars in the other', as when an ellipse 'expresses' a circle.[53] Not only do monads individually differ from each other in having different perceptions, that is, different points of view, they also differ in kind by having different degrees of clarity in these perceptions. Leibniz in fact grades them into 'bare monads', which have unconscious perceptions, 'souls', which have conscious perception and memory, and 'spirits', which have self-consciousness and reason.

Leibniz fills out the details of his metaphysical system by recourse to a further two logical principles, namely the 'Identity of Indiscernibles' and the 'Law of Continuity'. According to the 'Identity of Indiscernibles', 'there are not in nature two indiscernible real absolute beings'[54] or 'no two substances are completely similar, or differ *solo numero*'.[55] For the principle, which Leibniz calls 'metaphysically necessary', he gives at least four arguments, two of which seem to make it contingent and two necessary. Of the two which seem to make it contingent, the first is that to suppose two indiscernibles to exist is contrary to the principle of Sufficient Reason, for it would be to admit something without a reason.[56] If there were indiscernibles, God would have had no reason for choosing one rather than the other.[57] The second consists in an appeal to experience, whether to the impossibility of anyone's actually finding, for example, two identical leaves or to the discovery by the microscopists that two drops of water looking identical to the naked eye can be seen to be different under the microscope.[58] Of the two arguments which seem to make it necessary, one is that it follows from his principle that the predicate is contained in the subject;[59] while another is that if A were other than A', then A', which is allegedly indiscernible from A, would also have to be other than A', that is, other than itself — which is absurd. Using the principle of indiscernibles, Leibniz concludes that the world will be composed of a series of substances, each different from another and mirroring the world from a different angle, and, therefore, having different perceptions.

Leibniz's assumption of the Law of Continuity was possibly due to his interest in mathematics and the infinitesimal calculus. In many mathematical series, for example the series of fractions between nought and one, the items form a continuum. In opposition to the atomistic physics of his day, he believed also that in space 'nature never makes leaps'.[60] Hence, he concludes of the Law of Continuity, 'it takes its origin from the infinite, it is absolutely necessary in Geometry, but it succeeds also in Physics, because the sovereign wisdom, which is the source of all things, acts as a perfect geometer . . .'[61] It gives, he said, 'as much variety as possible, along with the greatest possible order'.[62]

Combining both principles, we get a picture of a universe in which each monad reflects the whole from one angle which differs to the very slightest extent from the representation given by another monad, so that the whole of nature is the infinite system of monads representing the universe from every possible point of view. As Russell summed it up, all created substances form a series in which every possible intermediate position is filled once (by the Law of Continuity) and only once (by the Law of Identity of Indiscernibles).[63]

Such a system, allied to the continual change on which Leibniz, as we saw, insisted, gives rise to an apparent difficulty. A change in one monad will necessitate a change in every other, since they only differ infinitesimally and we must not allow the existence of two indiscernibles. There must, therefore, be a corresponding change in every other monad. Since, however, monads cannot be influenced from outside, and, therefore, not by each other — they have, as we saw, no windows — how will these correlative changes take place? 'To act', Leibniz argued, only means to have distinct perceptions and to be 'acted on' only means to have confused perceptions.[64] Leibniz's solution, of which he was inordinately proud, is the doctrine of 'Pre-Established Harmony'. According to this, monads do not influence each other, but there is a pre-arranged plan by which a change in one monad is accompanied by a corresponding change in every other. The 'influence of one monad upon another', he says, 'is only ideal'.[65] In summary, 'the nature of every simple substance, soul or true monad, being such that its following state is a consequence of the preceding one; here now is the cause of the harmony found out. For God needs only to make a simple substance become once and at the beginning a representation of the Universe, according to its point of view; since from thence alone it follows that it will be so perpetually; and that all simple substances will always have a harmony among themselves, because they all represent the same universe.'[66] Leibniz compares this idea to, for example, two clocks set to keep perfect and perpetual time with each other or to 'several people agreeing to meet at a certain point on a certain day'.[67]

It is clear, I think, from this sketch of his metaphysical system that Leibniz, like Plato, Aristotle and Berkeley, starts with certain conceptual problems — of which the most important for him is to account for the truth of a proposition — for which he advances certain solutions, themselves depending on certain assumptions and principles, which seem to him to necessitate the positing of certain entities, that is, the monads, and a certain region for them to inhabit, which are metaphysical in the sense of being beyond what common sense and science either suppose or could encounter. Because many readers will, no doubt, think that for all its logical beauty this abstract universe of monads is rather implausible, it is worth examining the principles and assumptions which, I have argued, led Leibniz to think it necessary.

Using a geometrical or hypothetico-deductive procedure, Leibniz explains the world in terms of a set of basic individual substances, whose existence is to be proved by the principle that whatever actually exists can only exist because it is the best of all possible alternatives, and a set of consequences of these substances, whose existence is proved by the principle that 'every truth has its proof *a priori*, drawn from the meaning of the terms'.

Both these principles are ultimately exemplifications of the Principle of Sufficient Reason, namely that nothing ever happens without a reason. For this principle Leibniz really has no other grounds than, first, the pre-disposition of a very logical mind — exemplified either by the story of Buridan's ass which died of starvation because it could see no good reason for choosing between two equally succulent and equidistant bundles of hay[68] or by Leibniz's claim that Archimedes' work on the equilibrium of a balance used the principle when assuming that 'there is no reason why one side rather than the other should fall'[69] — and, secondly, the religious faith that the universe was created by an equally logical God.[70] Leibniz was convinced that logically any phenomenon, however irregular it looked, really exhibited an order which explained it, just as a scattered set of points in mathematics can be ordered and explained by a formula.[71]

Leibniz's belief that the sufficient reason for what actually exists is the operation of the principle of the best rests on his assumption of the existence of a creator who, by definition, is all good, all wise and all powerful and, therefore, always chooses the best. But, whatever Leibniz may have thought, neither the existence of such a creator nor his choice of the best is something which is necessarily so.

Leibniz's acceptance of the principle that the truth of every proposition depends on the meaning of its terms is open to at least three criticisms. First, he seems to have applied it exclusively to one type of proposition, namely, the subject–predicate proposition, because he accepted, at least in the case of individual substances, the Aristotelian tradition which reduced all propositions to this kind. An objection to this is that modern logic, for reasons we need not go into, has shown that various kinds of proposition, for example relational and existential, cannot be reduced to this form.[72] For example, the argument that if A is greater than B and B is greater than C, therefore A is greater than C, would have no common term if it were posed as a syllogism with 'A is greater than B' reduced to 'A is a-greater-than-B'. Nor does, for example, 'There is only one even prime number' attribute a predicate to a subject.

Secondly, the principle that the truth of every proposition depends on the meaning of its terms really assimilates contingent truths to necessary truths, despite Leibniz's attempts to argue that he has preserved the distinction. Certainly, he does see the distinction between what he calls truths 'necessary in themselves', that is, those whose denial is self-contradictory, such as 'A triangle has three sides', and truths which are 'hypothetically necessary', that is, those which follow from other truths, as when 'This figure has three sides' is deduced from 'This figure is a triangle' and 'A triangle has three sides.' He also sees the differences between explaining, by the law of contradiction, why a triangle has three sides, and explaining, allegedly by the law of sufficient reason, why this particular triangle is equilateral, that is, between what happens in all possible worlds and what happens in this particular world. He nevertheless insists that the explanation of the latter is, as much as the former, due to the meaning of its subject, that is, what he calls the concept of the subject, even though the latter, but not the former, may have to be traced back through an infinite series of predicates involved in its subject and its relations to everything else in the universe; a series which approaches asymptotically to necessity and which, because of its infinity, can be known only to God. Leibniz's view, moreover, appeals to more than the meaning of the terms in the proposition, even in an infinite analysis, for it becomes ultimately an appeal to the necessary choice by God of substances with certain characteristics rather than to the necessary characteristics of the concepts of the substances chosen. While necessary truths are 'founded on ideas', contingent truths are, he admits, 'founded on the decrees of God'.[73] 'The innocent are not eternally damned' is said to be hypothetically, but not absolutely, necessary, for though it does not have a self-contradictory denial, yet it would not be possible for God to allow its denial to be true.[74] In a sense, Leibniz is assimilating the way in which someone, for example God, can see as certain the contingent future conduct of a man from knowledge of his character and situation and the way in which someone can deduce as necessary the logical consequences of a concept from its nature. Added to this is a tendency on Leibniz's part, induced perhaps by the analogy from biology, to take too literally the metaphor present in the idea of a predicate being logically contained in its subject.

Thirdly, Leibniz's attempt to bring contingent truths under his principle that the truth of every proposition depends on the meaning of its terms rests on his appealing to the principle of the best. For God's choice of certain characteristics in the concepts of the initial individual substances, which determined their futures, itself proceeded on the principle of the best.[75] An *a priori* proof of the truth of a contingent proposition has to draw not only on the meaning of its terms but also on the assumption that all which happens is for the best. The necessity of contingent propositions is only hypothetical, the hypothesis being that what exists is God's choice of the best.[76]

Equally dubious are the two logical-mathematical-physical principles, those of the Identity of Indiscernibles and of Continuity, to which Leibniz gave a metaphysical use. These principles are certainly not necessarily true and their empirical truth has been disputed. Modern physics — like, indeed, the contemporary atomism of Leibniz's own day — by the introduction of the notion of quanta which can jump from one position to another without going through any intermediate stages, disagrees with the law of continuity. Kant objected that there could be two indiscernibly different drops of water, and modern chemistry and physics allow the idea of particles, such as photons, which are different from each other and yet indistinguishable.[77] It could also be argued without self-contradiction that two souls — with which Leibniz compared his monads — could be identical by having exactly similar perceptions.[78] The important point is that, whether or not these principles are true, they are empirical principles, which may or may not be applicable to mathematics and to physical and chemical phenomena. They are not *a priori* constraints on the nature of the universe.

Because Leibniz's metaphysical system is a conceptual, not an empirical, construction, its foundations merit logical, not experiential testing; a testing which, I think, it does not pass.

Notes

1. The abbreviations used in referring to Leibniz's works are: G. = C. J. Gerhardt (ed.) (1875–90), *Die philosophischen Schriften von G. W. Leibniz*; Couturat = L. Couturat (1903), *Opuscules et fragments inédits de Leibniz*; Corr = H. T. Mason and G. H. R. Parkinson (1967), *The Leibniz-Arnauld Correspondence*.

2. G. II. 62.

3. *Two Great Systems*, p. 86.

4. *Discourse*, VI.

5. *Tractatus*, sect. 122.

6. *Principles of Nature and of Grace* (henceforth *PNG*), sect. 6; Couturat, pp. 16, 20, 26; *Monadology*, sects. 66–7, 74.

7. *PNG*, sect. 13.

8. *Monadology*, sect. 76; *PNG*, sect. 6.
9. *Discourse*, XXVI.
10. *Discourse*, XXVII.
11. H. Ishiguro (1972), *Leibniz's Philosophy of Logic and Language*, Duckworth, Chapters 5 and 6, opposes much of the traditional interpretation of Leibniz's views on relations; cf. D. Wong (1980), 'Leibniz's theory of relations', *Philosophical Review*, 89, pp. 241–56.
12. G. II. 240.
13. G. II. 486.
14. *Corr* 50.
15. *Corr* 63.
16. *Discourse*, VIII.
17. *Corr* 64.
18. *Corr* 73.
19. *Corr* 41, 44.
20. *Discourse*, VIII.
21. *Corr* 45, 46.
22. *Discourse*, VIII.
23. *Discourse*, VIII; *Corr* 42.
24. *Corr* 47.
25. *Discourse*, XIII.
26. *Discourse*, XXX.
27. *Corr* 47.
28. *Corr* 162.
29. *Principia* II. 64.
30. *Discourse*, XII.
31. *Discourse*, XVIII.
32. G. II. 72.
33. *Discourse*, XVII, XVIII.
34. G. IV. 469.
35. G. II. 169.
36. *PNG*, sect. 2.
37. G. V. 96; III. 247.
38. G. IV. 493.
39. *Monadology*, sect. 19.
40. G. II. 43.
41. L. E. Loemker (ed.) (1956), *Leibniz: Philosophical Papers and Letters*, Chicago University Press, p. 149.
42. *Corr* 156, 151, 124.
43. *Monadology*, sects. 3, 1.
44. *Monadology*, sect. 4.
45. *Monadology*, sect. 7.
46. *Monadology*, sect. 8.
47. *Monadology*, sects. 31, 32.
48. *Monadology*, sects. 36–9.
49. *Monadology*, sect. 55.
50. e.g. G. VII. 301, 309.
51. *Monadology*, sect. 46.
52. G. VI. 599.
53. Couturat, p. 15.

54. G. VII. 393.
55. G. IV. 433.
56. G. VII. 394–5.
57. G. VII. 407.
58. G. VII. 563; *New Essays on the Human Understanding*, 2. 27. 3.
59. *Discourse*, IX.
60. G. V. 49.
61. G. III. 52.
62. *Monadology*, sects. 58–60.
63. B. Russell (1900, 1937), *A Critical Exposition of the Philosophy of Leibniz*, Allen and Unwin, p. 54.
64. *Monadology*, sects. 49–50.
65. *Monadology*, sect. 51.
66. G. VII. 412.
67. *Discourse*, XIV.
68. *Theodicy*, sect. 49.
69. G. VII. 356.
70. *Discourse*, I, IV, V, XIV.
71. *Discourse*, VI.
72. Ishiguro, Chapter 5 and 6, doubts that Leibniz tries to reduce relational to monadic predicates.
73. *Discourse*, XIII.
74. G.Grua, *Textes inédits* . . . . (1948), p. 300.
75. G. IV. 438–9.
76. Grua, p. 301.
77. Kant, *The Critique of Pure Reason*, A263/B319; cf. A. Cortes (1976) 'Leibniz's principle of the identity of indiscernibles: a false principle', *Philosophy of Science* 43, 491–505.
78. P. F. Strawson (1959), *Individuals*, Methuen and Co. Ltd, p. 125.

5

Bradley

Apart from Berkeley, who, ironical though it may seem, said his aim was 'to be eternally banishing metaphysics and recalling men to common sense', English-speaking philosophers have generally eschewed metaphysics and been noted for their down-to-earth, pragmatic approach to their subject. The one great exception to this is the nineteenth-century Oxford philosopher, F. H. Bradley, whose *Appearance and Reality* (1893), subtitled 'A metaphysical essay', is, perhaps, the last classical example of the grand traditional style of metaphysics. It is interesting that his metaphysics, as we shall see, was, like Berkeley's, a form of Idealism, that is, the theory which holds that only what is in some way or another experienced exists. As Berkeley claimed that 'to be is to be perceived', so Bradley insisted that 'anything in no sense felt or experienced, becomes to me quite unmeaning'.[1]

Though Bradley was very modest about the amount of success any attempt to discover metaphysical knowledge could have, he contended, as Kant with even more scepticism about such success had contended before him, that a desire to seek such knowledge is an instinctive part of human nature.[2] 'All of us,' Bradley said, 'are led beyond the region of ordinary facts. Some in one way and some in others, we seem to touch and have communion with what is beyond the visible world.'[3]

Bradley defined metaphysics, in the Aristotelian manner commonly reiterated in the many nineteenth- and early twentieth-century textbooks on the subject, as 'the study of first principles or ultimate truths, or again the effort to comprehend the universe, not simply piecemeal or by fragments, but somehow as a whole'.[4] For him such a comprehension of the universe became, for reasons we shall see, 'an attempt to know reality as against mere appearance',[5] an attempt 'to survey the field of appearances, to measure each by the idea of perfect individuality, and to arrange them in an order and in a system of reality and merit',[6] and 'to show how the world, physical and spiritual, realises by various stages and degrees the one absolute principle'.[7]

Like Plato, Berkeley and Leibniz, Bradley approaches his task armed with a chief principle of whose validity he is completely convinced. 'Thinking,' he says, 'means the acceptance of a certain standard, and that standard, in any case, is an assumption as to the character of reality'.[8] 'Ultimate reality,' he says, 'is such that it does not contradict itself; here is an absolute criterion. And it is proved absolute by the fact that, either in endeavouring to deny it, or even in attempting to doubt it, we tacitly assume its validity.'[9] Its great virtue is that it 'satisfies the intellect'.[10] This allows him to assert that it is logically impossible to doubt his conclusions.[11] The converse of this principle, which is what he usually uses, is that the self-contradictory cannot be real, but must be only appearance.[12]

He then proceeds to apply this 'absolute criterion' in its negative form to our various ordinary ideas about the world, that is, our various ways of regarding reality, and finds that it proves them all to be self-contradictory and, therefore, not real, but only 'appearance'. Such ideas include those of qualities and relations, space and time, primary and secondary qualities, substance, self, cause, change, motion and nature. As an illustration of how and why Bradley criticises these ideas, whose practical use and force he does not deny but whose metaphysical, and therefore ultimate, validity he calls in question, we can look, primarily, at the ideas of qualities and relations, whose self-contradictory nature and, therefore, whose 'theoretical unintelligibility' he particularly emphasises.

The conclusion of Chapter 3 is that 'Relation presupposes quality, and quality relation. Each can be something neither with, nor apart from, the other; and the vicious circle in which they turn is not the truth about reality.'[13] To establish this conclusion he takes in turn the four possibilities, namely that qualities are impossible either (i) without relations or (ii) with relations; and that relations are impossible either (iii) without qualities or (iv) with qualities. He tries to show that each of these is true and, therefore, the ideas of quality and relation are inconsistent. The proof of (i) is that the very existence of qualities implies some difference between them; but difference is a relation. On the other hand, the proof of its opposite (ii) is that qualities which are related must have a double character, both being that which has the relations and being what it is because of the relations. But such a diversity within a quality implies a new relation between the diverse elements, *ad infinitum*. Similarly, the proof of (iii) is that the very existence of relations implies some qualities to relate. On the other hand, the proof of the opposite (iv) is that if the relations are to be relevant to the qualities they must be related to them by a new relation and this by another *ad infinitum*. Hence, any way of thinking which uses the ideas of qualities and relations, however necessary for practical purposes, must give only appearance and not reality.

A similar examination aims to prove that space and time neither 'have nor belong to reality' by showing that each contradicts itself. For example, space, on the one hand, cannot be a mere relation since, unlike a relation, it is made up of parts which are themselves spaces. On the other hand, it is nothing but a relation, namely a collection or relation of spaces which are themselves relations of spaces *ad infinitum*. Again, space must be limited and yet without a space outside it; and this is a self-contradiction.

In successive chapters, Bradley argues that there are also self-contradictions or self-discrepancies in our ideas of thing and self, of cause, change and motion, of nature, God and man. The various regions or aspects of experience, such as pleasure and pain, perception and theory, aesthetic attitudes, will and thought, are all alleged to be in themselves discrepant and lacking in harmony.[14] Each has inconsistently both to embrace and yet be distinct from another. Therefore, none can as such be real, but only appearance.[15] Bradley is in fact attacking the piecemeal, pluralistic approach to the world and our knowledge of it which is characteristic of everyday common sense thinking. In his *Logic* he had argued that an apparently categorical judgement, for example that A is B, is really hypothetical, for example that if A is p and q, and . . . then it is B. For him reality is whole and indivisible and our knowledge of it a seamless garment. The attempts of common sense to view it as fragmentary, to carve it up, to distinguish relations within it, are argued to be full of inconsistencies.

We need not dwell on his specific arguments, which have not succeeded in convincing many scholars. Apart from a general suspicion about any arguments based on a logical dilemma, such as Kant used in his antinomies of reason, specific objections can be made to Bradley's individual proofs. Scorn has rightly been poured on his 'proof' that a relation between two qualities needs another relation to relate this relation to the qualities, as if — an analogy Bradley himself draws[16] — two links in a chain could only be related by a third link, and so *ad infinitum*.[17] Again, a modern physicist would probably meet his dilemma about space by invoking the notion of a space which is finite but unbounded. More generally, Bradley's wide view of self-contradiction assimilates not merely the contrary and the discrepant, but even the different.[18] Nor is there any reason to accept his theses that every fact depends on every other fact and that our knowledge of every fact depends on our knowledge of every other.

Though Bradley argues that all these ideas, because inconsistent and unintelligible, can only give us appearance and not reality, he emphasises that these appearances certainly exist.[19] 'Nothing,' he stresses, 'is actually removed from existence by being labelled "appearance".'[20] Furthermore, 'whatever exists must belong to reality'.[21] He sums up the results of the first and negative part of his enquiry thus: 'Everything so far, which we have seen, has turned out to be appearance. It is that which, taken as it stands, proves inconsistent with itself, and for this reason cannot be true of the real. But to deny its existence or to divorce it from reality is out of the question . . . And reality, set on one side and apart from all appearance, would assuredly be nothing. Hence, what is certain is that, in some way, these inseparables are joined.'[22] The task of Part II of his book is to see how.

It is clear from this that Bradley does not mean by calling anything, for example time, space, relations, etc., 'unreal' that it does not exist. He uses 'real' in an abnormal way to mean what is rational, self-consistent, coherent, harmonious and all-inclusive. Anything which falls short of this is 'unreal' and 'mere appearance'. His use of 'appearance' for anything which, on his own criterion, is 'not real' is also abnormal, though we can, perhaps, understand it if we bear in mind such an everyday phrase as 'It's not really so and so, it only appears to be.' Again, whenever in his *Logic* he denies some apparently obvious view, he phrases his denial in terms of what is 'really' so, for example all subject – predicate propositions are really identity-statements. It is because things can fall short of meeting these criteria to different extents that he introduces his well-known doctrine of degrees of truth or reality. For him, nothing is entirely false or unreal, just as nothing, except the whole, is entirely true or real.[23] The nearer anything gets to being coherent with everything, the nearer it becomes to being all-inclusive and harmonious and, therefore, to being true or real.[24] All appearances have degrees of reality; but some are more real than others.[25]

The other side of the coin that the self-contradictory is only appearance is that 'ultimate reality is such that it does not contradict itself'.[26] A thing is real, asserts Bradley, so far as its opposite is impossible.[27] Appearance cannot be reality, but, since appearances certainly exist, they must be related in some way to the real. The answer is that it is the character of the real to contain appearances and differences in a harmonious, inclusive, unified form.[28] Reality is present among its appearances in different degrees and with different values.[29] Bradley insists that reality — or the Absolute, or even the Whole, as he frequently calls it — is nothing apart from appearances; it 'appears in its appearances and they are its revelation'.[30] How this harmonising and transforming of discrepant elements takes place, Bradley confesses he does not know, but insists that it is possible and necessary and therefore is so. He in fact has recourse to a host of metaphors, for example appearances 'blend', 'are transmuted', 're-arranged', 'transcended', 'laid to rest', 'go home', etc., in the Absolute. Different properties, in themselves contradictory, can be combined if there is in their subject some internal ground of connection. By widening the subject — and Bradley thinks that it is reality which is the ultimate subject of all predicates — one can find a basis of union for all different properties; so that 'in the end nothing is contrary nor is there any insoluble contradiction'.[31] The existence of appearances is conditional on something else; that of reality only on itself. He repudiates as inconsistent the Kantian view that we know there are two distinct realms, that of knowable phenomena or appearances and that of unknowable things in themselves.[32] Reality is in some way nothing but its appearances.

Reality, as well as being rational, coherent, all-inclusive, harmonious, non-contradictory and containing all its appearances, must be supra-rational and, therefore, one.[33] It must be self-contained and self-consistent, for if it were externally determined or qualified by something else, we would have a conjunction of itself and this other; but it is such an external or bare conjunction which Bradley argues constitutes a self-contradiction, for it tries to unite what is separate. Unification needs an internal relation between the parts; and this is only possible in the whole. Therefore, only the whole is real.[34]

In matter or contents, reality, argues Bradley, is to be identified with experience, whether this be feeling, perception, thought or volition,[35] because experience gives us what we could not find in appearances, that is, an awareness of a non-relational whole or diversity in unity.[36] He is an 'idealist' because he holds that 'anything, in no sense felt or experienced, becomes to me quite unmeaning'.[37] There is for him no 'separation of feeling from the felt, or of the desired from desire, or what is thought from thinking'.[38] Nor is there any division, though of course there is a distinction, between the subject of experience and the object of it, between the experiencer and the experienced; all are parts of one whole.

From the necessary harmony of reality, or the Absolute, Bradley thinks it follows that it cannot contain any imperfection, which would import discord.[39] Hence, in it there will be a balance of pleasure over pain, for pain involves conflict and discord.[40] Moreover, such a reality, he contends, must satisfy our main, though not all, our wants, for example 'for truth and life, and for beauty and goodness'.[41]

For all its abstract and formal reasoning and results, Bradley's metaphysics starts, like those of the other metaphysicians we have considered, from what is given in ordinary experience, thought and language. Nor does he wish in any way to denigrate it for all practical purposes. He stresses that it is no part of the task of metaphysics to criticise or interfere with either the views of ordinary thinking or, much less, those of science. But, again like his predecessors, he finds that reflection on some of the problems involved in the ideas by which everyday and scientific thinking — and also aesthetic, religious and other modes of experience — approach the world, leads to a belief in something beyond and different from what is accepted by such thinking. We reach a 'knowledge of the Absolute, positive knowledge built on experience, and inevitable when we try to think consistently'.[42]

In such reflection he uses, as did in their different ways his predecessors, a principle, 'an absolute criterion', of whose validity he is convinced beyond all doubt. For Bradley this was the principle that reality does not contradict itself. Used negatively this showed that the ideas with which ordinary thinking approaches the world — such ideas as qualities and relations, space and time, thing and self, cause and change — breed self-contradictions and can, therefore, give us, not reality, but only appearance. Used positively the principle logically entails that, however impossible it may be for us to know the details of how this is accomplished, reality must be a coherent, self-consistent, all-inclusive unity in which all these appearances are somehow included, transmuted and transcended.[43] Though this Absolute is no more than its appearances and is, therefore, not a transcendent entity in the manner of Plato's Forms, Aristotle's Unmoved Mover, Berkeley's God or Leibniz's Monads, yet it is meta-empirical, not verifiable by the senses, reached by conceptual argument, beyond our personal experiences, though itself equal to experience; something in which appearances lose their special natures and are transcended.[44]

Bradley, perhaps the last of the great metaphysicians, exhibits, I suggest, an analogous pattern of thinking to Plato, perhaps the first.

Notes

1. 128. All references are to *Appearance and Reality*, 9th impression (Oxford, 1930).
2. 3–5.
3. 5.
4. 1, 398.
5. 1.
6. 433, 403.
7. 318.
8. 135, 454.
9. 120, 459–60, 463.
10. 491, 134–6, 502, 509.
11. 459.
12. 120, 167.
13. 21.
14. 405–12.
15. Chapter XXVI.
16. 33.
17. Cf. C. D. Broad (1933), *Examination of McTaggart's Philosophy*, I, 85.
18. 500 ff.
19. 65.
20. 12.
21. 114.
22. 114–15, 119.
23. 431–2, Chapter XXIV.
24. 322, 338–9.
25. 431, 433, 440.
26. 120–4.
27. 477.
28. 123, 127, 414.
29. 488.
30. 489, cf. 113, 213, 404, 431.

31. 505.
32. Chapter XII.
33. 104, 124–6.
34. 505–10.
35. 127–30, 405, 463–6.
36. 141, 494.
37. 128.
38. 129.
39. 137.
40. 138, 473.
41. 140, 440.
42. 142.
43. 119.
44. 172.

Part II
Rejections of Metaphysics

In the history of western thought there have been two major attempts to dismiss traditional metaphysics, not piecemeal because of specific errors in the reasoning of individual metaphysicians, such as those I have discussed in Plato, Aristotle, Berkeley, Leibniz and Bradley, but root and branch because of alleged misunderstanding of the nature of the whole enterprise. The first of these attempts was made by Kant in the eighteenth century; the second by the Logical Positivists in the twentieth century.

Kant argued that a misunderstanding of the nature of our concepts, especially those which are logically prior to experience, led metaphysicians to the illusory belief that one could by these have knowledge beyond experience. The Logical Positivists argued that a misunderstanding of the nature of meaning had led metaphysicians falsely to suppose that anything could be even sensibly said, let alone known, about anything beyond experience. Kant's argument, therefore, was based on a consideration of and a theory about the place which *a priori* concepts play in our reasoning, while the Logical Positivists' argument rested on a consideration of and a theory about our concept of meaning. For both the attack on traditional metaphysics was the negative side of positive views about knowledge and meaning respectively, deduced from an analysis of concepts. Both contrasted the legitimacy of reasoning which is related to experience with the illegitimacy of that which is imagined to relate to what lies beyond experience, though for Kant this illegitimacy was confined only to supposed knowledge of the transcendent, whereas for the Logical Positivists it encompassed even its intelligibility. Whereas the Logical Positivists rejected metaphysics *tout court*, Kant distinguished between an illegitimate and a legitimate form of it.

The more recent and not so much trumpeted rejection of metaphysics by Wittgenstein contained particular elements of both Kant's attack and that of the Logical Positivists. His case rested, especially in his earlier phase, partly, like Kant's, on a thesis about the limits of thought and partly, like the Logical Positivists', on a theory of meaning. More generally, just as the classical metaphysicians, on the one hand, and Kant and the Logical Positivists on the other, all advanced views which arose from their different theses about our most basic concepts, so Wittgenstein argued throughout his writings that it was a misunderstanding not only of individual key concepts — misunderstandings which gave rise to particular metaphysical fallacies — but of the very nature of a conceptual, as contrasted with a scientific, investigation, a 'grammatical' as opposed to an 'empirical' study, which is a source of traditional metaphysics.

In this Part I shall try to make quite clear what exactly were the grounds for the rejection of metaphysics by Kant, the Logical Positivists and Wittgenstein, and what criticisms can be and have been made of these grounds. After a consideration in the next Part of various attempts, not so much to criticise these grounds, but to bypass them, especially those of the Verificationists, as irrelevant, the final chapter will attempt to evaluate the methods of metaphysics.

6

Kant

The eighteenth-century German philosopher Kant is often, and I think correctly, supposed to have considered his central problem in philosophy to have been that of the status of metaphysics. The title of the book he wrote shortly after his great work *The Critique of Pure Reason*, and which was intended to provide a more readable and clear exposition of that work's thesis, was in fact *Prolegomena to any Future Metaphysics*. He followed Aristotle in characterising metaphysics as the study of 'whatever is insofar as it is', and kept close to its traditional etymological interpretation in allowing that its material was of what is 'beyond experience'. Because its subject matter is the properties of things in general, as contrasted with the particular subject matter of the particular sciences, it is 'a purely speculative science . . . entirely independent of the teachings of experience'.

Doubt was, however, thrown on the very possibility of such a science by its lack of success or of general acceptance, and by the destructive arguments of Kant's predecessor Hume. Therefore, the problem that Kant set himself was to show that this lack of success was due to a failure to distinguish between a legitimate and an illegitimate form of the subject, from which the past failure could be explained and a future genuine metaphysics set up. The clue to this distinction lay in the exact relation to experience of the two forms of metaphysics.

The past illegitimate form of metaphysics Kant classified as 'dogmatic' or 'transcendent', that is, going beyond experience, and his new legitimate form as 'critical' or 'transcendental', that is, independent of experience because giving the conditions in which such experience is possible. The former he compared to astrology and alchemy, the latter to astronomy and chemistry. The former was that which we have seen practised by Plato, Berkeley and Leibniz. Kant confessed he had himself followed it until awoken, in a way we shall see later, from his 'dogmatic slumber' by Hume's analysis of *cause*.

The difference between the two and, hence, the clue to the possibility of the second, that is, a new and reformed metaphysics to replace the old, lay, according to Kant, in their pretensions, their method and their subject matter. Though both, as befitted metaphysics, properly claimed to study *a priori* concepts, that is, concepts both logically and temporally prior to experience, rather than either the applied material of mathematics or the empirical material of science, dogmatic metaphysics makes the mistake of supposing that it could legitimately acquire knowledge from these concepts free from any consideration of their applicability to experience and, hence, supposedly in their connection with objects beyond any possible experience. Granted that connections between concepts are independent of experience, so that metaphysics is not an empirical subject, we must not, thinks Kant, fall into the opposite idea that they can provide knowledge on their own. Metaphysical judgements can be verified only by a recourse to the conditions for obtaining knowledge of things in general.

Kant's whole critical philosophy, therefore, consisted in an analysis of the general nature of our concepts, whose main feature was an account of the relation between these concepts and experience. Positively he tried to show that the very possibility of an experience depended on the existence and operation of such concepts, and, contrariwise, that the latter depended on the former; while negatively he argued that attempts to extend these concepts beyond experience resulted in illusion and fallacy. To suppose, as Plato and others did, that our reason could operate more powerfully if it were free of empirical restraints is as mistaken as if a bird were to think it could fly better in a vacuum.

One of his specific starting points in his enquiry into the conditions necessary for the possibility of experience was a consideration of mathematics and physics because they were two areas of thought and knowledge in which results were unquestionably possible because they were actual. A consideration of the ways in which we gained knowledge in these areas could, he argued, throw light on the way in which we can gain or fail to gain knowledge in metaphysics. We shall look at this in a moment.

His other specific starting point was a general consideration of the kind of knowledge which he thought is gained in mathematics or physics and sought after in metaphysics. He argued that in all three areas the required knowledge is of what is *necessarily* so. For example, in mathematics a straight line is necessarily the shortest distance between two points and 7 + 5 are necessarily 12. There are laws in what he called pure physics, such as, the quantity of matter remains unchanged, or action and reaction are equal, which as laws must hold necessarily. Finally, the connections between concepts which metaphysics investigates, and which are exemplified in the principle that every event has a cause, or the proposition that the world must have a beginning, are agreed by all to be necessary connections. A difference is that whereas in geometry, for example, we gain knowledge of the properties anything must have if it has a configuration, in metaphysics we seek knowledge of the properties anything must have generally.

Since it is not possible to get necessity from what merely happens or is experienced to be so, for 'experience merely teaches us what exists and how it exists, but never that it must necessarily exist so and not otherwise', our knowledge of what is necessarily so must be prior to experience, that is, *a priori*. Our problem, therefore, is whether and how it is possible to gain knowledge which is both of existing objects and yet prior to them. The clue, suggests Kant, lies in assuming that in certain respects objects conform to our knowledge rather than our knowledge to them.

Taking over from Aristotle the view that any proposition — or judgement, as he usually called it — must be of the subject – predicate form, Kant argued that the only two possibilities are, either that the predicate is contained in the subject and, therefore, expresses nothing which has not already been thought, explicitly or implicitly, in the concept of the subject, or that the predicate is not contained in the subject, and, therefore, expresses something not already expressed in the concept of the subject. The former kind of judgement he called explicative or analytic, and the latter ampliative or synthetic. An example of the former is 'All bodies are extended' and of the latter is 'All bodies are heavy.'

There are thus four possible kinds of judgement, viz. analytic *a priori*, synthetic *a priori*, analytic *a posteriori* and synthetic *a posteriori*. But on the principle that 'it would be absurd to base an analytic judgement on experience, as our concept suffices for the purpose without requiring any testimony from experience', the first and last kinds, that is, the analytic *a priori* and the synthetic *a posteriori*, can unquestionably be accepted and the third kind, the analytic *a posteriori*, ruled out. This leaves for discussion the second kind, the synthetic *a priori*.

Kant's main point is that it is this kind of judgement, the synthetic *a priori*, which is the clue to our whole solution. He considered that Hume's great contribution was to force metaphysicians to ask — unanswerably in Hume's view — how it is possible to explain the connection between, for example, any cause and its effect which, as contrasted with mere concomitance or regularity, is necessary and which, nevertheless, he had shown not to be analytically derivable from the relevant concepts themselves. In other words, to say, for example, that heat causes metal to expand seems to be to say something necessary, that is, something more than just that when the metal becomes hot it expands, yet the idea of expansion is not contained in the idea of heat in the way that, for example, the idea of extension is contained in that of body. Hume's conclusion from this was that any necessity here could only be subjective, Kant's that the relation between cause and effect has to be synthetic *a priori*. A similar problem arose and similar treatment was relevant, Kant argued, for every concept.

Kant thought that he had found legitimate examples of such synthetic *a priori* propositions in mathematics and physics.

As regards mathematics, he opposed the then prevailing — and now again currently accepted — view that their propositions, such as '7 + 5 = 12' and 'A straight line is the shortest distance between two points', which must be *a priori*, since they are necessary, are analytic. He argued, for instance, that 'the concept of twelve is by no means thought by merely thinking of the combination of seven and five . . . We must go beyond these concepts, by calling to our aid the "Anschauung" [commonly translated as 'intuition' though more easily understandable as 'perception'] corresponding to one of them, say our five fingers . . . and we must add successively the units of the five given in the intuition to the concept of the twelve.' Similarly, 'A straight line is the shortest distance between two points' was argued to be synthetic on the ground that the 'concept of straight contains nothing of quantity, but only a quality. The attribute of shortness is therefore altogether additional, and not obtainable by any analysis of the concept. Intuition, which alone makes the synthesis possible, must here also be brought in to assist us.' Similarly, 'All proofs of the complete equality of two given figures . . . come ultimately to superposition, which is evidently nothing else than a synthetic proposition resting upon immediate intuition.' Such intuitions, Kant allowed, can be by an imaginative rather than a perceptual representation.

His position on physics was similar. Such principles as 'The quantity of matter remains unchanged' or 'Action and re-action must always be equal' were, Kant said, generally accepted as being necessarily, and, therefore, *a priori* true. He argued that since, for example, 'in the conception of matter I do not cogitate its permanency, but merely its presence in space . . . I therefore really go out and beyond the conception of matter in order to think in it something *a priori* . . . The proposition is therefore not analytic, but synthetic.'

From all this he concluded that, since mathematics and physics provide us with undoubted examples of synthetic *a priori* propositions, what we need to ask before investigating metaphysics, which seeks to establish its own synthetic *a priori* propositions, is how these existing synthetic *a priori* propositions are possible. In Kant's expression of a thought which he credited to Hume, 'How is it possible that when a concept is given to me I can go beyond it and connect with it another, which is not contained in it and in such a manner as if the latter *necessarily* belonged to the former?' The answer to this question will consist in discovering what is the factor, independent of experience, outside the pure concept of the subject, which enables the predicate to be joined to the subject in a necessary connection. To discover this, we will have to find the necessary conditions by which, first, our senses yield an awareness, or intuition, of objects and, secondly, our thinking yields knowledge. We will find that all synthetic judgements are possible only through the reference of a concept to an intuition, which for *a priori* judgements must be pure intuition, and, in fact, the pure intuitions of space and time. In non-Kantian terms, he is saying that perceiving an external object, for example a tree, is only possible by having certain sense-impressions which we arrange according to an innate spatial and temporal system, adding certain appropriate images, and uniting all these according to certain innate principles of our understanding. It is because we cannot represent in pure intuition the concept of an object in general, or such concepts as reality, substance, cause in general, that metaphysics, unlike mathematics or physics, is impossible as a body of knowledge.

Applying this to mathematics — which Kant discussed in a section of his *Critique of Pure Reason* called the 'Transcendental Aesthetic' and in his *Prolegomena* sects. 6 – 13 — this outside factor which enables us to enlarge the subject is an immediate awareness — what he called intuition or perception (*Anschauung*) — which we get when our senses are affected by outside objects. Such an intuition, which is the only way that objects can appear to, and therefore be experienced and known by, us is made of three sorts of elements. First — which we will have to discuss later — that which is supplied by our understanding, for example whether it is a substance, is divisible, etc.; secondly, that which is supplied by sensation, for example its hardness and colour; and, thirdly, the form under which it is experienceable by us. This form, which Kant sometimes calls the 'pure form of sense intuition', sometimes the 'pure form of sensibility' and sometimes simply 'pure intuition', is an element, which, because it is merely the form under which what we experience through our senses is received by us, can be known *a priori*, that is, prior to any experience of what exactly is going to be received in that form and which, because it is not a mere concept, will also give rise to synthetical knowlege.

The two forms under which humans — whatever may be true of other beings — can experience things through the senses are, Kant held, space and time. Everything external must be represented as being in space and everything, whether external or internal, as being in time. It is not possible for anything to appear to us not in these forms. What will appear we do not know until it does, but we can know prior to experience that it will have to appear like this, because this is merely the form of our capacity to be affected. Moreover, since geometry is, according to Kant, based on the perception of space, and arithmetic on that of time, as we saw in the discussion of our knowledge of 'A straight line is the shortest distance between two points' and of '$7 + 5 = 12$', we can now see how the synthetic *a priori* propositions of these two disciplines are possible. They make judgements, not about specific objects we actually experience in the world nor, much less, about any unexperienced objects, but about the characteristics which whatever we experience must have, namely be spatial and temporal. In geometry, for instance, we verify as true or false a proposition in which a property is ascribed to a figure by representing in a pure intuition — either imaginary or perceptual — this figure and seeing whether the property is present in it. It is an accidental historical feature of Kant's view that he further thought that the details of such spatial and temporal forms were necessarily delineated in Euclid's geometry and in classical arithmetic, which seemed to him to be the final word on these subjects. Hence, he regarded 'Space has three dimensions', and 'Time has one dimension' as true synthetic *a priori* judgements. But his main point was that mathematical knowledge, which has to be synthetic *a priori*, is possible because it is about space and time, which are forms we impose on, and therefore know prior to, any experience we can have. A very important corollary of this, which we will emphasise later, is that the pure perceptions of space and time and, hence, the knowledge we gain in mathematics, are not about the objects as such which appear to us, but only about the appearances of themselves which they present to us. That is, it is not the objects in themselves, but only these objects as experienced, of which we can have any mathematical knowledge. There can be no possibility that mathematics will not be applicable to objects in space and time, since it is our mathematical thinking which imposes the forms of space and time on their presentation to us.

Though Kant's thesis that the propositions of mathematics are synthetic and not analytic is contrary to that now generally received, it is in fundamental agreement with the modern view that we get out of mathematics what we ourselves put in to it. Indeed, his great principle is that in all thinking 'we only know in things *a priori* that which we ourselves place in them'. In other words, the necessity of certain features of our experience is due to their subjective origin in us.

By showing how the possibility of synthetic *a priori* propositions arises in mathematics, Kant has also shown more generally the very possibility of experience. For he has argued that experience — with which he holds all our knowledge must begin — is only possible by a combination of external material caused to act upon us by some unknown and unknowable objects in themselves, and forms independently supplied by us to cope with that material. The forms cannot act upon the unknown causes of the material, and the material cannot act upon us except through the forms we impose on it. Our knowledge is, therefore, confined to what we can experience, though some things about this can be known *a priori*. Kant called this view transcendental or critical idealism to distinguish it from forms of idealism, like that of Berkeley, which he thought held not merely that only what appears can be known but that only this exists. Kant maintains, on the one hand, that space and time are objectively valid in respect of all objects which are presented to our sense, so that we could not experience any of these not in space and time. What we thus experience does not just appear to be in space and time, it really is so. On the other hand, space and time are purely subjective conditions of our human intuition, and, therefore, inapplicable to experienced objects in so far as these objects exist in themselves and unexperienced. He expresses this contrast by calling space and time empirically real but transcendentally ideal. Further, though Kant distances himself from Berkeley and idealists like him in his insistence that objects exist in themselves as well as being experienced, nevertheless he identifies real experienced objects in space and time, such as houses and trees, as contrasted with objects which only appear to us, for example in illusions, etc., to be real, as themselves only being certain combinations of experiences connected according to laws which somehow are supposed to make them at the same time outside of us and distinct from our experiences. For Kant to say that anything spatial and temporal — and, therefore, any physical object — exists independently of our experiencing it, for example things not actually or not yet or no longer experienced, is only to say that we could in certain conditions experience them (for example *Critique*, A 491–7/B 519–25). We can know nothing of things in themselves which may be the causes of what we experience or of what we would in certain circumstances experience.

Having dealt with the explanation of synthetic *a priori* propositions in mathematics, whose origin he finds in the contribution which our sensibility, that is, the passive faculty through which our senses function, makes to our acquisition of knowledge by its use of *a priori* forms of perception, namely space and time, Kant now turns, in his *Prolegomena* sects. 14–39, and in that part of his *Critique* called the 'Transcendental Logic', to the synthetic *a priori* propositions of pure physics. Their origin he will place in another alleged faculty, our active understanding, whose principal function he regards as the making of judgements. To know the very general laws of physics is, in his view, to know the principles of the connections of our representations which, we shall see, are the rules for uniting in judgements these representations in our consciousness. As the pure perception of our sensibility is the form in which something is and must be perceived, so the pure concept of our understanding is the form in which something is and must be thought. But though, for clarity of exposition, Kant treats these independently, he stresses that in the actual acquisition of knowledge they are combined. 'Concepts without perceptions', he said, 'are empty; perceptions without concepts are blind.' Our second task is, therefore, to show how our concepts can be made sensuous and how our perceptions can be brought under concepts.

The clue to the problem of how we think of objects is to be found in the nature of thinking. Thinking is, according to Kant, the use of the understanding, whose function is the making of judgements by synthesising various representations in one consciousness. Such unification may be done by bringing a perception under a concept, for example 'This is a body', or by bringing one concept under another concept, for example 'All bodies are heavy.' In other words, we think by classifying material and must, therefore, have both material, that is perceptions, and forms of classification, that is, concepts. Hence, an analysis of the various kinds of judgements would reveal to us the various kinds of concepts through which alone objects can be thought, for experienced objects are merely mind-imposed combinations of perceptions. Our task will be to show how these concepts can first be derived from the understanding and then applied to perceptions to give us that knowledge of what is represented to us in perception which has the necessity, objectivity and universality characteristic of the laws of science as contrasted with our merely successive series of experiences; a necessity and objectivity which, because it cannot be due to any things in themselves, must be due to imposed rules.

Kant alleges that there are in physics some very general principles, which, being necessary, are *a priori*, and not having a predicate derivable from the subject, are synthetic, such as 'Substance is permanent' and 'Every event has a cause'. Our problem, therefore, is to explain their synthetic *a priori* character.

For reasons similar to those already given, we must consider nature, that is, the subject matter of physics, as the complex of all the objects of experience, not of objects themselves. The possibility of experience will be the outside factor which makes some *a priori* judgements synthetic. Hence, we must seek the conditions under which alone such experience is possible. To which the answer is that every sense perception — which gives us only judgements of perception — must be subsumed under a concept, derived from our understanding, in order to give us an experience and a judgement of experience. This will be objective and, as such, a characteristic of an object, because it is necessary and universal, not because it tells us anything about the object in itself. To have knowledge of an object is to know the universal and necessary connections of the perceptions given to us. For example, the judgement of perception might be 'When the sun shines on the stone, the stone grows warm', which becomes a judgement of experience,

'The sun warms the stone', by adding the concept of cause, which necessarily connects the concepts of sunshine and heat. Indeed, we saw earlier that one of the elements in any perception is supplied by the understanding, so that even the judgements of mathematics rely on the concepts of the understanding. Thus, 'A straight line is the shortest distance between two points' presupposes that the line is subsumed under the concept of quantity. 'I cannot,' Kant said, 'know a line or anything else in space without drawing it and so producing a certain combination of various elements synthetically, so that the unity of this act is at the same time the unity of consciousness (in the notion of a line) and so alone can an object in space be known.'

A judgement of any kind is a function of unity. It is a uniting of representations, whether perceptions or concepts, in one consciousness. If it is a judgement of perception, the union is relative to an individual subject and is, therefore, contingent and subjective. If it is a judgement of experience, the union, which is bringing a perception under a concept, is synthetically necessary and objective. It is a general rule of nature, which, on the one side, is a unity of the experienced and, on the other, is a unity of the experiencing. It is, in one of Kant's best known phrases, 'the transcendental unity of apperception', that is, the kind of unity which exists among all the experiences of a single self-conscious person and enables him to call them 'his' and them to become objects for him. Kant also gives a synthesising function to the imagination, namely to bind together into a perception the separate data of sense. Since the rules for this are the same as for a judgement, we need not detail them here, though they also give necessary conditions for obtaining knowledge, since we can find connections among what is presented to our senses only by being aware of how they are connected in time, an awareness which we get from imagination.

From the traditional logic of Aristotle, Kant 'deduced' a list of general concepts which, because they combine together what we receive by subsuming perceptions under concepts, make experience possible. Following Aristotle, he called these 'categories'. And the exposition of the *a priori* way in which they are applicable to objects, and thus make our experience of objects possible, he called their 'transcendental deduction'. This showed that the manifold of intuitions can become a unitary representation only when it is subject to the categories of the understanding and they are applied to it. What Kant called the 'schematism' of the categories introduces rules by which the imagination subsumes under concepts through a common medium of time. These schematised categories then serve as a guide to a list of *a priori* synthetic principles which are the rules of the universal employment of the categories.

Examples of these principles are that all perceptions, conceived of as items in a unified spatio-temporal system, have a certain quantity and a certain degree; that they are necessarily connected; that however they change, these changes will be related causally and something will remain permanent; that they will be possible, actual or necessary. By the use of these principles we can distinguish between our temporally successive experiences and an objective experienced world of spatial-temporal, law-governed objects. Whether a particular subjective succession of perceptions is indicative of an objective succession of objects depends on whether the former is order-indifferent or not. Thus, in the perception of an event, for example a ship moving downstream, as contrasted with the perception of an object, for example the ship itself, there is always a rule which makes the order in which the perceptions, for example of the positions of the ship up and down stream as contrasted with the perceptions of the bow and the stern of the ship, follow one another in a necessary order, since under it the preceding time necessarily determines the succeeding time. Kant claims that this necessity is causal and that, therefore, one of the *a priori* conditions of experience is that every event has a cause. Such principles will, therefore, be confined to what is experienced, not to the inexperienced objects which cause them to appear to us.

An example of Kant's rather artificial way, via Aristotle's logic, of arriving at one of these principles is this. Taking the concept of cause and what he regards as a synthetic *a priori* principle of pure physics, namely that each perception is necessarily linked to another, he argues that to the representation that one perception is constantly followed by another but not conversely, for example the shining of the sun and the warming of the stone, is applied the logical form of a hypothetical, to give the judgement of perception which synthesises the two perceptions into 'If the sun shines, the stone grows warm.' In order for this to be treated as a law of physics, it must become a judgement of experience, necessary for any experience, by being subsumed under the concept of cause, furnished by our understanding, to give 'The shining of the sun causes the stone to grow warm.' Kant, of course, is not arguing that I can know *a priori* that the sun causes the stone to grow warm, but only that I can know *a priori* that something preceded the warming of the stone from which its warming follows according to a law. Such a principle applies only to experience but does not arise from it. Hence, both for the pure perceptions of space and time which lie in our sensibility, and for the universal — as contrasted with particular empirical — laws of nature, which lie in our understanding, we 'must seek nature,' says Kant, 'as to its universal conformity to law, in the conditions of the possibility of experience, which lie in our sensibility and our understanding'. In other words, 'The understanding does not draw its laws (*a priori*) from nature, but presents them to it.'

The great conclusion of Kant's enquiry into the nature of our acquisition of knowledge was that 'all concepts, and with them all principles, even such as are possible *a priori*, relate to empirical perception, that is, to the data for a possible experience. Apart from this relation they have no objective validity.'

All genuine, that is, synthetic as contrasted with analytic, knowledge has to be by observation. *A priori* synthetic knowledge is of what conditions enable us to get any knowledge by observation and is, therefore, only about what is a possible object of such knowledge. The first thesis of Kant's conclusion was, as we have seen, argued at length in the first two parts of the great *Critique of Pure Reason*, in the form of an investigation into the possibility of our actual knowledge of mathematics and science. As an examination of the actual and proper use of basic concepts this constitutes a legitimate metaphysics. The second thesis, though frequently expressed in the same parts, is argued at equal length in the third part of the work under the title of 'Transcendental Dialectic'. It takes the form of an investigation into the possibility of traditional transcendent metaphysics, which he himself had supported in his Inaugural Dissertation of 1770. Any such system will be shown to be pseudo-metaphysics. The examination of synthetic *a priori* propositions, that is, propositions which give us knowledge of what is necessarily so, as exemplified in mathematics and physics, has shown that such propositions are only verifiable by recourse to the conditions necessary for obtaining such knowledge. Just as it was shown that a mathematical proposition is true because of the necessary spatial and temporal ways in which we observe things, so a metaphysical proposition, such as 'Every event has a cause', is verifiable only by showing that its truth is a condition for obtaining any knowledge of events. This, believes Kant, genuine metaphysics can show by examining the nature of knowledge and experience, since the conditions for knowledge provide the synthetic factor, that is, the factor outside the given concepts, which connects those concepts necessarily. Apart from such conditions of knowledge, the proposition is unverifiable. What pseudo-metaphysics tries to show, but what cannot be shown, is that such a proposition is true not only for what can be known — which Kant has argued is confined to what can be experienced — but for anything which exists.

The nature of the pseudo-metaphysics is brought out by a series of interrelated contrasts. First, the contrast between thinking and knowing. We can think of what is unexperienceable, but not know it, since knowing, unlike thinking, requires intuitions to which the concepts of thought can be applied. Secondly, the contrast between the empirical and the transcendental uses of a concept or principle, that is, to objects of actual or possible sense-experience and to objects as they are in themselves, sometimes called objects of the understanding. For example, the concept of cause in the former contains the idea of a temporal sequence in accordance with a rule, but in the latter only the idea of deducing the existence of one thing from the existence of another. Hence, there is a legitimate application of concepts of the understanding to objects of experience but not to objects of the understanding. Thirdly, there is the contrast between 'concepts of nature' which apply only to experience and 'pure concepts of reason' which cannot be discovered or confirmed by any experience. Fourthly, there is the contrast between the understanding, which uses the former kind of concepts or categories, and reason, in whose nature the latter are inherent. Whereas the understanding unites the phenomena of experience by rules and is concerned with the synthetic unity of representations, reason tries to unite these rules of the understanding and is concerned with the unconditioned synthetic unity of all conditions. Hence, the latter never applies to experienceable objects, but to the concepts which the understanding applies to objects. The employment of the concepts of the understanding is immanent, that of the concepts of reason transcendent. Kant sometimes insists that reason does not have its own concepts, but converts the concepts of the understanding into ideas by trying to free them from the limitations of possible experience, by dealing with the unconditioned rather than the conditioned. The concept of a completed series or of a first event or of an uncaused event would be such a concept of reason. Fifthly, there is the contrast between the incomplete, partial, conditioned nature of any part of experience with which the categories of the understanding deal and the complete, unconditioned totality of all possible experience with which the concepts of reason deal.

Since reason is held by Kant to be the power of making mediate inferences, he derives the pure concepts of reason, which he calls 'Ideas', from Aristotle's traditional type of mediate inference, the syllogism, analogously and with the same artificiality to the way he deduced the categories from the kinds of judgement. The results are the psychological Idea of a complete subject, the Ego, the cosmological Idea of a complete series of conditions, the Cosmos, and the theological Idea of the complete complex of all possible being, God. Kant stresses that these Ideas are quite irrelevant in the explanation of the phenomena of experience and are abused if they are considered as applicable to objects beyond experience. In short, they have no legitimate application to any kind of object. Their purpose is regulative, that is, to urge completeness in the use of the understanding and its categories in experience; to lead us to the very boundary of experience and to strive for unity in our knowledge. Expressed in terms of the previous two parts of the *Critique*, Kant asks whether the synthetic *a priori* propositions of metaphysics are possible. Such propositions are the psychological, cosmological and theological variants on 'If the conditioned be given, all its conditions, i.e. the unconditioned, are also given.' Kant's argument is that such a proposition is not legitimate as a piece of knowledge, but only as a precept enjoining the pursuit of complete unity.

The Dialectic is given over to expressing the various contradictions which arise if these Ideas are taken as applicable to objects in themselves. For example, Kant argues that though there is a natural temptation to ask whether the world as a whole, as contrasted with some particular part of it, is infinite or bounded, no answer can be given. On the one hand, experience cannot answer the question since experience either of the infinite or of a boundary to space or time is impossible. On the other, the ideas of space and time are applicable only to what is experienceable, for they are, as we saw, only *a priori* forms of sense-experience. Similarly, Kant attacks the alleged knowledge of an immaterial, independently existing, non-composite, conscious self on the ground that experience cannot provide evidence for such a thing. Experience, we saw, is admittedly only possible on the supposition of a conscious unity of experience — his 'transcendental unity of apperception' — but this is no evidence for an alleged experience of a unified consciousness. I know the categories and through them all objects in the unity of apperception and, therefore, through myself, but I do not, thus, know myself through the categories. The self as a thing in itself is known only as a synthesiser of data according to rules; it is only the phenomenal self, that is, the self as it appears to me, which is known as something temporal which has experiences. Further, though the self can, as the ultimate subject of thinking, be regarded as a substance, yet the concept of the self as a substance is empty, Kant claims in one of his Analogies of Experience, unless it can be shown to imply permanence. Such an implication, however, holds only for objects of possible experience. Nor, of course, can we obtain knowledge of the self, or of anything else, other than by experience. Hence, the generally accepted view of metaphysics as seeking knowledge of the *whole* of reality, of the *ultimate* structure, the *original* cause or the *totality* of things is a view of what, according to Kant, is an impossible science.

Though Kant often speaks of objects in themselves, what he sometimes calls 'noumena', in a negative way as merely what cannot be objects of the senses and, therefore, cannot be known, he does not have any real doubt of the existence of objects beyond our experience. Their existence is necessary since objects of experience are the effects on our sense of objects beyond experience. Furthermore, on the one hand, he often characterises the contrast between the phenomenal, that is, the experienceable appearance, and the noumenal, that is, the intelligible thing in itself, not as a contrast between two sorts of objects, but as between two different ways of regarding the same object, in one of which ways it is subject to space and time and to such principles as causality, and in the other not. In the former, but not in the latter, way it can be experienced by and known to us. Yet, on the other hand, just as Locke thought matter — 'something I know not what', — Berkeley thought God, Plato thought Forms and other metaphysicians thought other unknowables necessary to explain the world we live in, so Kant undoubtedly felt a need for the existence of admittedly unknowable noumena. Apart from the argument that the experienced is only possible by contrast with the unexperienced, appearance by contrast with reality, it seemed to him that the existence of some unperceivable objects, such as the world, God and the self, is testified to not only by our natural predisposition to believe in them, but also by their indispensability for various practical matters, such as free will and the possibility of morality, and by their encouragement against the errors of materialism, naturalism and fatalism. Not only can we and must we *think* of them, they must *exist*. All that needs to be denied is that they can be *known*. But Kant seems to have held that, whereas the thought of how an object which presents itself is in itself gives us neither knowledge nor any idea of it, we do have a clear idea, though no knowledge, of such objects in themselves as God, the self and the world. Even though he constantly insists that a concept not applicable to or not applied to an intuition is only a logical function of unity, that is, a way of combining something, and has, in itself, no meaning, he also allows that such notions as first cause, immortality, God, etc. are not meaningless. He only holds that any proposition which asserts or denies their applicability to any objects is unverifiable and, therefore, invalid.

It is clear from all this that Kant's criticism of traditional metaphysics is based, like his opponents' advocacy of it, on his analysis of certain key concepts. The chief of these is the concept of *knowledge* and its subservient concepts of *judgement, experience, understanding* and *perception*. Others are certain specific concepts, such as *space* and *time, cause* and *substance*. The same basis supports his positive view of a reformed metaphysics. His investigations are designed to show that objects are perceivable, thinkable and knowable only under certain conditions, which can be ascertained by discovering the exact nature of *object, perception, thought* and *knowledge*. He himself said that, for example, his conclusion that the synthetic unity of consciousness is an objective condition of all knowledge and of the possibility of a perception's becoming an object for someone was analytically true. And all his philosophical conclusions are held to be *a priori*. Even if Kant sometimes overstepped the line between logic and psychology, and even if his picture of experience as a combination of externally given material and internally imposed forms often seems to offer a psychology of human cognition, he certainly intended his analysis of such fundamental concepts and, therefore, the conclusions he drew about limitations imposed on our knowledge to be an exercise in logic, not psychology.

Kant's main thesis is that, in addition to the unquestioned view that empirical knowledge can be had only of the empirical. *that is*, of the experienced, non-empirical or *a priori* knowledge is confined to the experienceable; that it is in fact knowledge of the forms of experience. This thesis follows from his belief that knowledge of objects is acquired by the use of concepts in judgements in which such concepts are given an application by collecting under them

102

temporally and spatially ordered sense perceptions. Concepts are forms of thought for the making of knowledge from given intuitions. Intuition is necessary to enable us to connect concepts together non-analytically, and thus obtain synthetic knowledge. We cannot, therefore, prove without intuition that, for example, everything must have a cause, and, hence, cannot prove this for the non-experienceable. Concepts, as he said, without perceptions are empty — a view of knowledge which he sometimes put in more psychological terms by saying that it needs contributions both from our sensibility and from our understanding. The Transcendental Dialectic is devoted to an exposé of the fallacies which arise from attempts to apply concepts to non-sensible objects; in psychological terms to a misuse of the alleged faculty of pure reason.

Kant's criticism of metaphysics is not as cramping as that either of Hume or of many later critics of metaphysics in that, unlike them, he allows not only purely analytic *a priori* knowledge of the nature of concepts — what Hume instanced as 'abstract reasoning concerning quantity or number' — and purely *a posteriori* synthetic knowledge of what we experience — what Hume called 'experimental reasoning concerning matters of fact and existence' — but also synthetic *a priori* knowledge which appears to assimilate the conceptual and the ontological. But he agrees with them that such knowledge is confined to the experienceable — for Kant, to the forms of such an experience — and gives us none of the information about the supersensible which metaphysicians claimed to exist. The genuine or transcendental metaphysical proposition that every empirically knowable event must have a cause can be established — and, of course, established *a priori* — but not the pseudo- — or transcendent — metaphysical proposition that every event must have a cause. Metaphysics can give us knowledge of the general characteristics of things only by showing what characteristics they must have in order for knowledge or experience to be had of them. Hence, a metaphysical proposition, such as 'every event must have a cause', can be verified — and, Kant thinks, is verified — only by proving that such a proposition is necessarily true if knowledge of events is to be possible at all.

We can, of course, limit Kant's criterion of possible knowledge even further, if we deny the existence of any synthetic *a priori* knowledge and argue — as one could plausibly do — that the advocacy of it is based partly on a mistaken belief in the necessary truth of Aristotle's logic, Euclid's geometry and Newton's physics. Kant's discussion of our knowledge of space and time denies —

what is allowed by most contemporary mathematicians — that the necessity of mathematics is due to its analytic character, and his discussion of our use of concepts often assimilates psychological theories to logical truths. Furthermore, his faith in the existence of a supersensible world, knowledge of which he has endeavoured to disprove and a belief in which largely depends on his thesis that it is necessary for morality, is not a legitimate substitute for an argued exception to what his criterion establishes. It has, moreover, various well known difficulties of its own, such as its use of the notion of cause — which, on Kant's thesis, ought to be applicable only to the experienceable — in assuming that things in themselves are the causes of the material which we receive in perception. Such a supersensible world is as much a consequence of his analysis of *knowledge* and of *experience* of objects as the combination of what is contributed by our mind and by an unknowable thing-in-itself as the supersensible worlds of Plato, Aristotle, Berkeley, Leibniz, etc. are consequences of their analyses of key concepts.

Both the critical side of Kant, which leads to his denial of the possibility of any knowledge of the supersensible advocated by traditional metaphysicians, and his liberal side, which leads to an insistence on the existence of such a supersensible, have the same source, namely, particular analyses of certain general concepts.

7
Verificationism

At the end of the nineteenth and the beginning of the twentieth century in Europe and the United States, philosophers with an interest in science, and scientists interested in philosophy, shared both a distaste for the speculations of metaphysicians who posed as super-scientists, and also a worry how to distinguish between genuine scientific hypotheses, such as whether light is corpuscular or wave-like, and whether motion is relative, and pseudo-science, such as whether waves travel through an aether, and whether there is a substance called 'phlogiston' or a power called 'animal spirits'. Their reactions gave rise in America to the Pragmatism of C. S. Peirce and William James, and somewhat later the Operationism of the physicist Bridgman and, in Europe, to the Positivism of the physicist Mach, followed by the Logical Positivism of the Vienna Circle, the scientific philosophy of the Berlin group, Reichenbach and Hempel, and the logic of the Polish thinkers Tarski and Kotarbinski. In England it was joined with an analytic and empiricist tradition, descended from Hume and going through Bertrand Russell and G. E. Moore at Cambridge, which was given popular expression by A. J. Ayer. A link between Europe and England was the Austrian philosopher Wittgenstein, who studied with Russell at Cambridge before the first World War and returned to settle there in the mid 'thirties.

If we rely mainly on two representative and clearly expressed manifestations of the majority feeling of these thinkers towards metaphysics, namely A. J. Ayer's book *Language, Truth and Logic*,[1] and R. Carnap's article 'The Elimination of Metaphysics through Logical Analysis of Language',[2] we find that the criterion used for judging the writings of metaphysicians is a Principle of

Verifiability supposed either to distinguish the meaningful from the meaningless, or even to define 'meaning' itself. Though this principle has been enunciated in various ways, usually in an attempt to preserve it from certain kinds of objections, we may take for our purpose Ayer's formulation, according to which 'a sentence is factually significant to any given person, if, and only if, he knows how to verify the proposition which it purports to express — that is, if he knows what observations would lead him, under certain conditions, to accept the proposition as being true, or reject it as being false'.[3]

It is important to note that this principle is deliberately limited in various ways and is not, despite careless remarks by both its advocates and opponents, intended to be a general theory of meaning. A minor limitation is its confinement to sentences, not single words and expressions. The latter are treated by examining the most elementary sentences in which they occur, for example 'X is a neutron (a belief, intention, etc.).'[4] Much more important is its limitation to sentences which attempt to say something true or false; a point which comes out clearly, though unwittingly, in a formulation by the Viennese Verificationist Schlick. He begins by saying that 'whenever we ask about a sentence "What does it mean?" what we expect is instruction as to the circumstances in which the sentence is to be used'. On this view, the principle would apply to any sentence, whether used to say what can be true or false or otherwise. However, he continues his formulation by equating this remark with 'we want a description of the conditions under which the sentence will form a true proposition and of those which will make it false'. Similarly, he explicitly equates 'stating the rules according to which the sentence is to be used' and 'stating the way in which it can be verified (or falsified)'. Wittgenstein had earlier said 'to be able to say "p" is true (or false), I must have determined under what conditions I call "p" true, and thereby I determine the meaning of the sentence'.

The Verificationists are usually careful to stress that their principle only covers what they call 'factual' ('literal', 'cognitive', 'theoretical', 'descriptive') meaning. But I do not think that this is intended as a different or additional limitation to that implied by 'true or false'. To say that a statement is factual and to say that it could be either true or false is, on this view, the same thing. This comes out in their treatment both of necessarily true statements — or 'tautologies', as they often call them — and, quite differently, of the evaluative statements of ethics and aesthetics. A tautology can only be true, just as a contradiction can only be false. Thus, whereas 'It will rain tomorrow' could be either true or false, 'Either it will rain tomorrow or it will not' cannot be false and 'It will rain tomorrow and it will not' cannot be true. Furthermore, a tautology does not say how things are, does not describe anything; you know nothing about the weather when you are told that either it will rain or it will not. Whether, therefore, we use 'factually meaningless' either of sentences which do not describe, do not state what could be a fact, or of sentences which do not say something which could be either true or false, sentences expressing tautologies — and contradictions — will be factually meaningless.

Wittgenstein said that sentences which do not 'picture' anything, as the expressions of tautologies do not, are 'senseless', but 'not nonsense'. This interpretation of 'factually meaningless' is in accord with the spirit of the Verificationists, for one of the things on which they often insist about many sentences used by theologians, such as 'God loves men', is that they are meaningless because they are held to express something true whatever the world is like and are not allowed under any conceivable circumstances to say something false. On the other hand, many Verificationists, such as Ayer and Carnap, who realise that it is highly misleading to call necessarily true statements — of which the whole of pure mathematics consists — 'meaningless', waver between confining the Verifiability Principle to sentences which express what can be either true or false, with the necessarily true in limbo, and widening the principle to cover sentences which express either what can be either true or false or what is necessarily true.[5] In choosing the latter alternative they are only following, as Ayer acknowledges,[6] the much earlier example of Hume who said, 'If we take in our hand any volume; of divinity, or school metaphysics, for instance; let us ask, Does it contain any abstract reasoning concerning quantity or number? No. Does it contain any experimental reasoning concerning matter of fact and existence? No. Commit it then to the flames. For it can contain nothing but sophistry and illusion.'

For different reasons, in discussing sentences used to make evaluations in morals (or aesthetics), such as 'Stealing money is wrong', Ayer concluded that they have no 'factual meaning' either because they 'do not make any factual statement' or because, what he thinks is the same, they 'say nothing which can be true or false'.[7] In his view, 'Stealing money is wrong' does not say, for example, that God or my neighbour or myself or the law disapproves of stealing or that there is any 'observable' property called 'wrongness' which the act possesses. But he never suggests that they have no legitimate use or are altogether meaningless.[8]

Not only was the Principle limited to sentences which express what can be true or false, that is, 'a genuine proposition about a matter of fact', it usually expressly confined its methods of verification to what could be observed by the senses. That is certainly clear and explicit in Ayer and Carnap and would, of course, be subscribed to by any philosopher of science. Though in practice, therefore, empirical verification was a necessary condition of being meaningful, in theory it is not, I think, part of the Principle; nor is it stated to be so in the formulations by Schlick, Wittgenstein, or, sometimes Carnap. Furthermore, the absence of any insistence on validation by the senses would allow the Principle to apply straightforwardly to mathematics, as, indeed, it was applied by such theorists as the Intuitionists. They suggested distinguishing genuine from pseudo-mathematical statements on the criterion of mathematical provability, and applied this criterion to such well-known, but still unsolved, problems as Goldbach's conjecture that any even number is the sum of two primes, or Fermat's last theorem that $X^n + Y^n \neq Z^n$ for $n > 2$.

In fact, the reason why empirical verification was by many philosophers included in the Principle was partly that most of its supporters were empiricists or even positivists, and partly that what they sought was a criterion to distinguish genuine scientific hypotheses from pseudo-scientific speculation. When, however, this Principle did include a demand for empirical verification, it was said to rule out metaphysics, which was held by the Verificationists to be, by definition, about what is outside or beyond experience.

Though the Principle was usually restrictive about the methods of verification, it is liberal about verification itself. First, it asks only for verifiability, that is, the possibility of verification, not for actual verification. Secondly, it asks only for logical verifiability, or verifiability in principle, not for verifiability in practice. In order to understand a sentence one does not have to know whether it says anything true or not, nor of any practicable means by which one could show which it does; one only has to be able to show what would count as a verification of it. A favourite example before the advances of space research was the sentence 'There are mountains on the other side of the moon.' Thirdly, an inherent scepticism in the empiricist and positivist holders of the Principle — irrelevant to the Principle itself — which made them deny that any empirical statement could be conclusively proved or disproved, led them to interpret 'verifiable' in a weak sense as meaning only 'confirmable'.

Doubt has often been expressed about the exact status or nature of the Verifiability Principle, usually as the objection that it does not seem, as it is claimed it should be, applicable to itself; that is, that the statement that all factually meaningful sentences should say something verifiable is not itself verifiable, and therefore the sentence used to state the Principle is not factually meaningful. The kind of answer that is made to this objection determines the status of the Principle. Some Verificationists have said, for instance, that it is illogical to expect it to be verifiable since it is not intended to be a factual statement, to be judged as either true or false, but to be either a definition stipulated by its makers, or a methodological postulate which is to be judged as useful or useless in distinguishing the factual from the pseudo-factual. Somewhat similarly it has been said that as a principle it cannot be self-applicable any more than the statement of the principle of causality that every event has a cause can itself be said to be a causal statement. It cannot be asked to pull itself up by its own bootstraps any more than a weighing machine can weigh itself. The difficulty with this type of answer, as some Verificationists have realised and as their critics have insisted, is that it makes the principle assume an uncomfortable air of arbitrariness. Other Verificationists have held that the Principle is indeed a factual statement verifiable by the actual use of, by the logical features of, language; and, furthermore, that such use shows it to be true. In so far as the Principle is giving not a theory of meaning but a criterion for saying whether a sentence is being used to make a factual statement, that is, something which says something either true or false, it is both verifiable and verified by such use. Since, however, a statement which is verifiable simply by the logical features of the language is an analytic statement, it seems best to take the Verifiability Principle as an allegedly analytic truth which follows from the meaning of 'factual statement'. The usual objection to its being verifiable is based on too narrow a limitation of the Principle to what is observable by using our sense organs together with the debatable view that the use of language is not thus observable.

Even if the Principle of Verifiability is considered, not as a theory of meaning or even of meaningfulness, but only as a theory about when a sentence does succeed in saying something which can be either true or false, it has some fairly well-known ambiguities which should be mentioned, but need not be discussed in detail, since their resolution does not alter the relevance of the Principle to the legitimacy of metaphysics. The first is an ambiguity in 'what would verify' what a sentence says between the *evidence* for the truth of what it says and the *conditions* under which what it says is true. For example, is what verifies what is said by 'Napoleon lost the Battle of Waterloo' the historical evidence for Napoleon's defeat or the actual defeat itself? Is what verifies what is said by 'The child is in great pain' its sleepless nights, its cries, grimaces, and shrinking from the touch, or the pain itself? Is what verifies what is said by 'An electron has passed through the cloud chamber' the trail of droplets, or some particle? Furthermore, would a difference in the evidence, contrasted with the necessary sameness of the conditions, imply a difference in meaning; for example the existence of three different pieces of evidence for the distance of the sun from the earth? For our purpose, however, the question is whether there is anything which would count *either* as evidence *or* as conditions for the truth of assertions about, for example, Plato's Forms, Aristotle's Being, Leibniz's Monads, Berkeley's God, Bradley's Absolute, or Kant's Noumena.

The second ambiguity, though also important for the credentials of the principle as a theory of meaning or of meaningfulness, is equally irrelevant to its bearing on the status of metaphysics. It is the ambiguity between *something's* and *somebody's* verifying what is said by the sentence, whether 'something' is taken as the evidence or the conditions. Thus, Wittgenstein, Schlick and Carnap emphasise the *conditions* or *evidence* which show that something is true, whereas Ayer and also Schlick and Carnap emphasise the *method* by which somebody shows that something true is said. The latter view found expression in the ambiguous slogan, 'The meaning of a proposition (sentence) is its method of verification.' Hence, the question arises whether what is said, for example, by the sentence 'Napoleon lost the Battle of Waterloo' is the same — as it could be if it depended only on *what* verifies it — or different — as it would be if it depended on *who* verifies it, a contemporary or myself. Similarly, is what is said by the sentence 'The child is in pain' the same for the child and the doctor? Equally, if two scientists use different methods for estimating the distance of the sun from the earth, are two different things being verified? Once again, however, though these questions caused great trouble to and provided much chopping and changing among various Verificationists, their resolution would not alter the relation of their Principle to the writings of metaphysicians.

Armed with the Principle of Verifiability, these philosophers declared that the utterances of metaphysicians, such as Greek speculations about the Principle (*Arche*) of the world or later hypotheses of a God, the supposition of an Ego or of the Absolute, the denigration of the world as only an appearance, controversies between rationalists and empiricists, realists and idealists, monists and pluralists, were meaningless, that is, did not amount to anything which could be either true or false. Indeed, the very enterprise of metaphysics which claimed that there could be knowledge of what was unexperiencable was declared, as by Kant earlier, to be nonsense. Since metaphysicians did not believe that these assertions were purely tautological, but claimed that they showed the existence of what is supersensible, they were open to the objection that they were unverifiable by experience and, therefore, on the Verificationists' Principle, meaningless. One could neither verify directly assertions about the existence of Plato's Forms or Leibniz's Monads — what would it be like to have experience of either of them? — as one could verify the hypothesis that there are mountains on the other side of the moon, nor verify them in terms of their implications — what difference would the presence or absence of Forms or Monads make to instances of justice or equality, to the nature of rivers or mountains? — as one could verify deductions made from the kinetic theory of gases or Einstein's theory of relativity. According to the Verificationists the sentences which occur in the writings of metaphysicians look like statements, but are not because they are unverifiable. What causes them to write such sentences and to believe that they express statements, is, it is alleged, linguistic mistakes, either grotesquely obvious, as when Heidegger, like the characters in *Alice in Wonderland*, treats 'nothing' as if it were, like 'cow', the name of something, or more subtle, as when the Ontological Argument for the existence of God treats 'exists' as if it were, like 'growls', a predicate. Most Verificationists did not bother to suggest an alternative function for metaphysical sentences, though Carnap maintained, as Lazerowitz did later, that it was to express the attitude or feelings of the metaphysicians. Thus, Monism might express a harmonious attitude.

In assessing the strength of the Verifiability Principle's attack on metaphysics, it is helpful, I think, to consider at least four pairs of contrasts, namely between what exists and what can be known, between having a meaning and being verifiable, between being either tautological or empirical and being of a third kind, and between being experienced by the senses and being experienced in some other way.

The difference between Kant's attack on metaphysics and that of the Verificationists is that whereas the latter denied the possibility both of knowledge of and of the existence of anything unconnected with our senses, the former denied only knowledge or verification of it. Kant, unlike the Verificationists, did not hold that talk about things-in-themselves was meaningless or said something neither true nor false. Indeed, he attributed to things-in-themselves such characteristics as being the cause of the material of our experience. Furthermore, he allowed that the ideas of God, immortality, the ego, etc. were genuine ideas. He did, however, deny that the existence of things-in-themselves was verifiable by sense-experience or that the Ideas of Reason had any application to experience. Therefore, the real difference between Kant and the Verificationists rests on a denial of their link between being meaningful and being verifiable (by sense-experience).

We saw that this link is confined by the Verificationists to sentences which purport to say what can be either true or false and, furthermore, reveals verifiability as at most a criterion of success in saying what is either true or false, and not as an equivalent of meaning. The strength of the link lies in the plausibility of the view that if something can be true or false, there must in principle be some conditions in which it is true or false and/or some method by which it can be shown to be so and, hence, that to know whether a sentence says something true or false — and, if so, what — is to know whether there are any such conditions or method — and, if so, what. It is easy to fool oneself that, for example 'The Form of Justice exists in another world' or 'What time is it on the sun?' must be meaningful because they look so like analogous phrases, such as 'Snakes exist in Ireland' or 'What time is it in San Francisco?' But trying to think how what appears to be expressed in these words would be investigated makes one pause. On the other hand, one feels that, for example, many mathematical formulae are so similar to other well recognised ones that one can see clearly what they mean even though one does not know how to prove or disprove them because they refer to infinite series, as in Fermat's theorem that $X^n + Y^n \neq Z^n$ for $n > 2$. And there is a highly technical argument by the mathematical logician Göbel which purports to show that one can formulate in arithmetic sentences which say something true but unprovable. Equally, a metaphysical thesis like Locke's hypothesis of 'matter' as 'something I know not what' or Aristotle's of the 'unmoved mover' seems to say something meaningful, however vague and general, even though no clue as to its verification is given.

Some who admit that whatever is true or false must be verifiable as true or false, nevertheless object to the Verifiability Principle. Their reason is that they refuse to confine what is true or false to the two classes alleged by Hume and the Verificationists, namely tautologies and empirical statements. A ground for this refusal is a belief in Kant's third class of statements, namely the synthetic *a priori*. But, though Kant would certainly agree that such statements are not verifiable *by* experience, to which they are prior, he also insisted that, like the concepts which comprise them, they are empty without reference to experience. A statement like 'Every event has a cause' is applicable only to the experienceable. Hence, even the acceptance of synthetic *a priori* statements does not constitute an objection to the central core of the Verifiability Principle, however much it disagrees with its explicit words. Others accept the criterion of verifiability, but dispute its relevance to metaphysics on the ground that what is most important in metaphysics is not something which can be true or false. We shall see that Collingwood, for example, held that the material which metaphysics studies, such as the principle that 'Every event has a cause', and which he called 'absolute presuppositions', is neither true nor false; while Wisdom suggested that the utterances of metaphysicians are paradoxes and, hence, not intended to be literally true. I shall, however, later give reasons for disputing both these interpretations of what is said by metaphysicians.

The essential dispute between the Verificationists and defenders of metaphysics is whether the only possible kind of experience is confined to the senses and whether, therefore, verifiability by the senses is the sole criterion of meaningfulness or of the capability of saying something true or false. Though the early Verificationists were strict about this, later exponents have shown some flexibility by widening the kinds of experience, at least to introspection. There are also good grounds for allowing verification by mathematical proof and by logical analysis. Nor does there seem in principle any objection to other kinds of experience, such as the mystical, the extra-sensory, the non-human, etc., provided clear proof of their existence and clear description of their nature can be given. Much of this, however, seems irrelevant to the conflict between the metaphysicians and the Verificationists, for there is no evidence that Plato, Aristotle, Berkeley, Leibniz, Bradley, etc. rested their assertions about their supersensible entities on such kinds of experience. Nor is it clear to what kind of experience, for example, Aristotle would have appealed for proof of the existence of Being as Being, Leibniz of his Monads, Bradley of the Absolute, etc. Plato gave no more clue than that the Forms are experienceable by the 'eye' of the mind or Berkeley than that God is something of which we can have a 'notion'.

More plausible is the claim that just as the existence of unobservables in science, for example molecules, genes, waves, is verifiable by their experienceable effects, however unexperienceable themselves, so likewise is the existence of unobservables in metaphysics, for example Forms, Monads, Noumena. Such a claim gains some credence from the fact that just as unobservables in science are introduced to explain some experienced physical phenomena, for example waves to explain the behaviour of sound and light, molecules to explain that of gases, so unobservables in metaphysics are brought in to explain some phenomena of daily experience, for example Platonic Forms to explain the existence of instances of justice, beauty and equality, Lockean Matter or Berkeleian God to explain the existence of the unperceived. I will consider this claim in more detail in the final chapter. Here it must suffice to mention briefly several objections. First, the metaphysical unobservables are postulated as the result of fallacious steps in the argument, whereas in science even the postulation of phlogiston and the aether was, perhaps, more false than fallacious. Secondly, and more relevant to our purpose, the introduction of these unobservables, unlike those of science, does not give rise to any possible further predictions. Whereas different implications follow from the postulation of a wave and a corpuscle, a virus and a bacillus, a neutron and a proton, Ptolemaic and Copernician astronomies, absolute and relative space, no experienceable difference distinguishes Aristotle's denial of Forms from Plato's assertion of them, Berkeley's hypothesis of God from Locke's hypothesis of matter, Leibniz's pluralism from Spinoza's Monism, Descartes' two substances from Hume's none. Equally, there is no kind of experience by which Zeno's world of eternal immobility can be distinguished from Heraclitus's world of unceasing change.

The conclusions of metaphysicians depend on and seemingly follow from their premises; they have no independent means of verification. Thus, Plato's Form of Justice is no more and no less than an indescribable something which is postulated to be the answer to at least the two assumedly legitimate questions, 'What is it which any instance (or example) of justice is an instance (or example) of?' and 'What is it which a less than perfect example of justice falls short of?' Berkeley's God is equally an indescribable something which is postulated to be the answer to the two questions, 'What is the cause of the sensations we have?' and 'What is it which perceives what is unperceivable by us?' No hint is given by either Plato or Berkeley of what it would be like to experience, by sense or in any other way, the Form of Justice or God or how our present experiences would differ if the seemingly contrary hypotheses of Aristotle or Locke were correct.

Whether or not we accept the Verificationists' link of either meaning or even meaningfulness to verifiability and follow them in dismissing the writings of metaphysicians as meaningless, we must, I think, agree that statements about the existence of metaphysical entities, such as Forms, the Unmoved Mover, Monads, God, Noumena or the Absolute have not been demonstrated by their proponents to be verifiable, that is, able to be shown to be true or false, by the senses or by any alternative kind of experience. We have already seen in practice, and will later have to examine the theory behind, the way in which beliefs about them are actually reached and whether the beliefs so reached are in some way verifiable or assessable.

Notes

1. A. J. Ayer (1936, 2nd edn. 1946) *Language, Truth and Logic*, Victor Gollancz.
2. R. Carnap (1932), 'Überwindung der Metaphysik durch Logische Analyse der Sprache', *Erkenntnis* II, reprinted in A. J. Ayer (ed.) (1959) *Logical Positivism*, Allen and Unwin, pp. 60–81.
3. A. J. Ayer (1946), pp. 35–41; cf. refinements on pp. 5–16.
4. Carnap, p. 62.
5. Ayer p. 34 contrasted with p. 54; Carnap p. 62 contrasted with p. 76.
6. pp. 31, 54.
7. Chapter 6.
8. Contrast Carnap, p. 77.

8
Wittgenstein

Wittgenstein's approach to metaphysics combined many of the features of Kant and of the Verificationists. Like Kant's, it sought the limits of thought, though Kant approached them through the medium of ideas and judgements, and Wittgenstein through words and sentences. Both insisted that thought and language should be kept to the areas where it normally operates, which for Kant certainly was and for Wittgenstein probably was the area of experience. Both contrasted the pseudo-metaphysics of traditional philosophy, which wrongly fancied itself as an investigation of the transcendent super-scientific, with a legitimate metaphysics which sought to deduce *a priori* transcendental or necessary features of the world from the nature of thought and language. In Kant, this legitimate metaphysics is exemplified by the philosophical deduction of the pure intuitions of space and time, and of the various categories of the understanding. In the early logical atomism of Wittgenstein's *Tractatus*, it is the derivation of the existence of objects and atomic states of affairs from names and elementary propositions. In his later work metaphysics is interpreted as a misleading formulation of what he called 'logical grammar', one of whose various purposes was to exhibit the relation between thought and reality.

The pseudo-metaphysics is accused by Kant of pretending to know what can only be thought of and by Wittgenstein of trying to say what can only be shown. It is accused by both of them of what Kant called a desire for the unconditioned and Wittgenstein a desire for generality. It is equated by both with the transcendent, and its pretence to be a science laughed to scorn.[1] For Kant it is the product of an illusion, for Wittgenstein the result of a bewitchment.

Yet neither denies the existence of the realm of the transcendent, which metaphysics wrongly tries to get to know or to speak about, as an area in which, for example, things ethical and religious abide.[2]

Like the Verificationists' approach, Wittgenstein uses, at least in his earlier work, from the *Tractatus Logico-Philosophicus* of 1921 — or even the Notebooks of 1914 — to the *Philosophical Remarks* of 1930, something like a principle of verifiability as a criterion by which to plot and measure the bounds of thought and language. Thus, the *Tractatus* insists that 'to be able to say "p" is true (or false), I must have determined under what conditions I call "p" true, and thereby I determine the meaning of the sentence'.[3]

This criterion, as we saw earlier, aims to distinguish genuine statement of empirical fact from anything else we say, whether nonsensical in the everyday sense or meaningless in a more restricted sense of not saying anything which could be true or false. In the *Tractatus* it shaded into a picture theory of meaning, according to which a sentence stating a possible empirical fact pictures a possible state of affairs in the way that either an ordinary picture portrays a scene, a map represents a country, a gramophone record holds a piece of music or a geometrical figure is a projective drawing of something. Only sentences which picture in this way have any sense. Thus, the sentence 'It is raining' has a sense because it tells us what the weather could be like, but neither a sentence expressing a tautology, for example 'Either it is raining or it is not raining', nor a sentence expressing a contradiction, 'It is raining and it is not raining', has any sense, because neither tells us anything about the weather. Equally, since whatever the world was like, it would make no difference to the alleged truth of 'An Euclidean triangle has the sum of its angles equal to two right angles', this sentence could give no picture of a state of affairs and is, like the whole of mathematics and logic, senseless. Equally, but differently, moral judgements do not picture what is, but only pronounce what ought to be, and the statements of theology speak of what is not in the world. Hence, neither has any sense.

More important for our theme is the peculiarity of a picture that it shares its *form* with what it pictures. Thus, in a picture of a cat on a mat, there is as well as a picture-element corresponding to a possible cat and another picture-element corresponding to a possible mat, a shared form — in this case a spatial form — between the elements of the picture and the elements of the pictured. As the cat is *on* the mat, so the pictured cat is *on* the pictured mat.

Wittgenstein insisted, first, that what is common to every picture and what it pictures is a shared logical form. Secondly, the picture does not *say* that this form is common to it and what it pictures, it *shows* it in the way that 'aRb' does not, according to Wittgenstein, *say* how a is related to b, but the positions of a and b around R *show* this. Moreover, no picture — and, hence, no sentence — could say that a particular picture (or sentence) had a form common to it and what it pictures, but would have, in its turn, to show this by sharing this form with the state of affairs it wished to picture.

At this stage in his life, Wittgenstein's main reason for dismissing metaphysics and, indeed, all philosophy, including that which he himself was writing in expounding this doctrine, was that it was attempting the impossible task of saying what could only be shown, namely how a picture is related to what it pictures, that is, how language is related to the world.[4] Hence, metaphysics — and all philosophy — is nonsense. It tries to express the inexpressible.

Yet, just as Kant did not deny the existence of that which could not be known but only thought of, namely the noumenal, so Wittgenstein did not deny — indeed, he emphasised — the existence of that which could not be said but only shown, namely form. It belongs to the essence of the world.[5] Furthermore, in the *Tractatus*, he thought, like Bertrand Russell, that a task for philosophers was the invention of an ideal language which, unlike ordinary language, would reveal the logic of thought and language rather than concealing it, so that from the appearance of the language the form of the thought would be clear.

Furthermore, just as Kant thought that deductions about the nature of the world could be made *a priori* from the nature of thought — that, for example, the world had to be composed of spatial and temporal objects subject to causal laws — so Wittgenstein argued in the *Tractatus* that the world was necessarily composed of atomic facts (*Sachverhalt*) which, in their turn, were combinations of objects (*Gegenstand*, *Sache*, *Ding*), because language and thought is composed of elementary propositions, which, in their turn, are combinations of names. Later, as we shall see, he argued that the logical grammar of a word, such as 'colour', 'pain', 'imagination', etc. tells us what kind of thing anything is; it gives us the essence of things.[6]

After the period of the *Tractatus* (1921) the 'picture theory' of meaning waned, but a general verificationism grew strongly until the *Philosophical Remarks* of 1930. In this work a sentence purporting to express a proposition is allowed to have a meaning only if a method of verifying the proposition is known, propositions with the same verification are said to have the same sense,[7] the meaning of a proposition is identified with its method of verification,[8] the verification is interpreted in terms of experience 'in some sense or another',[9] and the unverifiable and the metaphysical are identified with each other.[10] There is, indeed, the occasional later reference in such works as *Philosophical Grammar* of 1932 – 4 and even the late *Philosophical Investigations* of 1945 – 9 to the continued, though now confined, use of such a principle.[11] But it is now only one exemplification of what we shall see is Wittgenstein's later theory equating the meaning of a word with its use.[12]

Wittgenstein's employment of the Principle of Verifiability does not, however, raise for the status of metaphysics any problems not already encountered in its employment by the Logical Positivists, perhaps for the good reason that they may, as they often acknowledged, have borrowed it from him. The distinctive attack on metaphysics inherent in the distinction between *saying* and *showing* partly lapsed with the demise of the picture-theory of meaning and partly, as we shall see, became absorbed in the new theory.

What sounded the death knell both of the Principle of Verifiability and of the picture-theory was Wittgenstein's own realisation that the confinement of all the uses of language and, hence, of all its abuses, to the fact-stating is mistakenly narrow. Consequently narrow, therefore, was the current list of causes of meaninglessness in philosophers' utterances. A shift in emphasis took place from the complete sentence to the word or phrase and with it the recognition of the manifold variety of kinds of words, each with its own peculiar problems. The analogy shifted from that of a picture — which fact-stating sentences had been supposed to resemble — to tools and chess men.[13] The criterion and key to meaning was not verification, but *use*. The rules of a word's use were called its 'logical grammar'.[14]

'The meaning of a word is its use in the language' became the slogan.[15] No limit is laid down on the variety and types of use which different words may have — 'How it is verified' is now appropriate to only one example of the use of language[16] — but each word must have an ordinary, that is, a standard and explicable use. 'To say "..........." makes no sense is to exclude it from the sphere of language and thereby bound the domains of language.'[17]

What the metaphysician — and the traditional philosopher when he is mistaken — does, thinks Wittgenstein, is to get the grammar of his key words wrong; to misunderstand the use of these words as they occur in their natural habitat. 'When we do philosophy we are,' he says, 'like savages, primitive people, who hear the expressions of civilised men, put a false interpretation on them, and then draw the queerest conclusions from it.'[18] Wittgenstein conceives his task, therefore, as 'bringing back words from their metaphysical to their everyday use'.[19] As early as the *Tractatus* he advised that when someone 'wished to say something metaphysical', we should demonstrate to him that he had given no meaning to certain signs in his statements'.[20] Philosophical and metaphysical misinterpretations usually consist in treating the word (or concept) under consideration as if it were analogous in logical grammar to another word with which it is analogous in linguistic grammar,[21] in treating, in the language of the *Tractatus*, a similarity of sign as a similarity of symbol or, in the language of the *Philosophical Investigations*, in taking the surface grammar of a word to be its depth grammar.[22] A fundamentally mistaken example of this is the assimilation of the language of sensations to that of material objects. Describing one's state of mind is not like describing one's room.[23] Another is the supposition that, because 'thinking' and 'talking' are grammatically similar, they must both refer to activities, the latter physical and the former mental; and then to ask for the place of the thought as we ask for the place of the speech.[24] This, says Wittgenstein, is an error comparable to that of asking for the place of the king in chess analogous to the place of the wooden piece which represents the king. Similarly, because to pour out one's knowledge is assimilated to pouring out water, knowledge becomes 'the hypothesised reservoir out of which the visible water flows'.[25] A particularly common type of such error is the introduction of a substance, often of an aethereal kind, every time our language uses a substantive (a noun), for example for 'meaning', 'time', 'mind', 'thought', etc.[26] Mind, thoughts, meaning, etc. are considered to be kinds of entities. Even grammar, in the usual sense, can mislead, as when the use of the past tense in 'When I said "Queen Elizabeth" I *meant* Elizabeth II' tempts us to suppose that 'means' signifies something I did at the time of speaking.[27] In all this we are fighting against the fascination which linguistic forms of expression have on us.[28]

Though there are many causes of these logical assimilations of linguistically similar expressions, Wittgenstein was particularly struck by a few basic sources. First, there was what he called 'a one-sided diet', that is, the use of too few and too narrow a set of examples of the uses of the word under consideration (for example 'think', 'imagine', 'know').[29] For example, just as a scientist might conclude that all swans are white because he had only examined swans in England and not considered those in Australia, so a philosopher might think that imagination is necessarily tied to imagery because he had considered only visual imagining.

Secondly, metaphysical paradoxes, such as that everything flows, that all experience is vague, or that the floor we stand on is not really solid, are often due to using these words without any antithesis, that is, any idea of what is stable, precise or solid.[30] A third cause of metaphysical nonsense is a craving for generality, which, though permissible in science, is mistaken, Wittgenstein thinks, in philosophy. It is to this that he attributes a basic fallacy which has underlain much philosophy since Plato, namely the assumption that all things referred to by the same word, for example 'just', 'good', 'equal' must have something in common, or its variation that to grasp the meaning of a general word, like 'leaf', is to possess a general mental picture — for example Locke's 'abstract idea' — of a leaf. By contrast, Wittgenstein argues, as we saw in the chapter on Plato, that in the case of many words, such as 'game', 'number', 'colour', there need be no more than a family resemblance between the varied things to which the word can be applied.[31]

The most important cause, however, of metaphysics and of fallacy in traditional philosophy, which is also a cause of the philosophers' mistaken craving for generality, is the assimilation of philosophical problems to empirical problems, the failure to distinguish clearly between philosophy and the natural sciences, and the old belief that metaphysics is a kind of super-science.

As early as the *Tractatus*, Wittgenstein had insisted on a rigid separation of philosophy and science. 'Philosophy is not one of the natural sciences. It is something which stands above or below science.'[32] He allowed only the statements of science to say anything, and, therefore, to make sense, by condemning those of philosophy to the impossible task of saying what can only be shown.[33] Furthermore, he had hinted even there that a sure symptom of the misunderstanding of the nature of a proposition in logic was to give it the character of a proposition of natural science.[34] At the very end of the *Philosophical Investigations* he repeated 'We are not doing natural science.'[35] We have seen how often metaphysicians had tried to have the advantages of both the necessary and the empirical, of the conceptual and the ontological, to strive for what even Kant declared impossible in metaphysics, namely synthetic *a priori* propositions.

Throughout his writings Wittgenstein emphasised that 'The essential thing about metaphysics is that it obliterates the distinction between factual and conceptual investigations',[36] as in Cratylus' assertion that 'One cannot step into the same river twice'[37] or Berkeley's contention that 'The tree does not exist when no-one sees it.'[38] 'The character of a metaphysical question,' he declared, 'is that we express an uncertainty about the grammar of a word in the form of a scientific question',[39] as when we 'interpret a grammatical movement as the observation of a quasi-physical phenomenon'.[40] Thus, the philosophical question 'What is the object of a thought?' sounds like the scientific question 'What are the ultimate constituents of matter?', whereas it really seeks to understand the grammar of, for example, 'He thought of a solution', which will explain, among other things, how it is that we can think both of what does and of what does not exist.[41] Similarly, the philosopher talks as if 'I believe there are sense-data' is like 'I believe that matter consists of electrons'[42] or that 'Doesn't the child know that it is lying before I teach him the word?' is a question of fact.[43] Another example, not used by Wittgenstein, would be Locke's theory of ideas — the forerunner of sense-data — where, starting with the apparently harmless remark that an idea is 'whatever is the object of thought' and assuming that it would be generally accepted that in this sense there are ideas, he conducted his subsequent philosophical investigation into the origin and extent of our grasp of these ideas almost as if it were a piece of psychology; indeed, as if it were, in his words, an 'Essay on the Human Understanding'. But to Wittgenstein, to say, for example, 'Seeing is not an action, but a state' is to make a grammatical, not a psychological, remark.[44] This, he believes, is made clearer if we use what Carnap called the 'formal' for the 'material' mode and, for example, instead of asking 'Is understanding this activity?', we say 'Is "understanding" used for this activity?'[45]

Metaphysicians, according to Wittgenstein, failed to see that statements about the essence or nature of something, for example that pain is such that one person cannot have another's pain, are not empirical assertions about the nature of things in the world, but about the grammar of some key word, such as 'pain'.[46] Similarly, it is because to say, for example, 'Red is timeless' looks as if it were saying something about the nature of red that it is a metaphysical statement, whereas really it is a grammatical statement about the word 'red'.[47] In Wittgenstein's earlier writings the essence of things, which is the quarry of philosophical pursuit, was that which could be shown but not said.[48] Now, 'Essence', he says, 'is expressed by grammar.'[49] It is grammar which tells us 'what kind of thing anything is'.[50]

Hence, we must not try to solve philosophical questions as if they were scientific or experimental. We must not, for example, study our present headache to get clear about the philosophical problem of sensation.[51] To watch ourselves while we think in order to discover the nature or essence of thinking would be like watching the last move in chess to discover what check-mating is.[52] 'A machine cannot think' is not an empirical statement. We are not analysing phenomena, but concepts and, hence, the uses of words like 'feel', or 'think'.[53] For the puzzling thing about thinking is not how a strange mechanism works — which would be a scientific question — but a muddle caused by the mystifying use of language.[54] Hence, the metaphysical remark 'Thinking is an incorporeal process' would be a bad way of distinguishing the grammar of 'think' from that of 'eat'.[55]

A sure sign of a grammatical proposition masking as a scientific is the use of words like 'must' and 'can', as when the metaphysician insists, for example, that I *must* know what I feel.[56] This shows that what is at issue is a logical rule, not a matter of fact. It was not experience or scientific proof that persuaded Berkeley that a tree cannot exist when no-one perceives it, or Plato that because there are instances of justice there must also be justice itself. Berkeley's certainty came from his assumption about the nature of existence, that is, the grammar of 'exist', and Plato's from his analysis of the meaning of 'X is an example of justice.' 'If it's a logical "must",' says Wittgenstein, 'then it's a grammatical remark.'[57] Hence, one way of showing that a proposition, for example 'Only I can know whether I am in pain', is meant to be taken metaphysically is to ask whether it is empirical, that is, whether its opposite is conceivable, or whether it is asserting what must be so.[58]

The notion of logical grammar also allows Wittgenstein to explain what had been the typical metaphysical problem of the *Tractatus*, the impossible attempt to say what could only be shown, that is, the relation between language and the world. In *Philosophical Grammar* he holds that 'Like everything metaphysical, the harmony between thought and reality is to be found in the grammar of the language.'[59] Equally, the Verifiability Principle of meaning is now categorised as a contribution to the grammar of the proposition.[50]

The message of the *Tractatus* was that the essence of the world could not be stated in language, but only shown by the arrangement of its signs. Hence, we were told there that the right method of doing philosophy was to say nothing. In the *Philosophical Remarks* it is allowed that these arrangements of signs could be given in rules for the language which would exclude nonsensical combinations of signs.[61] Later the statement of such rules was identified with the logical grammar of the signs, so that now the unsayable essence of the world, whose grasp is the business of philosophy, became expressible in the grammar of the language. And metaphysics which had earlier been the result of attempts, such as that of Realism, Idealism, etc., to say the unsayable, became the misunderstanding of the grammar of the language and resulted in nonsensical arrangements of its words.

Since logical grammar gives us the essence of things, tells us what kind of thing anything is and allows us to express the relation between thought and reality, Wittgenstein's later views, like the early views of the *Tractatus*, contain a reformed metaphysics in the same sense in which the first two parts of Kant's *Critique*, that is, the Transcendental Aesthetic and the Transcendental Analytic, contained a metaphysics of experience. Wittgenstein, even in his later work, accepts the possibility of a correct *a priori* deduction of the nature of reality from the nature of thought or language, just as much as he rejects traditional metaphysics and philosophy as a fallacious inference of the latter from the former. Just as metaphysicians wrongly supposed that, because 'thinking' is linguistically analogous with 'talking', therefore 'thinking' is the name of an inner process as 'talking' is the name of an outer, so Wittgenstein argues that because 'thinking' is logically analogous to 'check-mating', therefore thinking refers to the circumstances in which some other activities take place just as 'check-mating' refers to the rules of chess and the position of the pieces which make, for example, a move in a particular game, from KB3 to QKt6, check-mate. Equally, 'A thing cannot be red and green all over' is a truth about reality derivable from the grammar of colour words.[63]

From his earliest to his latest writings Wittgenstein's attitude to metaphysics was, like Kant's, not so much an indiscriminate rejection of it, but an attempt to show that it had misunderstood its task and that it could, therefore, be replaced by a reformed discipline

— the study of logical grammar in Wittgenstein and the doctrine
of the Transcendental in Kant — of which Wittgenstein could say
what he had said of his philosophy, that it was an 'heir to what
used to be called philosophy'.[64]

Notes

1. *Notebooks* (1914–16), Basil Blackwell, p. 78.
2. *Notebooks*, pp. 78–9; *Tractatus* (1912), Routledge and Kegan Paul,
6.421, 6.432.
3. *Tractatus*, 4.063; *Notebooks*, pp. 67, 94.
4. *Notebooks*, p. 12; *Tractatus*, 6.53.
5. *Philosophical Remarks* (henceforth *PR*) (1930), sect. 54.
6. *Philosophical Investigations* (henceforth *PI*) (1945–9), sects. 371, 373.
7. *PR* sects. 36, 43, 59, 65, 114, 132, 149.
8. *PR* sects. 166, 232.
9. *PR* sects. 225, 65.
10. *PR* sect. 21.
11. *Philosophical Grammar* (henceforth *PG*) (1932–4), p. 227, 'our old
principle'; sect. 82; *PI* sect. 353.
12. *PG* sect. 82; *PI*. 353.
13. *Lectures on Aesthetics* (1936), 4.
14. *PI* sect. 29.
15. *PG* sect. 23; *PI* sects. 1, 9–11, 20, 30, 43, 138, 383, 421.
16. *PG* sect. 82; *PI* sect. 353.
17. *PG* sect. 137; *PI* sect. 500.
18. *PI* sect. 194; *PG* sect. 9.
19. *PI* sect. 116.
20. *Tractatus*, 6.53.
21. *PI* sect. 90.
22. *Tractatus*, 3.323–5; *PI* sect. 644.
23. *PI* sects. 290, 293.
24. *Blue and Brown Books* (henceforth *BB*) (1958), p. 7.
25. *PG* sect. 10; *BB*, pp. 130, 143.
26. *BB*, pp. 1, 5–6, 47.
27. *BB*, p. 142.
28. *BB*, p. 27; *PI* sect. 109.
29. *PI* sect. 593.
30. *BB*, pp. 45–6.
31. *BB*, pp. 17–20; *PI* sects. 65–73.
32. *Tractatus*, 4.111; *Notebooks*, p. 93.
33. *Tractatus*, 6.53.
34. *Tractatus*, 6.111.
35. *PI* p. 200.
36. *Zettel* (1929–48), sect. 458; *PI* sect. 392.
37. *Zettel*, sect. 459.
38. *BB*, pp. 56–7, 109; *Zettel*, sect. 427.

39. *BB*, pp. 35, 109; *PI* sects. 251, 253.

40. *PI* sect. 401.

41. *BB*, p. 35.

42. *BB*, p. 70.

43. 'Wittgenstein's Notes for Lectures on "Private Experience" and "Sense-Data"' (henceforth *Phil Rev*), *Philosophical Review*, 77 (1968), p. 302; *Zettel*, sect. 412.

44. *Zettel*, sect. 208; *PI* sect. 574.

45. *Zettel*, sect. 298; *PI* sect. 370.

46. *Phil Rev* pp. 277, 282; *BB*, p. 49; *PI* sects. 109, 295.

47. *PI* sects. 58, 199.

48. *PR* sect. 54.

49. *PI* sect. 371.

50. *PI* sect. 373.

51. *PI* sect. 314.

52. *PI* sect. 316.

53. *PI* sect. 383.

54. *BB*, pp. 5–6.

55. *PI* sect. 339.

56. *BB*, p. 55.

57. *PG* sect. 8; *BB*, p. 55.

58. *PG* sect. 83.

59. *PG* sect. 112; *Zettel*, sect. 55.

60. *PI* sect. 353.

61. *PR* sect. 54.

62. *PR* sect. 55.

63. *Zettel*, sect. 331.

64. *BB*, p. 28.

Part III
Rehabilitations of Metaphysics

After the attacks of the Verificationists in the twenties of this century, metaphysical system building of the speculative kind, which has only occasionally appealed to the English mind, went out of favour in English-speaking philosophy. Interest in this area of philosophy shifted, on the one hand, to that analytic examination of general concepts, such as identity, causality, existence, which we saw represented one main interpretation of metaphysics in Aristotle, and, on the other hand, to various attempts to save classical metaphysics from its critics, especially the Verificationists, by what amount to reinterpretations of its methods and objectives.

The three best known of such recent attempts to rehabilitate metaphysics, though vastly different from each other, share, as we shall see, two major common characteristics.

First, they all try to meet the rejection of metaphysics, especially by the Verificationists, by arguing that the attack is irrelevant because it wrongly supposes that the metaphysicians were advancing something which could be regarded as true or false and, therefore, could arguably be required to be verifiable. But in their opinion the assertions of the classical metaphysicians are not intended to be either true or false. Thus, R. G. Collingwood, who was Professor of Metaphysical Philosophy at Oxford from 1935 to 1941, held that what are typically, but wrongly, taken to be metaphysical statements, such as 'Every event has a cause' or 'God exists', are really what he called 'absolute presuppositions' which, he argued, cannot be either true or false. On the other hand, genuine metaphysical statements are purely historical statements that such pronouncements as 'Every event has a cause' or 'God exists' were the absolute presuppositions of a given epoch, area or thinker, and are, therefore, true or false historical statements. John Wisdom, who was Professor of Philosophy at Cambridge from 1952 to 1968, attempted to deflect the Verificationist attack as irrelevant by arguing that metaphysical statements should not be assessed as literally true or false because they are really paradoxes or verbal recommendations. The Verificationists' mistake was to suppose that the only way of revealing something new is either by deductive or by inductive reasoning which results in logically or empirically verifiable conclusions. But metaphysics, like psycho-analysis, art and some parts of science, tries, according to Wisdom, to illuminate by paradoxes the familiar in the hidden, the new in the old. The comparison of metaphysics with psycho-analysis is carried further by the contemporary American philosopher Morris Lazerowitz, whose argument for the irrelevance of the Verificationist attack is that metaphysical statements are simply the expressions or symptoms of deep-seated psycho-analytic needs, not statements of fact.

The second common factor shared by these recent rehabilitations of metaphysics is that they show, to different degrees, an ambivalence between asserting, on the one hand, that their accounts of metaphysical statements describe what the great metaphysicians of the past either thought they were doing or, whatever they thought, were actually doing, and asserting, on the other hand, that their accounts suggest how the sayings of these, and any other, metaphysicians should, and might profitably, be regarded. Within the first of these alternatives there is, as mentioned, a further ambivalence between claiming to discuss what the traditional metaphysicians said and thought they were doing and claiming to discuss what they actually were doing. Here the line is more usually taken that the practice of the metaphysicians, like that of many other people, belied their preaching and that they were not actually doing what they said and thought they were doing. This line is taken because of the sheer implausibility of supposing that the traditional metaphysicians said or thought they were doing what these rehabilitations allege they were. And it is, likewise, the very arguable implausibility of supposing that the metaphysicians were actually doing what their rehabilitators allege that leads the latter to adopt the third position, namely that their suggestions are how metaphysical sayings should, and profitably might, be taken.

9

Collingwood

R. G. Collingwood, like Kant, considered attempts by metaphysical arguments to reach what lies beyond experience as doomed to futility.[1] His own countersuggestion, in his *Essay on Metaphysics*, was that metaphysics is 'the attempt to find out what absolute presuppositions have been made by this or that person or group of persons, on this or that occasion or group of occasions, in the course of this or that piece of thinking'.[2] As such, 'All metaphysical questions are,' he said, 'historical questions, and all metaphysical propositions are historical propositions.'[3]

The psychological basis for this view was no doubt, as he himself records in his *Autobiography*, his own lifelong interest in the history of thought, which he regarded as 'my own subject'.[4] He admitted that his interest in philosophy was more in finding out historically what exactly Plato, Aristotle, Kant, etc. said and meant than in judging whether it was true or not.[5] Further, as we shall see, his theory that the truth or meaning of what is said depends on the question to which it is an answer involves a historical search for that question. He rejected the idea that philosophers at various times have tackled the same eternal questions; despite the similarity of their language, historical enquiries suggest that the problems are actually different.[6] Finally, it is significant that he was himself a distinguished historian and archaeologist of Roman Britain.

His early historical and archaeological work had convinced him of the practical maxim that 'one found out nothing at all except in answer to a question'.[7] He proceeded to raise this practical maxim to the status of a logical-psychological principle, namely 'Every statement that anybody ever makes is made in answer to a question', whether asked by himself or another.[8] This happens both in scientific and in lower-grade thinking, though only in the former is one necessarily aware of this, and only in the former is the question temporally as well as logically prior to the answer. He sometimes seems to have believed not merely that one could in principle always find a question to which any of one's statements is an answer, but that one actually did ask oneself such a question, even — strange as this is — if only unconsciously.[9] The cause of this belief may have been that he thought that assuming a question, which he supposed anyone who uttered a statement did, is a mental act.[10] We must object, however, that there are plenty of occasions on which we utter statements, e.g. quite gratuitously, in making claims, in expositions, etc., where no question, conscious or unconscious, lay behind them. In his *Autobiography*, he argues further that both what a man means, and what that which he says means, depend on the question to which what he says is an answer.[11] Thus the remark 'Number one plug is alright' is alleged not only to arise, but to take its meaning from, the question, 'Is it because number one plug is not sparking that my car won't go?' Secondly, he holds that no two propositions can contradict each other unless they are answers to the same question.[12] But it is absurd to suppose either that the meaning of the sentence 'Number one plug is alright' would be different or that the statement made by using those words would be different, if it were an answer, not to the above question, but to the question 'Are all the plugs in that packet from the shop alright?' Indeed, how could one discover what was even a possible question to which any given statement was the answer, unless one first knew the meaning of the words used to make the statement? It is equally absurd to suppose that 'Number one plug is faulty' does not contradict 'Number one plug is alright' if the first statement is an answer to the question about the plugs in the car and the second an answer to the question about the plugs in the packet. Of course, Collingwood would be quite right if all he was saying was that these two sentences do not make contradictory statements if the statements are about different plugs or about the same plugs at different times. But he clearly wants to do something much more novel than to make this well-known point.

Having put forward his first principle that every statement, or 'proposition' as he often calls it, is an answer to a question, he adds a second, namely that 'Every question involves a presupposition', conscious or not, from which it arises and which, by virtue of giving rise to the question, is said to be 'logically efficacious'.[13] A well-known illustration of this, which Collingwood mentions, is the recognition that to ask a man whether he has stopped beating his wife is to presuppose that he has been beating her.[14] More seriously, to ask what is the cause of cancer is to presuppose that it has a cause. A presupposition can, he argues, be either relative — that is, one which is both a presupposition of one question and the answer to another — or absolute — that is, one which, though a presupposition of a question, is never an answer to one. Thus, the proposition that cancer has a cause is a relative presupposition because it is not only a presupposition of the question 'What is the cause of cancer?', but also an answer to the question, e.g., 'Does cancer have a cause?' But, according to Collingwood, the presupposition that all events have causes is an absolute presupposition because, though it is presupposed by the question 'Does cancer have a cause?', it is not an answer to any question.

Since, as I quoted at the beginning, Collingwood regards metaphysics as a study of absolute presuppositions, it is important to get quite clear about these. The idea has a number of difficulties.

First, because he is wedded to his scheme of enquiry as a series of questions and answers, he defines an absolute presupposition as one which, though it is presupposed by a question, is never an answer to one. This gives an artificial air to some of his examples. Though he clearly wants to argue, quite sensibly, that there is an ascending order of presuppositions, so that a scientist who asks what is the cause of cancer presupposes that cancer has a cause, and he supposes this because he presupposes that everything in nature has a cause, Collingwood has to frame a series of separate questions.[15] Thus, the scientist's statement 'X is the cause of cancer' logically, and perhaps temporally, involves a prior question 'What is the cause of cancer?', which involves a presupposition 'Cancer has a cause', which should involve a prior question. But what is this question? Is it simply 'Has cancer a cause?' Sometimes Collingwood seems to take this line, as when he suggests that the prior question one has to find for the presupposition that a measuring-tape is accurate is simply 'a question admitting of the alternative answers "the tape is accurate", "the tape is not accurate" '.[16]

At other times, he changes the line of questioning, so that he does not look for a question to which, e.g., 'Cancer has a cause' is the answer, but shifts to the question 'Was the scientist sure that cancer had a cause?' with its answer 'Quite sure', and shifts again to the question 'Why was he sure?' with its answer 'Because every-thing that happens has a cause.' But, though he calls this last an absolute presupposition, it is clearly, in his own example, first, an answer to the question 'Why was he sure?' and, secondly, not a presupposition of any other question appearing in his set. Further-more, just as he allows 'Is the tape accurate?' as the question to which 'The tape is accurate' is an answer, and allows that 'Every-thing has a cause' can be an answer to the question 'Why are you sure that cancer has a cause?', why should he not allow that any of his own so-called absolute presuppositions, e.g. 'Everything has a cause', 'Mathematics is applicable to the world', 'Energy is conserved',[17] 'There exists a God', can be answers to the gram-matically corresponding questions 'Has everything a cause?', 'Is mathematics applicable to the world?', 'Is energy conserved?', 'Is there a God?' Indeed, Collingwood himself sometimes speaks more naturally not only of presuppositions being involved by questions, but also of their being involved also by statements and thoughts.[18]

A second, and major, awkward consequence of his insistence on the question-and-answer procedure is that absolute presuppo-sitions cannot be true or false or be properly called 'propositions'. This is mainly because, in his view, they cannot be statements, since every statement must be an answer to a question and absolute, as contrasted with relative, presuppositions cannot be answers to any questions.[19] A related reason for his denial of truth or falsity to absolute presuppositions is a peculiar change he advocated — though he sometimes suggested that this is in accordance with what is ordinarily meant — in the use of 'true', so that it would now apply, not to individual propositions, but to a complex of questions and answers.[20] Such propositions in this complex would now only be 'right' or 'wrong', that is, fruitful or not in advancing the question-and-answer technique. Similarly, he holds that absolute presuppositions cannot be verifiable, either in the ordinary sense he sometimes uses of being shown to be true or false[26] — since they are, by the previous argument, neither true nor false — or in a peculiar sense he sometimes introduces, namely 'that a question should be asked to which the affirmative answer would be that presupposition itself'[22] — since they are not possible answers to questions. Neither can they, for the same reasons, be proved or disproved or even justified.[23] They can only be dis-covered. Indeed, it seems doubtful whether absolute presuppo-sitions can, as Collingwood clearly wishes, even be meaningful.

For, first, on the doctrine of his *Autobiography* the meaning of what someone says depends on the question to which it is an answer, and an absolute presupposition is not the answer to any question. Secondly, on the Logical Positivists' theory of meaning, to which he shows himself sympathetic in his *Essay on Metaphysics*, what is not verifiable is not meaningful, and an absolute presupposition is not verifiable.

Quite apart from the impossibility of absolute presuppositions being true or false, Collingwood argues that such properties are unimportant to them anyway, since their importance lies in their 'logical efficacy', that is, their causing certain questions to arise — as the presupposition that it has a cause gives rise to the question, 'What is the cause of cancer?' Their logical efficacy, he holds, does not depend either on their being true or on their being thought to be true.[24] But, though he is quite right to argue that to presuppose that p is not to believe that it is true that p (or even to believe that p) any more than one need believe a known false assumption in *reductio ad absurdum* proofs, it does not follow, as he seems to have thought, that to presuppose that p is not to presuppose that it is true that p. It is difficult to see what presupposing that p could mean if it were not logically related — I do not say equivalent — to presupposing that it is true that p in the way that believing (thinking, assuming) that p is related to believing (thinking, assuming) that it is true that p.

It is, then, absolute presuppositions in the sense defined which Collingwood thinks it is the job of metaphysics to study. Clearly, since absolute presuppositions cannot be true or false, confirmed or disputed, contradictory of this or that, justified or evaluated except perhaps as being rich in giving rise to questions, any study of them cannot be critical or evaluative, but only historical. It can at most only discover them. A metaphysician is a historian or archaeologist, laying bare the presuppositions of a given system, such as the scientific systems of early Greece, of Newton or Einstein, or the historical systems of Thucydides, Gibbon or Mommsen. For instance, he suggests that an absolute presupposition of Newtonian physics was that some events have causes, while others have laws, of nineteenth century (or Kantian) physics that all events have causes, and of twentieth century (or Einsteinian) physics that no events have causes, but only laws.[25] The thinking whose presuppositions he thought it was the job of metaphysics to lay bare seems in fact usually, though not exclusively, to have been scientific thinking about nature. In such investigations the metaphysician plays as much the part of an analyst as that of a historian, since what the questions — to be identified historically — of a certain person, group or age absolutely presuppose is what asking these questions logically commits him or it to, and not what he consciously and explicitly may have thought he was assuming.[26] Nor can there be any attempt to decide between the relative merits of, e.g., the presupposition that every event has a cause, or that God exists, or that there is motion in the world. We can only point out when they were held. As we saw, this idea of absolute presuppositions has the curious result that such 'propositions' as 'Every event has a cause' or 'God exists' are neither true nor false, provable or unprovable or even contradicted by 'Not every event has a cause' or 'God does not exist.' Collingwood does frequently call an absolute presupposition itself, such as 'Every event has a cause', 'there is motion in nature', 'God exists', a metaphysical proposition.[27] But he says that this is short for a complex statement in which such a presupposition is prefaced by what he calls a 'metaphysical rubric', namely that 'in such and such a phase of scientific thought it was absolutely presupposed that . . .' It is strictly speaking only the resulting complex historical statement which is a metaphysical proposition.

A virtue of this view of metaphysics in his eyes was that by insisting that absolute presuppositions are neither true nor false, and that the assertions of this metaphysics are historical truths or falsehoods, this metaphysics was immune to the attacks of the Verificationists on metaphysics as traditionally conceived.[28]

In examining this view of metaphysics, we must first ask whether Collingwood thought it was a correct description of what metaphysicians, like Plato, Aristotle, Berkeley, Leibniz, Spinoza or Kant, have actually done, or whether he was only suggesting that this is what metaphysics should do or, perhaps as a consequence of his view of the nature of absolute presuppositions, the only thing they could legitimately do. The second, and more important, question is whether it is actually a correct description or, failing that, a helpful suggestion.

Collingwood is, in fact, quite ambivalent about how much a description of actual metaphysical practice his definition of 'metaphysics' is. He often claims that it is true of, and indeed derived from, the work of Aristotle, after which the subject was called.[29] More accurately, he claims that it is true of that part of Aristotle's work and of Aristotle's account wherein metaphysics is regarded as the study of first principles. Aristotle's definition of 'metaphysics' as the study of Being *qua* Being is dismissed, for reasons we need not examine, as nonsense. But, as I have argued in a previous chapter, the study of Being *qua* Being and the study of first principles are all part of the same examination of the most general concepts underlying our thinking, and pervasive throughout every particular enquiry: an examination which admittedly moves from the conceptual to the ontological, but which nevertheless need not distinguish between a study of Being and, e.g., a study of the law of contradiction or of the nature of identity, difference, unity, etc.

Similarly, he claims that what Spinoza does when he says that nature is the same as God is 'to state an historical fact about the religious foundation of seventeenth century natural science', while Aristotle 'describes the absolute presuppositions of Greek science in the fourth century BC';[30] that for Anselm and the Patristic writers, the remark 'God exists' is merely a statement that this is an absolute presupposition of Christian thinking;[31] that in Kant's metaphysics, especially that part of the *Critique* called 'Transcendental Analytic', he is merely 'stating as fully and accurately as he could what exactly the presuppositions were which in his work as a physicist [and that of all contemporary physics] he found himself making'.[32] At one place Collingwood roundly declares 'When I say this [sc. 'finding out what absolute presuppositions are in fact made'] is what metaphysicians do I mean this is what I find them doing when I read their works from Aristotle onwards.'[33]

On the other hand, he frequently admitted that both the pronouncements of metaphysicians and their practice failed to square with his definition. Sometimes he dismissed this on the ground that people's pronouncements often belied their practices and that it was only the former which contradicts his view. This was how he treated Aristotle's view that his examination of pure Being and of absolute presuppositions was the same; or the many Christian philosophers who often argued that there could be a proof of God's existence;[34] or Bradley who quipped that metaphysics is the finding of bad reasons for what we believe upon instinct;[35] or Samuel Alexander who held that every event has a cause can be proved from experience;[36] or Ayer who declared that metaphysical assertions are meaningless because unverifiable;[37] or Kant who tried to expose the basic errors of all previous metaphysics.[38] 'For a man of the twentieth century,' Collingwood said, 'it is inexcusable to take a metaphysician's word for what he is doing. You must settle that question for yourself by studying his work.'[39] This does not, of course, betoken any insincerity on the metaphysician's part, because, in Collingwood's view, they have genuinely not been aware of the truth of his doctrine that 'metaphysics has always been an historical science'.[40]

But this attempt, legitimate in itself, to distinguish what the metaphysicians said or thought they were doing, and what actually they were doing, is not only implausible in the actual examples taken, but it was not usually maintained even by Collingwood. Thus, he admitted that Aristotle actually did not only try to examine both the nature of being, and such presuppositions as the law of contradiction, but regarded these as parts of the same study;[41] that Spinoza's *Ethics* does constitute a quasi-mathematical attempt to prove his conclusions;[42] that Christian writers often produced proofs of the existence of God;[43] that Alexander and Bradley, wrongly in Collingwood's opinion, ended up with a variety of positivistic metaphysics;[44] that Ayer's whole thesis is an attack on metaphysical assertions as purported statements[45] — a mistake said to have been made earlier by Mill.[46] Furthermore, Collingwood's attempts to show Plato[47] and more particularly Kant[48] as believers in his view of metaphysics are, quite properly, hedged about with the *caveat* that those authors probably would not have accepted his interpretation.

Collingwood's usual position, however, seems to have been that not only the pronouncements of metaphysicians but also their practice only half fulfilled his notion of metaphysics. Thus, he frequently speaks of a 'reformed metaphysics' which is to be contrasted with the 'pseudo-metaphysics' which supposes that metaphysical statements can be deduced as conclusions in an argument.[49] 'The extent to which metaphysics has already been a science in the past,' he says, 'is governed by the extent to which it has already been history', and the way for it to become a proper science in the future is for it to become 'more completely and more consciously what in fact it has always been, an historical science'.[50] Collingwood's commentators and supporters clearly speak and think of his metaphysics as a 'reformed metaphysics'.[51]

There seems little doubt, as will be clear both to those who know at first hand the works of the classical metaphysicians and, I hope, to those who have read my interpretations of Plato, Aristotle, Berkeley, Leibniz and Bradley, that Collingwood's account of metaphysics has no historical basis whatsoever.

First, Plato, Aristotle, Berkeley, Leibniz and Bradley, do, as we saw in detail, argue for and think they have proved their conclusions, whether it be the existence of Forms, the Unmoved

Mover, a collection of Monads or God. Secondly, they neither think nor would they be right in thinking that these conclusions, which in fact posit a supersensible world, are the actual presuppositions of their or any age. They think, as Collingwood admits Kant did, that they are the necessary, but provable, conclusions of admitted premises analogous to the necessary and proved conclusions of scientists. They did not regard them as presuppositions any more than scientists regard the existence of atoms, absolute or relative space, genes, waves, the ether, phlogiston or gravity as presuppositions in Collingwood's sense. It would be ridiculous to suppose that Plato's Forms or Leibniz's Monads, whose postulation is the ultimate conclusions of their argument, are absolute presuppositions of any age. The sense in which, for example, Plato could be said to have argued that our recognition of imperfection presupposes our prior acquaintance with and, therefore, the existence of the perfect is not Collingwood's sense of 'presupposition', since Plato's presupposition is regarded as something true which is entailed by what presupposes it. Somewhat similarly, the scientist who thinks that the existence of genes is presupposed by the distribution of inherited characteristics thinks that his presupposition is true and at least empirically implied by the facts it seeks to explain. These are not even relative presuppositions, since they do not simply give rise to questions, but are allegedly implied, logically or empirically, by existing truths. Nor is the sense of Collingwood's 'presupposition' the same as that in which Strawson, and Frege before him, argued that the truth or falsity of a statement, for example that the present King of France is bald, presupposes — rather than, as Russell held, implies — that the object referred to by its subject term exists. For in this sense the presupposition which is made, for example that there is a present King of France, is something which must be true, if what presupposes it is to be either true or false. Furthermore, for Collingwood, but not for either Plato or Strawson – Frege, what presupposes something is strictly a question, or the asking of a question, not a statement. On the other hand, there may be some affinity between Collingwood's absolute presuppositions, which can be neither true nor false, and Wittgenstein's basic attitudes or beliefs which, in *On Certainty* he argued against G. E. Moore, are not based on evidence or grounds, and cannot be said to be known or, perhaps, even true, but feature only as the foundations of our shared forms of life. Another possible affinity with Wittgenstein is that between Collingwood's insistence that what is said only has meaning in relation to a question to which it is the answer, and Wittgenstein's view that without appropriate circumstances what is uttered has no meaning.

Thirdly, even if — which I dispute — some of the conclusions of metaphysicians, such as Berkeley's God or the principles of Kant's Transcendental Analytic, happen to be the presuppositions of the science of their contemporaries, they do not occupy in Berkeley or Kant the alleged place of historical truths. Collingwood is forced, in support of his thesis, to take the quite extraordinary view not only that what Anselm and the Patristics asserted in their metaphysics was not 'God exists', but 'Christian people believe that God exists', but also that the latter is what the former means.[52] Indeed, if the latter were what the former means the former would, contrary to Collingwood's view that absolute presuppositions cannot be true or false, itself be true, since the latter is admittedly true. Moreover, could A believe that p if 'p' could not express something true or false?

Fourthly, rival metaphysicians have always, despite Collingwood's claim that this is impossible, treated their conclusions as contradictory of each other.[53] Aristotle certainly thought that he had disproved Plato's theory of Forms, Berkeley explicitly took Locke's supposition of matter as the hypothesis which his theocentric metaphysics was designed to overthrow. Leibniz's pluralism and Spinoza's monism are, and were intended to be, alternative metaphysical systems, not rival historical theses about the presuppositions of their day. Fifthly, in examining some of the statements expressed by metaphysicians, such as Kant's statement that every event has a cause, Collingwood asks, for example, why did Kant believe it.[54] Yet he is clearly not asking, as on his own view he should, why did Kant believe the historical statement that the presupposition that every event has a cause underlies nineteenth-century physics, but why did Kant believe that every event has a cause — something which, on Collingwood's view, could not be true or false, or believed or not believed. Similar remarks apply to his examination of Aristotle's arguments for his 'metaphysical proposition' that there is motion in nature, of the presuppositions of positivism, and of the whole concept of cause.[55] Collingwood himself not only criticises and condemns many of the presupposition of the past, but some of his sympathetic commentators contend that he rightly argued that this is a legitimate part of the task of a historian of ideas.[56]

Finally, I have suggested an alternative explanation of how

the classical metaphysicians have arrived at their conclusions, an explanation which, I have argued, is supported by the actual argument used in their works and which pictures them as reaching — admittedly illegitimately[57] — supersensible conclusions from an analysis of those basic ideas which Aristotle, the eponym of metaphysics, set up as the proper subject matter of their subject.

Collingwood's 'reformed metaphysics' as a history of ideas, namely those ideas and principles which either actually have been or logically ought to have been presupposed in the thought of any given period or thinker, is a perfectly legitimate study. It is not surprising that such a study should have proved attractive to the historian and archaeologist in Collingwood. But it is not, as he usually reluctantly admits, the study which one can see pursued in the work of the great metaphysicians from Plato to Bradley, nor is there any reason why it should replace it or usurp its name.

Notes

1. R. G. Collingwood (1939), *An Autobiography*, Penguin Books (henceforth *A*), 48.
2. R. G. Collingwood (1940), *An Essay on Metaphysics*, Oxford University Press (henceforth *M*), 47.
3. *M* 49, 62; *A* 52.
4. *A* 7, 75.
5. *A* 23–4.
6. *A* 45–51.
7. *A* 21.
8. *M* 23.
9. *M* 24.
10. *M* 24–26, 42–3.
11. *A* 26–7.
12. *A* 27.
13. *M* 25–6.
14. *M* 25–6.
15. *M* 21.
16. *M* 29–30.
17. *M* 264–8.
18. *M* 21.
19. *M* 32.
20. *A* 29–31.
21. *M* 31–2, 147.
22. *M* 30.
23. *M* 45–6.
24. *M* 28–9, 52–3.

25. *M* 49–51.
26. *M* 214.
27. *M* 217, 238.
28. *M* Chapters 14, 16.
29. *M* Chapters 1–2, pp. 41, 61.
30. *M* 71.
31. *M* 186–90.
32. *M* 240, 243, 249.
33. *M* 54.
34. *M* 188.
35. *M* 153–4, 162.
36. *M* 175–6.
37. *M* Chapter 16.
38. *M* 237.
39. *M* 235.
40. *M* 58.
41. *M* 54, 61.
42. *M* 68.
43. *M* Chapter 18.
44. *M* 176, 162.
45. *M* Chapter 16.
46. *M* 165.
47. *M* Chapter 15.
48. *M* Chapters 23 ff.
49. *M* 61–7.
50. *M* 77.
51. e.g. A. Donagan (1962), *The Later Philosophy of R. G. Collingwood*, Clarendon Press, Oxford; D. Rynin (1964), 'Absolute Pre-suppositions, Truth and Metaphysics', *Review of Metaphysics*, 18, 301–33; L. Rubinoff (1970), *Collingwood and the Reform of Metaphysics*, University of Toronto Press.
52. *M* 188.
53. *A* 43, 50.
54. *M* Chapter 33.
55. *M* 216–18, 143 ff., Part IIIc.
56. e.g. Rubinoff, pp. 260–4.
57. cf. *A* 48.

10
Wisdom

In his Presidential Address to the Aristotelian Society in 1950, John Wisdom repeated a thesis he had held since at least the late 1930s, that the questions and doctrines of metaphysics are paradoxes.[2] Both earlier and later he made it clear that this was only part of the wider thesis that philosophy in general — and, indeed, much of what poets, novelists and psycho-analysts give us — consists of a series of paradoxes.[3] As paradoxes, they belong to the even wider class of unconventional utterances; a class which includes the metaphors and figurative language of poets.[4] Such utterances range from the poetic, 'The red rose is a falcon and the white rose is a dove', through the epigrammatic, 'Poverty is a crime' and the aphoristic, 'Everyone who looks at a woman to lust after her has already committed adultery', to the psycho-analytic, 'We are all mad' or, 'You hate your sister.'[5] Metaphysical examples are 'Infinite numbers are not really numbers', 'No-one knows the past', 'Ethical statements are neither true nor false', 'Tables and chairs are not really solid', 'One can never know the mind of another', ' "It is so" means no more than "It seems so" '.[6] Wisdom is using 'paradox' in its wider, though etymological and original, sense of something against received opinion, rather than in the narrow sense of self-contradiction used by philosophers in talking of the 'logical paradoxes', for example of Burali-Forti or Russell. Yet he rightly supposes that merely being against what we ordinarily believe would not be sufficient. One would not call 'The earth goes round the sun', 'The earth is flat', 'There is no God', 'Man is unselfish' paradoxes, even if these contradicted almost universal belief, whereas one might call 'To be is to be perceived' or 'One cannot know what another feels' paradoxes because they suggest either necessary conjunctions between the apparently opposite or necessary disjunctions between the apparently similar. It is in this sense that Zeno's famous conclusions against motion and plurality are called paradoxes.

Similarly, Wisdom likens metaphysical questions to puzzles and riddles to which there is no clearly right answer.[7] For example, he takes the question 'If when a dog attacks her, a cow keeps her horns always towards him, so that she rotates as fast as he revolves, does he go round her?' as analogous to the philosophical question whether the sentence 'There is cheese here' means, as Berkeley and the phenomenalists would have insisted, the same as any set of sentences about what we see, smell, etc., or would see if we looked, smell if we sniffed, etc.[8]

The point and use of paradoxes, as of metaphors and other figures of speech, in any field, is, according to Wisdom, to illuminate in a way which cannot be done by a straightforward statement of fact. This is partly because their paradoxicality catches our attention by shocking us, as does the critic who says 'George Forsyte wasn't really a Forsyte' or the woman who dissuades her friend from purchasing a hat by exclaiming 'It's the Taj Mahal.'[9] It is mainly, however, because the paradox or metaphor directs our attention to similarities which we are inclined to overlook or away from differences we are inclined to over-emphasise, as when the native calls a motorcycle a kind of horse, the sociologist calls poverty a crime or Christ called lust adultery.[10]

So, argues Wisdom, in metaphysics to say, for example, that one can never really know that another is in pain calls attention by its very paradoxicality to the difference between knowing this and knowing that oneself is in pain, namely that the idea of being mistaken is appropriate with the former but nonsense with the latter.[11] Similarly, to say that even in the most favourable circumstances we don't *know* that there is cheese on the table is, he holds, to emphasise the similarity between this situation and occasions when we have suffered from illusions, hallucinations, perspective, etc., and the difference between this situation and occasions when we undoubtedly do feel pains or have sensations.[12] To say that the laws of logic are really rules of grammar is to distinguish them from the empirical laws of science and to assimilate them to the regulative rules of a game.[13] Metaphysical questions, such as Berkeley's 'Can two people see or feel the same thing?', to which there is, according to Wisdom, no clearly correct affirmative or negative answer, are really requests for a description of the features which would incline one to answer 'yes' — for example, the ways in which the question is like 'Can two people hit the same thing?' — and of the features which would incline one to answer 'no' — for example, the ways in which the question is like 'Can two people play the same game of patience?'[14] The power of the paradox and, hence, of a metaphysical statement, is its ability to penetrate to these similarities and differences.[15]

It is clear that Wisdom is distinguishing, quite rightly, between an objective, namely the uncovering and highlighting of known but commonly unnoticed similarities and differences between items, and the means of reaching such an objective, namely the use of unconventional, figurative and particularly paradoxical language. While the paradox is the means which philosophy in general, like poetry, psycho-analysis, etc., and metaphysics in particular, uses, the particular objective of philosophy is the investigation of certain kinds of similarities and differences. The metaphysician tries 'to bring out relations between categories of being, between spheres of language',[16] 'between the manner in which sentences are used',[17] e.g. between statements about material objects and statements about hallucinations on the one hand, and between the former statements and statements about one's own feelings on the other.[18] The 'metaphysical character' of a statement is its 'fundamental logic'.[19] Metaphysical questions are defined as 'paradoxical questions with the peculiarity that they are concerned with the character of questions, of discussions, of reasons, of knowledge' about 'time and space, good and evil, things and persons';[20] items which are elsewhere called 'ultimate classes of fact',[21] whose peculiarity is that they are in a way already very familiar to us.[22] Their 'illumination' is the philosopher's job.[23] Indeed, it is the very fact of their familiarity which calls for a paradox to highlight a similarity or a difference which we knew about, but whose character or importance the utterer of the paradox wishes to draw to our attention.[24] Agreeing that the philosopher's job is 'to give their (i.e. these concepts') place on the language map', he adds that this cannot be done with 'a plain answer, a single statement', and, therefore, calls for a paradox.[25] Wisdom often goes so far as to say that 'a philosopher since he has no news . . . must be either paradoxical or boring',[26] though in a later paper he does express a belief in the continuity of an analytic examination of concepts throughout the whole history of metaphysics.[27]

So it is a philosopher's puzzlement about these relations which *causes* him to utter paradoxes, while it is his desire to underline certain features of these relations which is his *reason* for such utterances.[28] Wisdom thus distinguishes his view from that of Wittgenstein who, he thinks, noticed the causes of the paradoxes, but not the reasons for them.[29] Wisdom's view of the objective of philosophy, namely the investigation of conceptual similarities and differences, continued the same from his earliest writings, though there he had characterised it as an attempt to promote insight into the ultimate structure of facts.[30] It was his view of the means of doing this which changed; from his earlier advocacy of analysis, in a special form he called 'Ostentation', to his later support for paradox.

In giving the investigation of conceptual relations as the job of every philosopher, and consequently of the metaphysician, Wisdom is simply following the tradition which I have tried to show runs through the whole history of the subject from Plato onwards. It is, therefore, his claim that the way the metaphysician does or, indeed, must do his job by the utterance of paradoxes, which marks out Wisdom's peculiar contribution to the debate about the nature and methods of metaphysics. This is also his escape route from the Verificationists' attack on metaphysics as meaningless because unverifiable.[31] Hence, it is this claim we must examine more closely.

Paradoxes as such are not, as Wisdom rightly insists, true or false. If taken literally, they are, however, false. Moreover, it is only because we are inclined to take them as being meant to be literal and, therefore, as apparently glaring falsehoods, that we are surprised or shocked enough by them to give them further attention. Wisdom himself, in fact, insists on the importance of taking both them and their opposites literally so as to see exactly which similarities and differences they do highlight. Thus, it is only by taking literally the sceptical paradox, advocated by Hume (and by Plato and Parmenides before him), that claims as to how things seem provide *no* reasons for claims as to how things are, and the opposite reductive paradox, advocated by Berkeley (and by Protagoras before him), that they provide *every* reason for how things are, that we can appreciate the similarities and differences between statements about what seems to be and statements about what is.[32] By examining Hume's reasons we see the differences between deductive and inductive reasoning, while by examining Berkeley's we see the similarities between the evidence for something and the thing itself: similarly, with the paradoxes that infinite numbers are not really numbers or that one cannot know the mind of another.[33]

It is important to stress here that just as Wisdom is not saying that a paradox cannot be literally false, so he is not saying that the statements of metaphysicians cannot be literally false. He clearly thinks that both the sceptical and the reductionist views about the relation between what seems to be and what is are wrong.[34] He castigates them as confused and fallacious.[35] Equally false is the premiss — that it makes sense to talk of someone's knowing another's feelings as the other does — behind the metaphysician's paradox that no-one can ever know another's feelings.[36] What Wisdom wishes to hold is, first, that unless the literally false statement of the metaphysician is seen as a paradox, it will be dismissed without our looking more clearly at the correct and important points to which it is drawing attention, that is, to the undoubtedly existing similarities and differences which are being overlooked. And, secondly, that the opposite statement, put forward by a rival metaphysician who sees the falsity of the original, is equally false. This is the point behind his comparison of metaphysical questions to questions to which both an affirmative and negative answer can be given, like the question whether the dog goes round the cow. Similarly, both the sceptic who says that how things seem is *no* reason for how things are, and the reductionist who says that they are *every* reason for how things are, are mistaken.

In comparing metaphysical questions with questions to which both an affirmative and a negative answer are equally false, and in comparing rival metaphysical statements with opposing paradoxes, Wisdom has, I suggest, confused contraries with contradictries. Contraries can both be false, but one or other contradictory must be true. The Berkeleian and Protagorean position that what seems gives *every* reason for what is, and the Humean and Platonic position that it gives *no* reason are contraries, both of which are false. The intermediate position which contradicts both contraries, that it gives *some* reason, is true. Similarly, the reductive metaphysician who says that the mind is 'nothing but' a pattern of bodily behaviour, or that thinking is nothing but talking, and the transcendent metaphysician who says that the mind is 'something over and above' the behaviour of the body, or that thinking is an extra inner activity, take contrary positions both of which are false.[37] This does not show that there cannot be a literally true intermediate position which contradicts both, for example that the mind is related to the body as, for example, vision to the eye, and that thinking is related to talking as doing something (e.g.

teaching, working, practising, obeying an order, killing someone) is related to that by which one does it (e.g. saying so and so, delivering milk, playing the piano, standing to attention, shooting a man).

Sometimes Wisdom's reason for supposing that what the metaphysician or philosopher says should not be taken as true or false is that it is 'a verbal recommendation in response to a request which is really a request with regard to a sentence which lacks a conventional use whether there occur situations which could conventionally be described by it'. Thus, the sceptic is said to recommend that we shouldn't say we 'know' so and so where we admit we could be wrong, but only that we 'think' so and so; and that we shouldn't say that something 'is' so, but only that it is 'probable that it is so'.[39] The philosopher who compares questions of right and wrong to questions of taste is, according to Wisdom, only trying to throw light on the former by suggesting a possibility.[40]

The recommendation takes the form of a paradox which, says Wisdom, is a 'penetrating suggestion as to how it [sc. the language] might be used so as to reveal what, by the actual use of language, is hidden'.[41] Thus, to say 'No man can do what another does' — or, as Berkeley, 'No one can perceive what another perceives' — 'introduces a new logic to show up a hidden feature of the old, uses language oddly in order to show up an oddity in our usual use'.[42] Though in the usual usage of language the answer to the question 'Does "It's raining" mean to everyone "It here and now looks to *me*, feels to *me*, as if it's raining"?' is 'no', a metaphysician like Berkeley or Protagoras will paradoxically answer 'yes', thus suggesting that we should change the use of 'is' so that it means 'is perceived' or 'it seems'. If the metaphysician's remark is only a recommendation or suggestion and not a statement or thesis, then clearly it cannot be true or false, but only useful or useless, illuminating or misleading. Thus, though Wisdom argues that many of the pronouncements of the great metaphysicians are illuminating, he admits that much metaphysics is misleading or useless, as when it is said that 'Good is an ultimate predicate' or 'A proposition is a subsistent entity' or 'We can never know the real causes of our sensations.'[43]

Having sketched Wisdom's view of metaphysics, let us ask, as we did of Collingwood, first, whether it is offered as a description either of what metaphysicians believed themselves to be doing, or of what they were actually doing, or as a recommendation of what metaphysicians should be doing; secondly, if it is intended as a description, is it a correct description of either the metaphysician's preaching or of his practice, and, if it is a recommendation, is it useful? Wisdom nowhere draws any clear distinction between metaphysics and the rest of philosophy, even calling the philosophical investigation of the nature of metaphysics the 'metaphysics of metaphysics';[44] hence, he applies his thesis of paradoxicality to all philosophers.

Wisdom was certainly under no illusion that the metaphysicians of the past had ever thought of their pronouncements as paradoxes, intentional or unintentional. He allowed that they may insist that they are speaking literally and even offer the most conventional reasons for their views.[45] In a section of a 1938 paper devoted to the question 'What is a metaphysical theory?', he argued that at that time the two most commonly held views of the nature of metaphysics were either that it consists of super-scientific discoveries or that it is a branch of logic engaged on an *a priori* science of definitions, that is, conceptual analysis.[46] This is the pair of alternatives which I have argued constitutes the conflicting strands of traditional metaphysics. He did, however, declare that these and other views are mistaken and belied by the practice of the metaphysicians themselves. Because he thought that his own view expressed what they were really after, he was able to say that 'to give metaphysicians what they want, we have to do little more than remove the spectacles through which they look at their own work'.[47] 'The peculiarity of philosophical conflicts has', he held, 'only lately been grasped.'[48] Like Collingwood, he reasonably argued that metaphysicians are no better than the rest of us at giving a correct account of what they are doing.[49] He even ventured the further claim that in general we do not adequately recognise 'how often and how usefully people speak paradoxically' not only in metaphysics and in philosophy in general, but also in psycho-analytic theories and in the whole of literature.[50]

Wisdom had moreover to defend this alleged contrast between the preaching and the practice of metaphysicians not only against the general pronouncements of other philosophers about metaphysics and philosophy as such, but also against the metaphysicians' expressed goals in their detailed work. Thus, though he argues that Moore legalistically misunderstands what his opponents are doing,[51] he cannot deny that Moore does explicitly — and rightly — argue that what they say is literally false, and that he 'insists on knitting his brows' over the problems as if they were ones to which one correct answer could be given.[52] Wisdom also allows that Wittgenstein treats his opponent's theories as 'merely symptoms of linguistic confusion';[53] that Broad and those who debate with him whether 'being intelligent' simply means 'behaving intelligently' do think that they are contradicting each other;[54] that the Anti-positivists took quite literally the Verificationists' declaration that metaphysical questions are meaningless, and argued that it was either false or dependent on a technical use of 'meaningful'.[55] It is quite clear from Wisdom's account that the jurist Glanville Williams thought that certain legal questions, such as whether such and such actions constituted negligence, are quite literally questions of words, not questions of fact, in the way that lawyers also quite literally contrast questions of law with questions of fact.[56]

Apart from Wisdom's own examples there are many reasons for saying that traditional metaphysics was certainly never intended to be, nor treated as if it were, nor played the role, however unconsciously, of a set of paradoxes. First, even Berkeley, who was once caricatured by Leibniz as 'one of those who wishes to be known for his paradoxes', argued for his paradoxical-sounding thesis that what is is what seems (or *esse* is *percipi*), and held that it was literally true. Nor did he merely recommend that people should say that things are not at a distance or not without the mind, or that no two people perceive the same thing; he insisted that in 'strictness of speech' these are literally true. Similarly, Zeno's paradoxical thesis that nothing moves was regarded by him — and has been so regarded by a host of critics since — as the intended conclusion of a strict deductive argument, whose logical fallacy the efforts of many generations have not entirely clarified. Zeno not only thought it was literally true, he and other Eleatics suggested that the contradictory view comes to be held only as the result of an unwarranted faith in the evidence of one's senses. Heraclitus did not regard his equally paradoxical contrary thesis that everything moves as a paradox, but as a scientific truth based on a close examination of natural phenomena, just as Eddington defended his 'paradox' that tables and chairs are not solid as a discovery of physics. Wisdom's argument that the metaphysician cannot really want just an analysis of a concept because what he wants, namely an analysis which both contains and does not contain the original concept, is logically impossible, is no better than an argument that no-one could really have wanted to square the circle or build a perpetual motion machine since these are impossible.[57]

More importantly, even if there are some metaphysical theses which are undoubtedly paradoxical, at least in the sense that they go glaringly against what we commonly say, there are many which have neither this aim nor this characteristic. There is nothing paradoxical, however wrong, about Plato's belief in a world of Forms, Aristotle's assumption of an Unmoved Mover, Berkeley's God or Leibniz's world of Monads. Still less is there anything paradoxical about many of the statements of other parts of philosophy, from which Wisdom does not usually or explicitly distinguish metaphysics. Plato's analysis of knowledge as true belief together with *logos*, Aristotle's account of *akrasia*, Descartes' description of the relation between the mind and the body, Locke's distinction between primary and secondary qualities, Mill's utilitarian doctrine of ethics, etc., are by no stretch of the imagination either paradoxes or paradoxically sounding pronouncements. Aristotle's thesis that statements about the future are neither true nor false at the time they are made is not either in fact or in intention any more a paradox than is the same judgment pronounced by the English courts, who as a result held that such statements — for example that there will be a swimming pool at your Majorca hotel or an available seat on your international flight — do not offend against the Trade Descriptions Act of 1968. Even if one wants to regard the thesis as a paradox rather than as literally false, the bad arguments which Aristotle and his legal successors advanced for it were aimed at showing that it was literally true.

Wisdom's own examples, frequently exhibiting various forms of scepticism that one cannot really know so and so, constitute a one-sided diet from which he has overhastily drawn a general conclusion about philosophy in general and metaphysics in particular.

One of Wisdom's most frequent reasons for holding that metaphysical statements must be paradoxical is that metaphysics reaches its conclusions neither by deductive nor by inductive argument, but by calling attention to the known but overlooked, by revealing the familiar in the hidden.[58] By his characterisation he hoped to deflect the Verificationists' attack on metaphysics as meaningless, for such an attack, he argues, is based on the mis-assumption that only what is verifiable and, therefore, capable of being literally true or false is meaningful.[59] Wisdom's premisses about metaphysical reasoning are partly correct, but his conclusion does not follow. Plato thought that the theory of Forms, the theory that the reason why X's things are X (just things are just, beautiful things are beautiful) is because they copy or partake in

Xness (justice, beauty), was obviously correct; and Berkeley upbraided himself because he had not seen the 'obvious truth' that to be is to be perceived. But Plato did not consider that his principle that just things are just because they share in justice, nor Berkeley that his principle that to be is to be perceived, was a paradox. Neither are they. They are simply mistaken analyses.

Certainly, what philosophy often does is to draw attention to what something amounts to, in the way that a series of lines amounts to a certain pattern,[60] a series of incidents to negligence, a piece of behaviour to rudeness, a flow of words to thinking, that is, places it in a setting — 'discovers by reflection' as Wisdom says[61] — rather than reaches a deductive or an inductive conclusion. Philosophers from Plato to Moore agree that in some sense philosophy largely consists in bringing to our attention what we already know, whether we interpret this in the Platonic idiom of reminding us of what we learnt in a previous life,[62] in the Aristotelian formalisation of our valid patterns of everyday reasoning,[63] in the Moorean distinction between knowing the meaning of what we say and needing to be shown the correct analysis of it, or in the analytic contrast between being able to use a concept correctly and being able to give a correct account of that use. This is the truth in Wisdom's thesis that metaphysics, and philosophy in general, argues neither by deduction nor induction, but calls our attention to what is known but overlooked. But none of this shows that the resolution of our ignorance has to take, or ordinarily does take, the form of a paradox. Indeed, Wisdom finds the same method of highlighting a hitherto unrecognised pattern in the well-known in Newton's discovery of gravitation and Einstein's Relativity Theory, as well as in the conclusions of psycho-analysts and in works of art and literature.[64] Yet the scientists' conclusions are, despite what Wisdom sometimes holds, certainly not paradoxes;[65] on the contrary, they are literally verifiable. Furthermore, Wisdom also contends that metaphysical assertions have their own appropriate kind of assessment procedure.[66] Since what the procedure in fact amounts to is an examination of their logic, what he calls the 'metaphysics of metaphysics',[67] he is verifying his alleged paradoxes by the same tests as analytic philosophers commonly verify conceptual statements, namely by the touchstone of the actual behaviour of the concepts analysed.

Even if we confine ourselves to Wisdom's own examples, they do not prove his thesis. They are, in fact, of various kinds. One group arises from the problem of deciding which class to put something into or to give, as he puts it, a description of a class, such as 'Are infinite numbers really numbers?', 'Are ethical pronouncements true or false?', which, like the question 'Is poverty a crime (or a disease)?', 'Is lust adultery?', 'Is a flying boat a plane (or a ship)?', are questions to which there is a case for giving both the answer 'yes' and the answer 'no', and about which there is an air of paradox in giving perhaps either, but certainly in giving an affirmative, answer. But there is nothing either peculiarly metaphysical or philosophical or even literary about such questions. They occur in every area, including science, where there are borderline cases which share some of the attributes of one class and some of another; for example, Is light wave-like or corpuscular? Is psychology a natural or a social science? Unless one decides on the set of defining criteria, there will always be such disputes. It is not true here that the ordinary use of the language gives one answer and the metaphysician or other thinker para-doxically recommends the opposite.

Another group of examples is formed by those questions to which Wisdom's answers are, as we saw, not contradictions but only contraries, and, therefore, possibly both wrong. For example, the sceptical doctrine of Hume which holds that what seems is *no* reason for what is, and the reductionist thesis of Berkeley which holds that it is *every* reason. Here there is a generally accepted view, namely the intermediate view that what seems provides some, but not the whole, reason for what is, in contrast to which both of the metaphysical answers are paradoxical and wrong.

A third group, which overlaps with the previous two and which predominates in Wisdom's examples, is that of the sceptical philosopher who holds that there are no such things as the past, other people, anything other than sensations, etc., or that no-one can ever know that there are such.[68] It is, however, not surprising that the sceptic's views will be paradoxical since he is, by defini-tion, denying what everyone else accepts and, therefore, by defini-tion, uttering a paradox, that is, going against received opinion. Yet, even the sceptic does not think he is making paradoxes. Wisdom, indeed, often maintains that he is uttering tautologies; tautologies which are 'caricatures of logic' and, hence, the 'monsters of metaphysics'.[69]

A fourth miscellaneous group is formed by questions to which Wisdom's belief that contradictory, or even contrary, answers are both plausible is simply mistaken due to an ambiguity in the question. Thus, it is incorrect to suppose that the question 'Does the word "here" used of different places, the word "now" used of different times, the word "I" in the mouths of different speakers have different meanings?' has no unequivocal answer.[70] The answer 'no', as well as the temptation by some people to say 'yes', can be explained by pointing out the difference between the meaning and the reference of a word. Though 'here', 'now' and 'I' can be used to refer to different places, times or people, they no more have different meanings than, for example, 'Saturday', 'summer' have different meanings when used of different Saturdays or different summers. A possible reason for the mistake is that one can certainly say, for example, 'By "Saturday" I meant "Saturday 21st June" ', and 'By "in the summer" I meant the summer of 1970', just as one can say, 'By "the last book from the end" I meant that one.' Even with examples like 'Does "It is raining" mean "It looks to me as if it is"?' Wisdom admits that the metaphysician knows that there is only one correct answer, which he advocates changing.[71] I would not have thought that Wisdom would claim that what he himself admits was a traditional philosophical problem, namely 'How can what does not exist be thought of or talked of?' is either a puzzle to which there is no one answer or to which the answer is necessarily a paradox. Yet, he suggests, surely implausibly, that even the analysis of 'A will be hungry' in terms of A's symptoms and his sensations, and the Humean thesis that causation is nothing more than regular sequence, are paradoxes.[72]

Nor does any of the philosophers of the past either think or argue as if he thought that all he was doing was recommending a new way of speaking or simply attempting to throw light on a matter by suggesting possibilities. They are clearly arguing that their opponents have misclassified the item under consideration by failing to see similarities and differences whose existence demands a reclassification of the item in the way that a zoologist demands that a whale be classified as a mammal and not as a fish. It is simply not true, as Wisdom alleges, that the sceptic merely recommends that we don't use 'know' in 'He knows there is cheese on the table', but only in 'He knows he is in pain', so as to draw attention to the fact that one can be mistaken about the existence of the cheese but not of the pain. The sceptic in fact says we cannot know there is cheese on the table because he (wrongly) believes that it is part of the concept of *knowledge* that it excludes not only actual mistakes but even the possibility of mistakes, and that this is something which the everyday use of 'know' has overlooked. Even the Verification Principle, which some of its adherents admittedly did, like Wisdom,[73] regard as a recommendation — though only, I think, to avoid the apparently awkward consequent of making it subject to its own criteria — was generally taken as a true or false definition or description of the meaning of 'meaning' as applied to sentences which purport to express something true or false.

Just as Wisdom often seems to stretch the idea of paradox in characterising many metaphysical statements as such, and in suggesting that the idea is closely linked to the idea of highlighting an unnoticed feature of the familiar, so he misuses the contrast of appearance and reality in his claims that the metaphysicians' use of this contrast corresponds to his contrast of the unfamiliar in the familiar, and that it was intended by them to be provocative.[74] This is certainly not true of either Plato's or Bradley's use of the contrast.

Since it is clear both that traditional metaphysicians and philosophers in general never intended their utterances to be taken as other than literally true, and that their practice does not belie their intentions, we should finally consider Wisdom's advocacy of metaphysical statements as paradoxes as a recommendation of how to take them. This is justified in that he himself admits that his thesis is itself a paradox, albeit an illuminating paradox and, therefore, not literally true.

My submission is that there is no particular virtue in this recommendation. First, it is not at all clear that treating, for example, 'Nothing moves', 'What seems is what is', 'One can never know what another feels' as paradoxes catches and holds our attention more than treating them as literal statements. Nor is there anything in the history of metaphysics to suggest that those who treated them literally considered them less carefully because of this. Secondly, Wisdom himself admits that paradoxes have also to be, and are best, treated literally in order to see exactly what similarities and differences they are drawing attention to.[75] What is interesting, for example, about Zeno's paradox that nothing moves is quite independent of what is interesting about Heraclitus' opposite paradox that everything moves. What led Hume to suppose that what seems is no reason for what is has little in common with what led Berkeley to hold that what seems is every reason for what is. Hence, the alleged superiority of the paradoxical over the literal, namely that it saves us from missing the wood for the trees, is non-existent.[76]

Thirdly, the investigation of similarities and differences between concepts, which Wisdom admits to be the aim of metaphysics, need no more be conducted by, and is no more illuminated by, paradoxical statements rather than literal statements, than the investigation of similarities and differences between various sorts of items which the various sciences carry on. Whether a sponge is a plant or an animal, whether light travels in waves or corpuscles, whether a whale is a fish or an animal, or whether a tomato is a fruit or a vegetable, are questions to which alternative answers each have a plausibility which can be considered without dressing them up as a paradox.

Fourthly, though there are many metaphysical theses whose expression does wear a paradoxical air, this, as we saw, is quite untrue of many others. One could not sensibly recommend that Plato's theory of Forms, Aristotle's views on substance or an Unmoved Mover, Berkeley's belief in God as a cause of our perceptions, Leibniz's system of Monads, Collingwood's list of absolute presuppositions, Bradley's committal to the Absolute, be viewed as paradoxical, however incredible and implausible they are held to be by the majority, and however false they literally are.

Finally, it must once again be stressed that Wisdom's recommendation is about the methods of metaphysics, not about its nature, which he agrees is the illumination of the relations between concepts. Furthermore, he does not distinguish metaphysics from the rest of philosophy by its methods, which he claims are common to both but, presumably — though he has almost nothing to say on this — by its precise subject matter, that is, the relations between ultimate concepts or, as he sometimes puts it, 'ultimate classes of fact'.[77]

It is not insignificant that Collingwood's thesis that metaphysical statements are historical statements comes from a historian, or that Wisdom's thesis that metaphysical statements are paradoxes comes from one whose own literary style is flowery, figurative and full of paradoxes.

Notes

1. In the references, the date refers to the original publication, but the pages to its place in one of the following collections. *Other Minds* (1952), Basil Blackwell, collects items dated 1940–3, 1946a, 1950a, 1950b; *Philosophy and Psycho-Analysis* (1953), Basil Blackwell, those dated 1933, 1934, 1937, 1938, 1944, 1945, 1946b, 1947, 1948a, 1948b, 1950c, 1953; *Paradox and Discovery* (1965), Basil Blackwell, those dated 1950d, 1952a,

1952b, 1956, 1957, 1959, 1961a, 1961b, 1962. The dating will enable the reader to check changes in Wisdom's views over time. A chronological bibliography of Wisdom's publications is given in R. Bambrough (ed.) (1974) *Wisdom: Twelve Essays*, Basil Blackwell.

2. 1950b. 258–9.
3. 1946b. 176–7; 1953. 264.
4. 1953. 249, 254, 264, 266.
5. 1937. 40; 1938. 63; 1944. 122; 1953. 263, 273.
6. 1950b. 247; 1950b. 258; 1953. 243, 269; 1953. 272; 1953. 255; 1950b. 244.
7. 1950b. 256.
8. 1938. 96; 1946b. 176.
9. 1953. 254, 264.
10. 1937. 40; 1944. 112.
11. 1937. 42–6; 1950b. 247.
12. 1937. 46–7.
13. 1937. 48.
14. 1938. 100; 1944. 112.
15. 1937. 41, 46; 1953. 281; 1961b. 102; 1962. 150.
16. 1937. 39, 42; 1938. 89; 1940–3. 83; 1948b. 228; 1956. 45–8; 1961a. 66–7.
17. 1937. 50; 1957. 126.
18. 1937. 46–7; 1950b. 247.
19. 1957. 130.
20. 1950b. 259; 1956. 45–8; 1957. 120; 1961a. 66–7.
21. 1938. 90; 1957. 128–30.
22. 1944. 112; 1957. 120.
23. 1937. 37.
24. 1937. 39, 46; 1953. 249.
25. 1937. 50.
26. 1953. 255; 1937. 38, 50; 1944. 102; 1950b. 258; 1951d. 1; 1953. 270.
27. 1961a. 75.
28. 1937. 42, 39.
29. 1937. 41.
30. 1933.
31. 1953. 265–6.
32. 1950b. 247.
33. 1950b. 247; 1953. 254–60.
34. 1950b. 238 ff.
35. 1937. 42–6; 1950b. 244–5.
36. 1953. 258.
37. cf. 1938. 99–100.
38. 1937. 36, 45.
39. 1950b. 238–9; 1937, 42.
40. 1961a. 78–80.
41. 1938. 100.
42. 1946b. 177.
43. 1937. 40, 42; 1950b. 250; 1953. 281.
44. 1965. 133.

45. 1957. 125.
46. 1938. 56 ff.
47. 1938. 101.
48. 1946b. 176 – 7; 1937. 49 – 50.
49. 1957. 96, 118; 1961a. 75.
50. 1953. 272 – 3.
51. 1944. 115 – 17.
52. 1937. 41; 1944. 115.
53. 1937. 41.
54. 1938. 98.
55. 1953. 273.
56. 1953. 249 – 54.
57. 1938. 65 – 76; 1961a. 67.
58. 1944. 112 – 15; 1946b. 178, 181; 1950d. 1 – 6; 1953. 248, 260, 263, 266; 1957. 120, 126; 1961a. 80.
59. 1953. 265 – 6; 1957. 133.
60. 1945. 153; 1953. 265.
61. 1953. 266.
62. cf. 1953. 249.
63. cf. 1965. 143.
64. 1948a. 242; 1948b. 224 – 6; 1950d. 6; 1953. 252; 1956. 52; 1961b. 96.
65. 1961b. 96.
66. 1950b. 258 – 9; 1957. 133 – 8.
67. 1957. 133.
68. 1961b. 101.
69. 1950a. 233; 1950b. 246, 258.
70. 1950b. 255.
71. 1950b. 255.
72. 1946a. 203 – 4; 1937. 49 – 50.
73. 1938. 53.
74. 1937. 50; 1948b. 226.
75. 1950b. 256.
76. 1944. 117.
77. 1938. 90.

11
Lazerowitz

Dissatisfied, like Kant and, indeed, many philosophers since Descartes, with the lack of progress in metaphysics as contrasted with the triumphs of science,[1] an American philosopher, Morris Lazerowitz, offers an explanation of its sad state. His views are given, with much repetition, in three collections of essays, *The Structure of Metaphysics* (1955), *Studies in Metaphilosophy* (1964) and *Philosophy and Illusion* (1968). His explanation consists in a theory about its nature for which the negative argument is that no other theory explains equally well either its methods, its lack of results and agreement, or its resilience, and the positive argument is a piece of speculative psycho-analysis. Unlike Kant, Collingwood and Wisdom, he does not advance his theory as a reformed metaphysics which should replace the old nor does he, on the other hand, follow Kant, and sometimes Collingwood and Wisdom, in pretending that the traditional metaphysicians would ever accept it as a true account of their actual practice. He does, however, insist that it is a description of what they have in fact done, though they were, he not only admits but indeed claims, unconscious of doing so.[2] Like Wisdom, he frequently and sometimes explicitly widens his thesis to cover not merely metaphysics but the whole of philosophy.[3] His theory, he claims, 'alone can discover what philosophical utterances really say'.[4]

Lazerowitz's theory of the nature of metaphysics was intended to apply to that practised by such traditional figures as, for example, Zeno, who said that motion is impossible, Heraclitus, who, on the contrary, argued that everything flows, Berkeley, whose key principle was that *esse* is *percipi*, Kant, who held that every event necessarily has a cause, Plato, who believed in the

159

existence of universals or Forms, and Locke, who advanced the hypothesis that the qualities of material objects inhere in an unknown matter. According to the theory a metaphysical doctrine consists of three layers.[5] First, there is the conscious, but mistaken, belief that a metaphysical assertion is saying something about the world and its characteristics analogous to the way in which scientific statements do; that, for example, Zeno's assertion that nothing moves is a more general form of a scientific assertion that the sun does not move, or that Berkeley's question whether the rose can blush unseen is like a scientist's question whether it has a smell in a vacuum. Secondly, at the pre-conscious level the metaphysical assertion is the stipulation of a new use for one of its key terms, as when Berkeley decides to use 'exists' to mean 'perceived', or Hume to use 'cause' as equivalent to 'regularly precedes'. Thirdly, the stipulative definition expounded in the second layer of the metaphysical assertion is the expression of an unconscious wish, such as Zeno's desire for conservatism,[6] Bradley's need to overcome his 'melancholic discontent'[7] revealed by his attack on the finite, Spinoza's unsatisfied 'childhood curiosity and dependence' expressed in the place of power given in his metaphysics to God,[8] Kant's fear of space manifested by his thesis that space is a mind-dependent form of perception.[9]

It is only in the supposition of a third layer that Lazerowitz's thesis has any novelty, though even here it is, as he acknowledges, anticipated to some extent by both J. T. and J. O. Wisdom[10] and by Freud.[11] The first layer, with its suggestion that metaphysical assertions appear to be, but are not really, statements about features of the world, either sensible or supersensible, is the stock-in-trade of most twentieth-century discussions of metaphysics, including, as we saw, that of Wittgenstein, who accused metaphysicians of confusing problems about the logical grammar of words with problems of science. I have partly discussed it already in hinting at my view that a metaphysician draws a conclusion about an alleged supersensible feature of the world from premises, one of which is a factual assertion of the existence of something in the world, e.g. the existence of instances of justice or equality or of a red rose in the desert, and the other a conceptual premiss about the nature of the concept involved, e.g. 'being an instance of' or 'exists'. I shall discuss it further in the concluding chapter.

The second layer, with its suggestion that the metaphysician's assertions are not true or false statements about the use of words, but express decisions to use them differently, though also largely anticipated by J. T. Wisdom in his thesis that metaphysical statements are paradoxes, merits further consideration because it is the element to which, in practice, Lazerowitz gives the most attention, and it is in order to explain its existence that the third layer is posited. Furthermore, though this is only occasionally stressed, it can be regarded as an attempt, analogous but different in kind to those of Collingwood and Wisdom, to escape the Verificationists' rejection of metaphysics as meaningless because unverifiable.[12] For, though Lazerowitz agrees that, as the Verificationists claim, metaphysical utterances express neither empirical nor *a priori* statements and, therefore, say nothing either true or false, he argues that their legitimacy is preserved by their two-fold function of making a (verbal) recommendation and expressing an (unconscious) desire.[13] If, as I shall try to show, the second layer is non-existent, then the main reason for the introduction of the third layer vanishes. But before examining the alleged second layer, let us look at the supposed third layer, since it is in this that the main new claim of Lazerowitz's theory lies.

Lazerowitz's positive arguments for his theory of the nature of metaphysics as a structure with an unconscious third layer are very slight. They consist, first, in the supposition that only an unconscious desire or need could account for the phenomenon commented on by G. E. Moore that 'philosophers have been able to hold sincerely [and Lazerowitz adds 'tenaciously'], as part of their philosophical creed, propositions inconsistent with what they themselves knew to be true';[14] secondly in the well-known psychoanalytic theory about the place of the unconscious and of wish fulfilment in human nature; and, thirdly, in several such theories about particular metaphysicians. The weakness of this third argument stems from his and our ignorance of the lives, particularly the infantile and the unconscious lives, of such philosophers. Not surprisingly, therefore, Lazerowitz rarely even attempts to make plausible any psycho-analytic explanation of why a particular metaphysician holds the position he does; why Plato, but not Aristotle, should believe in the independent existence of universals, why Berkeley, but not Locke, should deny the existence of matter, or why Zeno, but not Heraclitus, should think that nothing moves. On the few occasions when he does refer to the unconscious wishes of specific metaphysicians, as when he attributes a need for reassurance to Descartes, a 'fear of Medusa' to those who advocate a representative theory of perception, a 'melancholy discontent' to Bradley, 'unsatisfied childhood curiosity' to Spinoza, and agoraphobia to Kant, Zeno, Bradley and Russell, no evidence is, or probably could be, produced to show that these were characteristics of these philosophers other than, in Kant's case, the belief that he never travelled far from Königsberg.[15]

The only sustained attempt known to me by any philosopher to give a detailed list of links between the overt symptoms, that is the public writings, of a metaphysician, and their alleged hidden causes is in J. O. Wisdom's book *The Unconscious Origin of Berkeley's Philosophy* (1953), Hogarth Press. But the details given there of Berkeley's childhood are so slight and the links alleged between it and his writings so fantastically speculative that the hypothesis has, rightly, never been given serious consideration by any professional philosopher.

What, on the other hand, Lazerowitz does in the few cases I have mentioned is to work backwards from the symptoms of the specific writer to an alleged condition by using generalisations about the known psycho-analytic causes of certain types of symptoms. This is, indeed, part of his general technique. For usually he does not deign to enquire into the psychology of the individual metaphysician, but defends his general hypothesis by the argument that psycho-analysis — and, indeed, common sense — can offer a plausible explanation of why anyone should have certain sorts of beliefs. It is, for example, perfectly plausible that someone who denies motion should be expressing a fear of change, that someone who has recourse to a deity feels a need of a father figure, or that someone who says that all is appearance or illusion should be displaying a melancholic, even neurotic, disposition. But without either a general psycho-analytic law that all denials of motion, all hypotheses of a deity or all arguments for the universality of illusion are symptoms of the supposed unconscious troubles, or specific proof that a given advocate of one of these views was a victim of the corresponding hidden emotion, there is no argument for attributing the cause of the former to the latter in any of the metaphysical systems before us. Furthermore, anyone who has taught groups, however psychologically heterogeneous, of first-year students knows how easy it is with the appropriate arguments to render plausible such metaphysical positions as Zeno's denial of motion, Plato's hypothesis of Forms, Locke's belief in matter, or Berkeley's principle that to be is to be perceived or perceivable. It is beyond belief that it is any psycho-analytic

162

connection between the metaphysical positions and certain unconscious mental elements, rather than the subtlety and the seductive-
ness of the arguments, which leads the students to accept them at
least temporarily.

What all this suggests is that it is not any positive psycho-
analytic evidence which lends weight to Lazerowitz's hypothesis
about a third layer, but the negative fact that he finds none of the
usual explanations of the alleged barrenness, yet permanence, of
metaphysics convincing.[16] Such a suggestion is supported by his
own frequent assertion that his hypothesis is the only viable
alternative when he has, as he thinks, effectively disposed of the
usual explanations.[17] However, as I mentioned earlier, the need
for a psycho-analytic explanation only arises on the supposition
that the metaphysician does not, as he and most of his opponents
think, say anything true or false, but only proposes a new use of
language. Though even here there could be alternative explanations for such a proposal; for example, Wisdom's thesis that a new
use of words is recommended to draw attention dramatically to a
known but hitherto insufficiently noticed similarity or difference.

Since this alleged change in the use of a word is made in what
Lazerowitz calls the second, pre-conscious, layer of the metaphysical assertion, under the guise of a statement about the non-
linguistic world, let us now examine this layer. Lazerowitz's
position is that the metaphysician who asserts that, for example,
nothing moves, or that abstract words are proper names, which
Lazerowitz takes to be the essence of 'There are universals', or
who, like Berkeley, denies substance or, like Bradley, the reality of
physical things or, like Kant, that 'existence' is a predicate, or, like
the emotivists, that 'beautiful' is an attribute, is not saying anything true or false about the use of these words or the concepts they
express, but is altering their use, recommending a revised use or
announcing his decision to use them differently.[18] Lazerowitz
admits that the metaphysician is quite unconscious of what he is
doing. The metaphysician thinks that he is asserting either something linguistic or something non-linguistic to be so. But,
Lazerowitz argues, even in the face of an explicit denial to the
contrary — as when Bradley roundly declares that it is the
ordinary use of 'physical thing' which is mistaken,[19] Berkeley
advises us to think with the learned even though we may speak
with the vulgar, Ayer castigates metaphysics as literally nonsense,[20] or Moore, in direct answer to Lazerowitz, says quite
explicitly that recommending a change in the use of words was

not something he ever thought or now thinks he is doing[21] — that what the metaphysician really does is to alter the use of the words, though his decision is expressed as if it were the stating of a fact.[22]

Sometimes Lazerowitz gives as the metaphysician's reason for this supposed alteration of the use of a word that which Wisdom had been inclined to give, namely the need to come to a conclusion in a case where there is no 'yes' or 'no' answer. Thus, the metaphysician has to decide whether or not to use 'meaning' in such a way that the answer to 'Are self-contradictions meaningless?' will be true, since the ordinary use of 'meaning' gives no unequivocal answer.[23] Similarly, it is alleged that a philosopher, like Mill, who wishes to call attention to the similarity between 'All cats are animals' and 'All cats are mousers' stretches the meaning of 'empirical generalisation' to cover the former.[24] A philosopher who wishes to emphasise the difference between utterances about the value of things and other kinds of utterances contracts the application of 'statement' so as to exclude the former, while another stretches the meaning of 'means the same' so as to assimilate value-utterances and utterances stating one's likes and dislikes.[25] The point about this kind of explanation, however, is that it contains no hint — and if it did it would be implausible — that the metaphysician's reason for changing the use of a word is unconscious, much less due to psycho-analytic causes, though, of course, Lazerowitz does argue that the metaphysician usually does not realise that he is making a change, but thinks that he is only stating a fact. Lazerowitz's rather ambivalent position on how conscious a metaphysician is that he is altering language is shown by his use of such curious phrases as 'deliberate, if not conscious'.[26]

Sometimes Lazerowitz attributes to the metaphysician a reason for his alleged changes which has a more psychological flavour about it, though at a rather superficial level.[27] Thus, the metaphysician who claims that motion is impossible is alleged to be altering the use of, for example, 'instant', 'now' and 'moment' because of a 'linguistic grievance' that these words should 'wear the cloak of a time interval denoting substance and not be one in fact'.[28] An existentialist metaphysician who talks seriously about 'The Nothing' is alleged to be showing that he is 'seriously dissatisfied with the fact that the word "nothing" has the grammatical function of a substantive but does not, so to speak, get enough linguistic credit for its grammatical work'.[29] Logical Positivists are said to 'covertly redefine' the word 'nonsense' in

applying it to metaphysicians because of 'an attitude of dis-
approval of anyone doing metaphysics'.[30]

Lazerowitz's usual thesis, however, is that no such obvious
reason can be the explanation for the metaphysician's unwitting
alteration of the use of words which he wrongly supposes to be a
factual assertion about the constitution of the world.[31] The reasons
for such a piece of self-deception must be psycho-analytic.[32] They
must be one or other of the kinds which we have already seen
Lazerowitz hints at for particular theories, such as 'Motion is
impossible', 'All is appearance', etc. For example, he surmises
that Parmenides, Zeno, Bradley and Russell, who have in some
way or other denied the reality of space — or, as he would say,
altered the use of the word 'space' — must all suffer from some
form of agoraphobia.[33]

Underlying Lazerowitz's conjectures about the metaphysician's
reasons for altering the use of a word is, of course, the assumption
which gives rise to the need for such reasons, namely the assumption that what the metaphysician in fact does is to alter, albeit
unconsciously, the word's use, rather than attempt to state its
correct use. This is the alleged second layer of metaphysics. Is
there any good reason for this assumption? Lazerowitz's main
reason is a negative one that it is too incredible to suppose that the
metaphysician should not realise that his remarks about the use of
the word are a demonstrably false account of how the word is
correctly used.[34] Surely, insists Lazerowitz, Zeno knew that
'moves' can be correctly applied to some things, Anselm and
Descartes knew that 'existence is not a characterising attribute', all
moral philosophers know that 'This is good' makes a statement,
the advocates of universals know the meaning of common abstract
nouns. Since all this must have been so obvious to them, they
cannot have been disputing about the correctness of such assertions, but must have been proposing a change.

To this there are various answers. First, as we have seen and as
Lazerowitz sometimes admits, many philosophers from Berkeley
to Bradley have explicitly stated that the ordinary use of the word
(or concept) under consideration is incorrect.[35] The metaphysician
contrasts a 'strict' or 'philosophical' use of language with the
practical, perhaps loose, use sufficient for everyday affairs. Thus,
he asserts, that whereas we can ordinarily say that so and so is such
and such, that so and so is known to be so, that we can both see
and hear a train or that two people can see the same train, strictly
speaking we ought to say only that so and so is probably such and

such, that so and so is justifiably believed to be so, that what we see is only the colour of the train, and what we hear only the sound of the train, and that what two people see is only the different appearances, one of which the train presents to each. Even non-philosophers commonly adhere to the mistaken assumption that there is a difference between the correct and the ordinary use of a word.[36]

Secondly, the types of argument used by metaphysicians like Plato, Zeno, Leibniz, Berkeley or Bradley are not of a kind which could possibly be used to alter use. They are, as many generations of students will testify, very convincing 'proofs' of either convincing or, more usually, unconvincing conclusions.[37] They have the characteristic which Hume attributed to Berkeley's arguments, 'that they admit of no answer and produce no conviction'. Plato's (and Descartes') argument that we could not recognise imperfection unless we were able to compare it with perfection, the idea of which we must, therefore, already have, or his similar argument that there could not be instances of justice or equality unless there were something, namely justice or equality itself, for these to be instances of, are subtle, however mistaken, arguments, not for changing the use of the phrase 'abstract noun', but for supposing that abstract nouns are the names of things which were later called 'universals'. Many people have been unable to see the fallacy in Zeno's argument that one cannot move from A to B without first, apparently *per impossibile*, going through an infinite number of subdivisions of the distance between A and B. Bradley's puzzle about the 'temporal contents' of 'now' led him, wrongly, to the assertion that there was something self-contradictory about the notion. It did not lead him, as Lazerowitz claims, to recommend its abolition.[38] For each one of Lazerowitz's examples of metaphysical assertions which are alleged to be proposed alterations of the meanings of a word, it would be easy to show how subtle and initially plausible an argument a great metaphysician has given for concluding that the ordinary use of the word and the accompanying common belief in some state of affairs is mistaken.

Thirdly, the force of Lazerowitz's argument that no intelligent metaphysician could fail to see that his assertion — or at least some rival's assertion — about the correct use of a word (the nature of the concept) was demonstrably false loses its force when one realises that typical metaphysical assertions are not, in the way Lazerowitz alleges, straightforwardly linguistic and, therefore, easily verifiable by a glance at the ordinary meaning of a word known to all. Lazerowitz himself sometimes admits this. Thus, though he says that 'There are universals' and 'Abstract words have meaning' are the same, he admits that there can be and is a dispute whether universals exist but none whether abstract words have meanings.[39] He admits that 'the ordinary use of the word ['meaning'] tells us nothing about whether it is correct English to apply the word to expressions classified as self-contradictions'.[40] Similarly, 'ordinary', non-philosophical grammar provides no such subclassification for the class of adjectives which will enable us to say whether or not 'beautiful' is a property-denoting adjective.[41]

Usually, however, he contends that the disputants are in fact disagreeing about the meaning of the terms at issue while at the same time knowing them perfectly well. But here he confuses a dispute about the meaning of the word and a dispute about the analysis of that meaning. Thus, he argues that it is impossible to know the meaning of a term, e.g. 'beautiful', and not know whether the term 'denotes a property', the latter being what the rival philosophers are ostensibly disputing about.[42] But this is simply a mistake. Most English adults know the meaning of 'beautiful', but whether it is used in the same way as 'yellow' or not is something they would be puzzled about. The history of thought shows clearly that though we all know the meaning of, for example, 'mind', 'think', 'promise', we do not know whether 'mind' operates similarly enough to 'body', 'think' to 'talk', 'promise' to 'say' to make it correct to allow that 'mind' denotes a specific substance, 'think' an activity and 'promise' an act. Similarly, Plato's disagreement with Aristotle on the separate existence of universals was not a disagreement inconsistent with their agreement on the meaning of 'justice';[43] nor does the ordinary use of the word 'substance' show whether Locke or Berkeley was correct in the dispute as to whether a table is no more than the sum of its perceivable qualities.[44] The long-lasting discussions about how propositions are related to the sentences and how numbers are related to the numerals which express them are not merely linguistic discussions about the use of the English words 'proposition', 'sentence', 'number' and 'numeral' — though a knowledge of such use is indispensable to progress here. Nor can it be argued that the philosopher who says 'Propositions are sentences' is saying something which both he and his opponent know already from their facility in English to be obviously true (or false); nor that there is no such thing as finding out by examination whether 'proposition' or 'meaning' is used to refer to an entity additional to a sentence; and that such questions, therefore, have no true or false answers.[45] Even when Lazerowitz allows the distinction between knowing the meaning of a word and knowing the correct analysis of the meaning, he thinks the latter too easy a topic to account for the failure of philosophers to agree on a solution to it;[46] but his own subsequent survey of various analyses of the meaning of 'logically necessary' gives the lie to this opinion.[47]

Fourthly, even if we waive this third objection and allow that the metaphysician is saying something which he not only knows to be in conflict with the ordinary use of the words, but also with what he himself adheres to outside his philosophy, we find that he frequently offers a plausible explanation of this conflict.

Sometimes, as I have mentioned, he makes a distinction between the 'strict' use of the key word appropriate in his philosophical work, and the practical, perhaps loose, use sufficient for everyday affairs. Sometimes attention is drawn to the indistinguishable features of the rival positions. Thus, the perceivable features of the Lockean world where a physical object's qualities are held together by a material substratum, and of the Berkeleian world where they are held together by a spiritual being, are the same. Sometimes the bolder position of Hume or Moore is advocated. Hume said of his sceptical doubts, 'When after three or four hours' amusement I return to these speculations, they appear so cold, and strained and ridiculous, that I cannot find in my heart to enter into them any further.' Moore accepted as a psychological fact that people are capable of holding 'sincerely, as part of their philosophical creed, propositions inconsistent with what they themselves *know* to be true'. One of the commonest attempts at reconciliation is what Lazerowitz admits is the frequent metaphysical move of drawing a distinction between what is really so and what only appears to be so. This is the move made by Plato, Zeno, Leibniz, Bradley and many others, who respect pure reason more than the senses. Lazerowitz's answer is briefly this: he argues that if it is logically impossible for so and so to be such and such, e.g. for anything to move, for space to exist, for something to be known, etc., then it is equally logically impossible for so and so to appear to be such and such. As Wittgenstein once said, 'We could not say what an "unlogical" world would look like.'[48] From this Lazerowitz concludes, first, that the metaphysician cannot, therefore, reconcile his position with what he and we ordinarily believe by allowing that what we believe just appears to be so. Secondly, that the impossibility of the logically impossible's appearing to be so is so obvious that no metaphysician can have failed to see it, therefore he cannot seriously have been trying to reconcile the two positions; therefore he cannot have thought his position inconsistent with the ordinary, therefore he must have been, not asserting the correctness of his new position, but proposing that the ordinary position be changed to it.[49]

To this argument we must answer that, though the premiss is strictly correct, the first conclusion can be not too loosely taken in ways which allow exceptions; and, more importantly, that the second conclusion neither follows from the premiss nor is it true in itself. As regards the first conclusion, there is a use of 'appears', namely that akin to 'inclined to think', in which, for example, a circle may appear to be equal in area to a square though this is logically impossible. Furthermore, the so-called 'impossible figures' of psychologists might be said to 'show' not merely what is spatially impossible, but what is logically impossible. Finally, though it is logically impossible for a rabbit which was not in a hat to come out of the hat, magicians commonly make it appear that this happens, just as mathematical jokers can make it appear that one is equal to two. In these ways the logical impossibility of motion would not preclude its appearing to be logically possible. More important for our purposes is the falsity of the second conclusion, namely that the impossibility of what is logically impossible's appearing to exist is so obvious that any metaphysician who held that so and so was impossible must have seen that it could not even appear to be possible. In the first place, it is difficult to see how metaphysicians could have used so often the argument that what is impossible could and does appear to be possible, if its fallaciousness is so obvious. Secondly, it is clear, as Lazerowitz allows, that many philosophers have in fact either overlooked the fallacy or even disputed it,[50] perhaps because they assimilated by analogy the fallacious argument to the perfectly respectable argument that what is physically impossible can appear to exist. Thirdly, it is most significant that, despite Lazerowitz's insistence that the fallacy of allowing that though so and so is logically impossible, yet it may appear to exist, is clear and obvious, he returns to its proof and explanation time and time again and at great length.[51] 'Methinks the lady doth protest too much.'

Fifthly, it is significant that metaphysical assertions are commonly made, as the Verificationists gleefully pointed out, in areas where proof and disproof are difficult or dubious. How is the existence of the self or of God, the immortality of the soul, the origin of the universe, the objectivity of morals, to be proved or disproved? Lazerowitz makes metaphysical controversies seem too simple and soluble.

A sixth point to be made in support of the view that the traditional metaphysicians were not altering language, consciously or unconsciously, but giving analyses of the ordinary meanings of certain words with the realised consequences that their analyses were in conflict with what was ordinarily believed, even by themselves, is that their arguments only proceed on the assumption that their unacceptable and bizarre conclusions use the key words in the same senses — and these the ordinary senses — as do the premisses from which they are deduced. Thus, Zeno clearly used 'moves' in the same sense in his metaphysical, but mistaken, conclusion that nothing moves as he did in his correct premiss that in order to move from A to B one must move from A to a position half-way to B. There is no indication that the meaning of 'space' changes during Kant's argument for his conclusion — which Lazerowitz thinks an alteration of the meaning of the word 'space' in order to express an unconscious agoraphobia — that space is an *a priori* form of perception.

A seventh relevant remark about Lazerowitz's thesis that the metaphysician is not making an assertion about the use of words but is announcing an alteration in his use of them is that the latter view seems to have the same important consequences as the former, namely that there is something wrong about the ordinary use of the words. And what could relevantly be wrong with them except that they allegedly state something to be so which is not so, or fail to state something which is so; for example that things move or are known, that existence is an attribute, that there are universals, etc. So Lazerowitz admits that the metaphysician who says 'Time is unreal' proposes that we should not use 'now' because it is wrongly thought to be a unit of time.[52] Why should a philosopher propose, as Lazerowitz suggests that he does, that abstract words should be classified with proper names, unless he thought this more correct than the ordinary classification?[53] A zoologist who reclassifies whales with mammals rather than with fish, or sponges with animals rather than with plants could, perhaps, be said to be recommending a change. But he is doing so because he thinks the previous classification to be wrong; and his reclassification can be assessed as true or false by his fellow scientists.

Finally, there are, as we shall see later, many possible explanations of why metaphysical assertions should have seemed so plausible despite either their implying the existence in the universe of some highly speculative and, perhaps, fantastic features, or their flying in the face of common sense and ordinary language. Such explanations often also account for their long life. These explanations refer not only to the fact already alluded to that, though metaphysical assertions arise from conceptual and linguistic mistakes, they are not merely assertions about the use of well-known words, but also to the natural inclination to certain ways of thinking to which our language leads us, and to the one-sided diet of examples on which metaphysicians have typically fed.[54]

Whether the metaphysician is altering the use of words, or only giving what he argues is their correct use, he is finding fault with the ordinary use and with some of the beliefs which are commonly expressed in it. He is saying, for example, that it is wrong to suppose that things move, exist unperceived or in space, that we know them as they really are, etc. Furthermore, he gives arguments, however bad, for these conclusions, however mistaken. Whether or not his conclusions and arguments also express his unconscious desires that his particular conclusion should be correct, that is, that nothing should move, that space should not be independent of him, that there should be a God, etc., is quite another matter, which, though it may explain some of the tenacity with which he holds his views — just as our desires can explain some of the tenacity with which many of us hold many of our everyday views — is independent of the truth or falsity of the views themselves. It is also something for which Lazerowitz has provided no evidence other than the plausibility of the general psycho-analytic thesis, for example that those who deny what seems obvious to others may have some hidden reason for doing so, and, of the particular theses, that a denial of motion may be linked with a fear of change, a denial of space with agoraphobia, the exaltation of God with a feeling of dependence, etc.

Lazerowitz can, and does, dismiss all his potential critics with the suggestion that their disagreement is due, not to any weakness in his arguments, but to their unconscious desire to save their pride in their work.[55] He is happy to dismiss support for rival explanations of metaphysics because they satisfy the unconscious needs of their advocates, but does not query his own explanations for the same reason.[56]

Notes

1. *The Structure of Metaphysics* (henceforth *SM*), Routledge and Kegan Paul, 23, 181, 256, 272; *Studies in Metaphilosophy* (henceforth *M*), Routledge and Kegan Paul, 8; *Philosophy and Illusion* (henceforth *P*), Allen and Unwin, 9, 82, 99, 110, 210.
2. *SM* 104, 108, 156, 164, 219, 225, 258; *M* 107, 155, 171.
3. *M* Chapters 1 and 5; *P* Chapters 4 and 5.
4. *M* 256.
5. *SM* Chapter 2, pp. 26, 57–66, 71, 230; *M* Chapters 4 and 5, pp. 71, 181, 217, 226, 230–5, 239, 249, 256; *P* Chapters 4 and 5, pp. 110, 124.
6. *SM* 68–70.
7. *M* 248–9; *P* 117.
8. *M* 255.
9. *M* 181.
10. *SM* 67, 102; *M* 238.
11. *P* Chapter 4.
12. *SM* 49–57, Chapter 4.
13. *SM* Chapter 1, 106; *M* 241; *P* 83–4, 120, 225.
14. *SM* 95, 108, 131, 139, 184–5, 272; *M* 20, 66, 90, 184; *P* 204.
15. *M* 59; *P* 215; *M* 248–9; *M* 255; *M* 181.
16. *SM* 257, 272.
17. *SM* 26 ff., 57–8, 101, 187, 272; *M* 171, 223–4, 241; *P* 55, 112.
18. *SM* 19, 23, 104, 108, 149, 156, 164, 174, 192, 197, 219, 222, 257, 272; *M* 66, 71, 105, 153, 177, 201, 207–8, 218, 153; *P* 88, 109, 139, 161, 165, 225, 235, 247.
19. *SM* 219–20.
20. *SM* 108.
21. *M* 155.
22. *SM* 104, 108, 156, 164, 219, 225, 258; *M* 107, 155, 171.
23. *SM* 242–3.
24. *SM* 242–3.
25. *SM* 272.
26. *M* 108, 120.
27. *SM* 63, 156, 168, 225; *M* 107.
28. *SM* 32; *P* 20.
29. *SM* 174.
30. *SM* 116.
31. *SM* 227.
32. *SM* 66–71, 79, 224, 227–9; *M* 66, 69, 151, 171; *P* 99–101, 139–40, 215.
33. *M* 180.
34. *M* 66–7, 95–6, 100; *SM* 95, 131, 184–5.
35. *SM* 104, 108, 164.
36. cf. *SM* 48–9.
37. cf. *SM* 104–5.
38. *SM* 20–2.
39. *SM* 85; contrast 95.
40. *SM* 242.
41. *M* 104–5.

42. *M* 79.
43. *SM* Chapter 3.
44. *SM* Chapter 7.
45. *P* 85 ff.
46. *SM* 186–7.
47. *SM* 256–8.
48. *Tractatus*, 3.031.
49. *SM* 170 ff.
50. *SM* 43, 233 ff., 265 ff.; 160, 219; *P* 24, 154.
51. *SM* 43, 168, 170–1, 187, 207–15, 231–47, 265; *M* 125, 130, 139, 146, 157, 160, 219; *P* 24, 115, 133, 136, 154.
52. *SM* 22; cf. 104 on universals.
53. *SM* 101, 106.
54. *SM* 45, 91–2; *M* 166–8.
55. *M* 215–6; *SM* 68, 226.
56. *SM* 58; *M* 61, 215; *P* 83.

12
Conclusion

My aim in the first part of this essay was to show by a critical exposition of the arguments of such acknowledged classical metaphysicians as Plato, Aristotle, Berkeley, Leibniz and Bradley, that the history of metaphysics from the earliest to the latest times reveals the subject as having a certain consistent pattern of methods, canons, results, etc. underlying quite different exemplifications.

A metaphysician, such sketches show, is faced at the first stage of his enquiry, as is a philosopher in any area, with the task of explaining the nature of a certain concept or set of concepts. What differentiates his particular concepts from those studied in other branches of philosophy is their generality. Part of the truth underlying the common traditional characterisation of metaphysics as dealing with what is most general, most comprehensive or most fundamental — as dealing, in a frequent phrase, with 'reality as a whole' — is this generality of the metaphysicians' concepts. Such concepts as existence, reality, substance, truth, similarity, difference, identity, contradiction, necessity and causality are common to our thinking in every area, whether it be ethics, science, politics, art, etc.

The most fundamental of these general concepts is that of existence or being. What exactly does it mean to say of something that it is or that it exists? This is a concept in whose nature every metaphysician has been primarily interested. A grandiloquent word, from the Greek, for the study of the nature of existence or being is ontology. Hence, there is a sense in which metaphysics can truly be said, as it frequently is said, to be about ontology. We have seen that there is also another sense in which metaphysics can also be said, as it even more commonly is said, to be about ontology, namely as a study of the things which exist, including those supersensible things which metaphysicians commonly postulate.

For Plato the conceptual interest in ontology assumed the following general form. When we say that such and such is so and so, for example that 'This is a man, a bed, a bee' or 'This is just, courageous or holy' or that 'Courage is good' or 'Justice is different from holiness', what exactly is the relation or relations expressed by 'is' between such and such and so and so? More particularly, when we say 'This and this and . . . are each so and so', for example 'X and Y and Z are all just (or bees)', which we might also naturally put as 'X and Y and Z are all instances of, examples of, cases of, justice (of bees)', what is the relation, expressed by 'is' or by 'is an instance of' or by 'is an example of' between the instance or example and that of which it is an instance or example? In general, what is the relation between any instances or examples and that of which they are instances or examples?

Aristotle is famous for having explicitly posed as the prime problem of metaphysics the study of Being as Being, by which he meant to distinguish between it and the various sciences on the grounds that while they seek knowledge of what it is for various particular kinds of things to be, whether these are perceivable objects, such as animals, plants, stars and planets, or abstract objects, such as numbers or figures, metaphysics asks what it is for being to be. While science studies the being of this or that, metaphysics studies the being of being.

We saw that Berkeley frequently asserted that his prime aim was to get clear about the concept of existence, whether it was used of such physical objects as trees and tables, or such non-physical objects as minds and numbers. His metaphysics, or part of it, has commonly been summed up, both by himself and by his commentators, in a slogan, 'to be is to be perceived', which puts the nature of existence at its centre.

Leibniz, a logician of great originality, assuming that all truths are expressible in the Aristotelian subject – predicate form, took as his basic problem the discovery of the reason why any such proposition could be true. In other words, why is it that when it is truly said that 'X is Y' then X *is* Y. His answer, as we have seen, is that in all such cases the predicate Y, whether it mentions a present or a future attribute of X, is in a sense included in the subject X.

Bradley, who repeated Aristotle's definition of 'metaphysics' as 'the study of first principles or ultimate truths', differed from him in emphasising a contrast between 'mere being', which he considered too empty and negative, and 'reality', which joins existence and content, what he called the 'that' and the 'what'. He argued that in every judgement, such as 'X is Y', the subject indicates the 'that' and the predicate the 'what'. Bradley saw his task as discovering the nature of this Reality.

Furthermore, various philosophers and metaphysicians, whom I have not discussed, such as Parmenides, perhaps the founder of metaphysics, Aquinas and his followers, and twentieth-century Existentialists, have put the topic of being or existence at the head of their studies.

All these metaphysicians begin, I have suggested, with a conceptual problem often centred on the concept of *being* or existence, and, therefore, in one sense 'ontological'. The second characteristic stage in their common pattern of approach is, I claim, commitment to some prime principle which seemed to each of them, in his different way, to offer a solution to his conceptual problem. Here we see that desire for generality which Wittgenstein considered a virtue of science, but a vice of philosophy.

Thus, Plato's overriding conviction was that to say that this and this and this are all so and sos, for example that X and Y and Z are all men or are all just, was, first, to say that *that* which these many all are or *that* which these many are all instances or examples of is *one*; secondly, that that one which these are, or are instances of, is something additional to those which are, or are instances of, it; and, thirdly, that it is something which explains them. It seemed obvious to Plato that there could not be instances or examples of something, for example humanity or justice, unless as well as the instances or examples there exists also that of which they are instances or examples. Thus, the universe must contain both instances or examples and that of which they are instances or examples; what later philosophers called particulars and universals.

Fundamental to Aristotle's attempt to discover the nature of Being was his idea that, though 'being' has various senses — one corresponding to each of what he called categories, such as qualities, relations, locations, etc. — these senses all centre round one sense, called *ousia* or Existent. Just as each thing is to be explained in terms of its own *ousia*, so existence itself is to be explained by a primary instance of *ousia* in the way that, for example, the healthiness of exercise or of a complexion is to be explained by the primary instance of healthiness, that is, the healthiness of a person. As Plato looked for the explanation of everything in his idea of the 'one over many', Aristotle sought it in his idea of the 'many towards one'.

Berkeley regarded his analysis of existence in terms either of that which exists being perceived (*esse est percipi*) — which holds for physical objects — or of that which exists perceiving (*esse est percipere*) — which holds for spirits — as his great discovery and as the key to unlock all the difficulties which he thought he saw in the received views of Locke and his scientific friends. This was the principle about which he wondered, not so much as to his eventually discovering it, but to his not having seen it sooner.

Leibniz's reflections not only on the subject – predicate form of propositions, but also on the principles of deductive logic and of mathematics, backed up by the theories of contemporary biologists, convinced him of his 'great principle' that 'every truth has its proof *a priori* drawn from the meaning of its terms' and, therefore, that 'the present is big with the future, the future might be read in the past, the distant is expressed in the near'.

Bradley claimed that thinking meant the acceptance of a certain standard which amounted to an assumption as to the character of reality. Such a standard would be one which satisfied the intellect. His belief was that 'ultimate reality is such that it does not contradict itself; here is an absolute criterion. And it is proved absolute by the fact that, either in endeavouring to deny it, or even in attempting to doubt it, we tacitly assume its validity.'

The third stage of enquiry which I claim is characteristic of the pattern of argument used by the classical metaphysicians is the drawing of certain conclusions about the existence of non-empirical and transcendent entities from a combination of the bases provided by their original logical problems and their guiding principles. In thus hypothesising the existence of such extra entities, whether Plato's Forms, Aristotle's Unmoved Mover, Berkeley's Infinite Mind, Leibniz's Monads or Bradley's Absolute, they qualify as proponents of ontology in a sense not restricted to the logical analysis of the concept of existence, but embracing a belief in the actual existence of particular kinds of objects. This is the traditional sense in which it has commonly been claimed — and I think rightly claimed — that ontology is a hallmark of all the classical metaphysicians. Metaphysicians, like scientists, have always typically held that there are more things in heaven and earth than are dreamt of in the ordinary man's philosophy.

Thus, Plato argued that that one of which there are many instances, for example that justice, that humanity of which particular just acts or particular men are instances, must be an entity existing additionally to the entities which constitute its instances. Furthermore, it must be an entity existing beyond the area in which, and in a different manner from, that in which its instances exist, since, in the normal world which we can experience, we find only instances of, for example, justice or humanity, that is, individual just acts and individual men, but never justice or humanity itself. Moreover, Plato had, as we have seen, additional arguments, such as his argument from our experience of and our ability to recognise imperfection to the supposed necessity of an innate idea of perfection, for the existence of these transcendent entities.

Aristotle's move from his belief in a primary concept of existence, that is, *ousia*, on which all other senses of 'existence' depended, to a belief in the existence of a primary supersensible entity, which was the basic cause of all other entities, stemmed partly from several conceptual shifts. First, he easily shifts, perhaps because of an adherence to an Object Theory of Meaning, between regarding Being as a concept and regarding it as an entity and, hence, assimilates metaphysics as the study of the concept of Being to metaphysics as the study of an entity called 'being'. A particular and important instance of this is a shift from the notion of *ousia* or Existent to actual *ousiai* or existents. Secondly, he did not always clearly separate an entity, its essence and its being from each other, and so moved from conclusions about one of these to conclusions about the others. Finally, apart from particular arguments, such as that from the existence of motion to an unmoved mover, he seems to have argued from the study of being to that of a primary instance of being, namely *ousia*, hence to a primary instance of *ousia*, namely separate *ousia*, and finally to a primary instance of separate *ousia*, namely separate and immovable, and therefore, divine *ousia*.

Berkeley's belief in his cardinal principle that to be is to be perceived led him inevitably by two routes to postulate the existence of an entity additional to those encountered in this world. The first route joined his principle of *esse est percipi* to the common-sense belief, which he did not wish to dispute, that the common objects of the world, such as trees and mountains, tables and chairs, continue to exist when no human being is perceiving them. From this he concluded that they must at these times be being perceived by a non-human mind; therefore, we must postulate the existence of an infinite mind to hold in existence whatever is not being perceived by any finite mind. The second route joined his principle to the fact that what we do perceive cannot be caused by our own minds — as contrasted with the way in which what we imagine or dream or hallucinate may be our own creations — but yet must, like images, dreams, etc., be created by some mind and not by the inert, inactive matter believed in by Locke and his scientific friends. From this he concluded that it must be created by another, infinite, mind. In short, it seemed to Berkeley that the existence of an infinite mind was necessary to explain the existence both of the perceived and the unperceived world about us.

Because Leibniz was captivated by his principle that all the consequences, whether these be logical conclusions, material effects or simply the future, of anything must already be contained in that thing in the way that the predicate of a proposition is, at least in the obvious example of an analytic proposition, contained in the subject, he was driven to introduce entities, created at the beginning of the world, each constantly unfolding its future without any mutual influence, but in a pre-arranged harmony with each other to give the world as it is at any time. His acceptance of certain other logical principles, such as the identity of indiscernibles and the law of continuity, together with analogies with mathematical points, physical centres of force and human selves, gave these entities, his Monads, such various characteristics as simplicity, variety, infinite plurality, etc.

Bradley uses his criterion of non-self-contradiction in a negative way to show that the ways in which we ordinarily view the world, that is, as made up of things, qualities, relations, space and time, change, cause, etc. all breed contradictions and therefore cannot tell us what *really* is, but only what *appears* to be. The positive use of the criterion shows that 'ultimate reality is such that it does not contradict itself'. We must, therefore, suppose reality to be an absolute or whole which is rational, coherent, all-inclusive, harmonious, non-contradictory, in which appearances are 'transmuted' and 'transcended'.

The introduction of entities not actually experienced in order to explain what is experienced is, of course, quite common in many areas. Sometimes this introduction takes only the simple form of introducing what is not experienced but quite easily could be, as when strange footprints are explained by a known fox or by an unknown abominable snowman. Sometimes it takes the form of introducing what is not in practice or at the time experienceable, as when the aberration in the path of the planet Uranus is explained by the hypothetical presence of another planet of an estimated size and position — observed a hundred years later as Neptune — or, perhaps, when another's pain is supposed to explain his grimaces, or some Freudian element in one's unconscious is supposed to explain one's abnormal actions. Sometimes what is introduced in science to explain certain phenomena is at the time of its introduction at least disputably inexperienceable even in principle, as when hereditary characteristics are explained by genes, certain diseases by viruses, and light and sound by waves. Scientists and philosophers of science differ on how far some of the entities introduced in scientific explanations could ever, even in principle, be experienced in themselves, for example gravitational attraction, neutrinos, the super-ego, etc. and certainly scientists have often — though, in the opinion of their successors, illegitimately — introduced such unexperienceable entities as phlogiston, coronium and the aether. It is partly the introduction of unobserved or unobservable entities by such early Greek thinkers as the Milesians and the Atomists which makes it difficult to decide whether to call them scientists or metaphysicians. Equally in the nineteenth century it was the nature, and the untestability, of such entities as the aether and caloric fluid which later led the Logical Positivists to castigate some scientists as merely metaphysicians.

There are, however, several important differences between the introduction of entities in any of these ways by common sense or science and the introduction of metaphysical entities. The first, and perhaps the most important, difference is this. Whereas the scientist or common man introduces so and so as a *sufficient* explanation of such and such, claiming only that it could account in an empirical way for the existence or characteristics of that which is to be explained — for instance, shadows by straight lines of light — the metaphysician introduces his entities, whether Platonic Forms, Leibnizian Monads or a Berkeleian God, as not only a sufficient but also the *necessary* explanation to account in a logical way for the existence of what we normally experience. Plato, for example, contends that only the existence of justice itself could explain both the existence, and our recognition of the existence of, just acts. In his view the latter implies the former. His early dialogues are devoted to discussing and dismissing alternative candidates to play the role of that which could be common to and explain the existence of instances of, for example, holiness, courage, justice, etc. Only the Form of Courage can account for instances of courage. Berkeley argues that nothing but an infinite spirit could explain either what we actually perceive or what we could in certain circumstances perceive. Locke's introduction of matter is dismissed as nonsensical. In other words, whereas the scientist introduces entities to account for our actual experience, the metaphysician introduces them to account for the very possibility of such experience. To this extent it can, I think, be properly said that whereas the scientist uses empirical arguments for the introduction of his entities, the metaphysician uses what Kant called transcendental arguments — transcendental, not because they introduce transcendent entities, though they do, but because they insist that these entities are logically necessary for the very possibility of what they explain. Kant would agree with the metaphysicians that if their theses are to be properly metaphysical theses, unlike the statements of scientists, they must be in some way necessary. Wittgenstein frequently emphasises as a hallmark of philosophical theses in general and of metaphysical theses in particular that they do not arise from looking and seeing whether something is so, but from insisting that it must be so; for example that there must be an intrinsic difference between memory images and dream images,[1] that if we can display our knowledge we must have it stored somewhere,[2] or that I must know what I feel.[3]

A second difference between the scientific and the metaphysical introduction of unexperienced and/or unexperienceable entities is this. The scientist commonly reaches his conclusion for the existence of such an entity from two premisses, one of which states the occurrence of what is given and the other of which states some general empirical scientific law which he has either discovered or accepted. Thus, the postulation of the planet Neptune resulted from a combination of a given path of the planet Uranus and Newton's law of gravity that bodies attract each other proportional to their masses and inversely to the square of the distance between them. Light was conjectured to consist of corpuscles because of a given set of data about interference and the rectilinear propagation of light. The postulation of Mendel's genes resulted from a combination of the given statistical distribution of the characteristics of the offspring of the mating elements and an assumption that like parental characteristics determined this distribution. The metaphysician, on the other hand, reaches his conclusion about the existence of unexperienced entities by combining one premiss, which, like that of the scientist, states the admittedly given, and another which, unlike that of the scientist, states his allegedly necessary conceptual premiss. Thus, Plato concludes that since there are just acts, that is, instances of justice, and since there cannot be instances of anything without that of which they are instances, there must exist justice itself. Berkeley concludes that since there admittedly exist unperceived objects and since to be is to be perceived, there must exist an omnipresent perceiver. Thus, though the pattern of argument for the existence of scientific unobserved objects and for metaphysical unobserved objects is the same, and rightly so in order to give a valid argument, their arguments differ in the character of their second premiss, which for the scientist is an empirical law of his system, and for the metaphysician an apparently obvious or proved conceptual principle of his. In either case a disproof of the second premiss would disprove the conclusion. Often in science this is what happens. Equally I have tried to show in the individual chapters — what would be generally accepted — that none of the principles used by Plato, Aristotle, Berkeley, Leibniz or Bradley is acceptable. That is, that the principle of the 'one over many', of '*esse est percipi*', of 'the present is big with the future' and of the equivalence of incompleteness and unreality are all false. Therefore, in none of these cases does the metaphysical conclusion follow. This is not to say that no metaphysical conclusion could ever follow. In principle, the pattern of argument which relies on one premiss, which is true because it states what is given, and on another which is true because it states a true principle — whether it be a law of physics, such as the inverse square law, or a conceptual principle, such as the one over many, can lead to a perfectly true conclusion. It seems to me, therefore, that in this respect the type of argument used by the metaphysician is as good, because the same, as that of the scientist. Though one cannot, as the Logical Positivists insist, deduce the super-empirical from the purely empirical, one can do so with the help of an extra premiss. The pattern of argument can be illustrated, perhaps, by using a simple philosophical, though non-metaphysical, example which is perfectly valid. If it is true as a matter of experience that most men are interested in women, then since it is conceptually true that whoever is interested in something will be or feel inclined to give attention to what he is interested in, then it will be true that most men will be or feel inclined to give their attention to women. Similar arguments are used in the application of the conceptual truths of mathematics.

Thus, given that a bath is being filled by so many men at such a rate and emptied by others at another rate, the addition of elementary mathematical principles allows us to deduce when the bath will in fact be full. The objection which has been brought against the classical metaphysicians in the earlier individual chapters is not to the pattern of their argument, but to its particular second premiss. It is because, I believe, no conceptual premiss yet advanced by any metaphysician is correct, that I conclude that no introduction of any metaphysical entity has yet been proved valid. It is conceptually false that there cannot be instances without any entity of which they are instances, or that *esse* is *percipi* or that the predicate is contained in the subject of every true proposition.

The very assurance and tenacity with which all metaphysicians have advanced their various theories and have defended the existence of the entities which they have introduced stem, I think, from this fact that they have all used, and have been properly convinced that they are using, a valid pattern of argument which had a statement of the indisputably given as one premiss, and a supposedly indisputable principle, whose truth they all claim to have proved or to have shown to be obvious, as the second premiss. It was, as their writings show, their conviction of the obvious truth of their particular principle, which they differently offered, which made them adhere so confidently to their conclusion.

The difference between the empirical laws or theories commonly used by scientists as the second premiss in this pattern of argument, and the conceptual principles used by metaphysicians, provides one ground for the objection, raised in different ways by Kant and the Logical Positivists, that the statements made by metaphysicians are not verifiable by any experience. If these principles are, as I have argued, purely conceptual, then, of course, they are not verifiable or falsifiable by experience, since that is the nature of a conceptual principle. It is not experience which shows us, for example, that what is known must be so, while what is believed can be not so. The metaphysicians themselves adopt a slightly ambivalent position in regard to these principles. They all are struck by and insistent upon what they think are their obviousness and their indisputability. Often, as in Berkeley's *esse est percipi*, they say quite explicitly that they are meant to be analyses or definitions of some concept. Yet, they also refer to common experience to support them. Plato's dialogues are often intended to show that nothing but, for example, justice itself, could explain what is common and necessary to all instances of justice, and Berkeley advances various arguments, especially in the discussions between Hylas and Philonous, to convince the reader that nothing can exist unperceived. Leibniz clearly took not only logic and mathematics but also biology both as the inspiration of and as a support for his doctrine that all the consequences of anything are in it from the beginning, and Bradley frequently stressed that his criterion of non-contradictory 'satifies the intellect'.

This ambivalence can, I think, be understood and accepted by a comparison of these metaphysical principles with simple mathematical statements. Though such a statement or formula in mathematics as $n(a+b) = na + nb$, or $2 + 2 = 4$, is conceptually true and not true because of any of the features of the world of physical objects, such as coins or apples, it is commonly suggested, at least in the elementary teaching of these to children, that they are confirmed by what happens with coins and apples. But the fact that three heaps of two apples and four bananas is the same as three heaps of two apples and three heaps of four bananas does not confirm the formula $3(2+4) = 3 \times 2 + 3 \times 4$; it only illustrates it. Experience does not verify the formula, it only makes clear what the formula is saying. Similarly, the references to experience which the metaphysicians make in trying to persuade the reader to accept their principles, whether of the one over many, that *esse* is *percipi*, that the present contains the future, or that the incomplete is not real, illustrate various supposedly true conceptual principles.

If the metaphysicians' principles are, despite some of the language which they use about them, intended to be conceptual, not empirical, then it is, although true, not a fair objection that, in this respect, metaphysical statements are unverifiable by experience. Further, if the enunciation of such principles as the one over many or *esse* is *percipi*, as contrasted with hypotheses introducing extra entities, as Forms, the Unmoved Mover, God or Monads, can count as metaphysical statements, then there certainly are verifiable or falsifiable metaphysical statements. Indeed, I have suggested that they are all in fact false. But such statements are verifiable only at the cost of being purely conceptual rather than existential, and thus at the cost of not being capable of telling us anything about what the universe may be like.

A third difference between the scientific and the metaphysical introduction of unexperienced and/or unexperienceable entities is this. Evidence, of an empirical kind, is usually provided by the scientist to establish not only that the introduced entities can account, usually causally, for the phenomena to be explained, but that they can account for further phenomena in some ways unlike the original phenomena. Hence, two rival scientific hypotheses, for example the Ptolemaic and the Copernican explanations of the paths of the planets or the wave and the corpuscular theories of light, should and will provide not merely different explanations of the given phenomena, but different predictions about phenomena not yet tested. The theory whose predictions are wrong will be wrong. Though it is sometimes alleged that, for example, Darwin's theory of evolution, at least initially, was explanatory of zoological and fossil data without being predictive of any novel facts, it seems that predictive powers, exemplified in the part which interference phenomena played in deciding between the wave and the corpuscular theories of light, are a vital requirement of scientific theories. Metaphysical theories share with scientific theories the desire to explain by their introduced entities all the phenomena we encounter. They differ, however, in that, though such rival systems give different accounts of the original phenomena, they do not suggest different predictions for new material. For example, though Plato held that what is common to all instances, for example of justice or of man, is something additional to and existing apart from its instances in another world, Aristotle argued that what is common did not exist other than in its instances. Yet nothing can be predicted about any other phenomena in the world which would be different on the Platonic and on the Aristotelian hypotheses. Again, though Berkeley and Locke differed about the cause of our having the perceptions we do have when, as we say, we perceive some object such as a tree — Locke supposing it was something in the tree called 'matter' and Berkeley supposing it was a power in an infinite mind — no test of anything we encounter was or could be suggested by either metaphysician which would enable us to differentiate between the two hypotheses. Leibniz's theory denied the commonly accepted view that various objects and events are related by cause and effect, but he can suggest no way in which what happens would be any different if such events are related, as he holds, by a pre-established harmony between them.

This difference provides a second ground for the criticism of Kant and the Logical Positivists that the statements made by metaphysicians are not testable by any experience. The metaphysician may claim that his hypothesis is proved by our actual experience, since it is supposed to be logically implied by what is given in experience, together with some supposedly proved principle, such as the 'one over many' or '*esse est percipi*'. So, according to Plato, just acts cannot exist without the Form of Justice or, according to Berkeley, humanly unexperienced objects cannot exist without a non-human perceiver. Yet, as we have just seen, there is no further and different experience which is relevant to confirming these theories or to deciding between them and their rivals in the way that a scientist would claim that his theories are verifiable or falsifiable by testing the predictions which one can make on the strength of them.

Yet, even if it is admitted that metaphysical hypotheses are unlike scientific hypotheses in that no testable predictions can be made on their basis, does this show in any way that they are not perfectly meaningful and, indeed, even testable? Does there not seem to be a clear and understandable difference between the Platonic supposition that justice is something separate from and additional to acts of justice, which perhaps those acts copy, and the Aristotelian supposition that it is something present in each act; or between the Lockean supposition that the cause of our perceptions is some material substance and the Berkeleian supposition that it is an immaterial mind; or between the Leibnizian supposition that the relations between different objects are pre-arranged coincidences and the rival supposition that they are causal connections?

Part of the reason for this feeling, I think, is that the metaphysical hypothesis trades on a picture it conjures up which is analogous to a testable suggestion. Thus, we can clearly see the difference between, for example, a situation in which we have one original painting and a set of exact copies of it, and a situation in which we have a set of exactly similar paintings all with identical labels on them. Hence, we think we have an analogy with the Platonic one over many and the Aristotelian one in each. Or again, we clearly see the difference between our having sensations caused by a material object emitting sounds and smells and our having images or thoughts induced in us by telepathy and by the suggestive powers of others. Hence, we think we have an analogy with the Lockean and the Berkeleian hypotheses. Or we clearly see the difference between a railway system in which all the apparent interrelations between the trains are due to a pre-established computerised signal system at headquarters controlling each train, and a system in which each train is affected in causal ways by the other trains which approach it, so that in the former system crashes at intersections are avoided by prior timing of all the trains, while in the latter they are avoided by causal sensors on the trains themselves. Hence, we think we have an analogy with the Leibnizian pre-established harmony and its rival causal theories.

When, however, we press these analogies we find that they break down. First, Plato himself realised that none of his attempts to say exactly what the relation was between an individual just act and the Form of Justice seemed very plausible. It was not the relation of part and whole nor that of copy and original. What would one expect to find in the Aristotelian analogy corresponding to the common labels on the paintings? Secondly, if we were genuinely puzzled whether our seeming to see a familiar object was due either to it or a trick of light, on the one hand, or to a hallucination induced by a hypnotist or by our own wishful thinking, on the other hand, one could think of tests to resolve this doubt, but how can we show whether what we seem to see is produced by Locke's Matter or by Berkeley's God? Finally, though we can examine the trains in the railway system to see if they are fitted with sensors to avoid each other or if their mutual avoidance is due to the signal system of the central communications office, we have no analogous tests for deciding between Leibnizian and causal theories.

The way in which an analogous picture can seem to give meaning to something we say, although in fact there is no real connection between what we say and the picture we rely on, can be brought out by an illustration offered by Wittgenstein. Because I can sensibly ask 'When it is noon in London, what time is it in New York or in Sydney?' it may look as if we can equally sensibly ask 'What time is it then on the sun or on the moon?' Part of the reason for our accepting the latter question may be because we can picture people supposedly telling the time on the moon or the sun in the way they normally do in New York or Sydney, for example by looking at their watches, or we can introduce a new way of telling the time, for example by reference to some atomic clock. But in fact the method we actually use to decide the time in London, New York or Sydney is by reference to the angle the sun's rays make with the surface of the earth at each of these places. But there is no test for the relative angle the sun's rays make with the surface of the moon and there could be none for the angle they make with the sun itself and, therefore, any question about the time on the moon or the sun does not at present have, even in principle, any test or any answer.

Similarly, whereas to ask about the temperature of an individual molecule seems to make as good sense as asking about the temperature of a single gas ring, in kinetic theory such a question is as senseless as asking what is the average of an individual person. Though 'exceeding the speed of light' seems an intelligible phrase, the special relativity theory holds that it is in principle impossible to verify or falsify any statement that a body did exceed the speed of light.

A fourth difference between the metaphysical and the scientific introduction of unexperienced entities lies in the possibility of the entity itself being experienced. Sometimes what scientists introduce to explain puzzling phenomena are objects which they believe to be only practically inexperienceable, as when Neptune was hypothesised a hundred years before its observation by telescope to account for an aberration in the path of Uranus. Sometimes what they introduce are objects, which at least at the time of their introduction they admittedly have no clue as to how they could even in principle be experienced, as in the introduction of genes, chromosomes, molecules, atoms, neutrinos, electric fluid, etc. It is a matter of debate among scientists and philosophers of science whether any of these latter entities are in principle inexperienceable, and whether recourse to such instruments as electron microscopes, X-ray plates, cloud chambers, Geiger counters, etc. gives direct experience of them, or only experience of some of their effects. On the one hand, one of the reasons for scientific rejection of such 'occult objects' as coronium, phlogiston, the aether, a *virtus dormativa* and, more recently, the ego, super-ego and id, seems to have been their inexperienceability. Furthermore, even those who express doubts about the experienceability of any of these scientific entities talk as if they exist in space and time. On the other hand, some argue that statements about such theoretical entities only form part of a model of, or way of looking at, the world, and do not give descriptions of any underlying reality. They argue that their value is usually assessed in terms of their explanatory and predictive powers. It is, they say, not the non-observability of phlogiston, caloric fluid, the aether, etc. which led to their abandonment, but their lack of these explanatory and predictive powers. Practising scientists are, indeed, usually not very interested in whether, for example, molecules are really like billiard balls, but in whether to assume that in some respects they are is helpful in explaining what is given, and in producing further suggestions for enquiry. But whatever view is taken about scientific 'theoretical entities', it seems agreed by scientists that if these really exist and are not merely items in a model, then they must be experienceable either directly by the use of various scientific instruments, or indirectly by their effects, though the kind of link between the theoretical entity and its verifying experience may be very different for different kinds of such entities.

In all such discussions of the experienceability of the entities introduced by science, experience is limited to sense-experience. Similarly, when the impossibility of their being experienced is raised as an objection by Kant and the Logical Positivists either to the very introduction of metaphysical entities, as by the Logical Positivists, or at least to the possibility of any knowledge about them, as by Kant, what is at issue is their experienceability by the senses.

Now all metaphysicians admit — indeed, most of them insist — that the entities they introduce to explain what we experience are not experienceable by the senses. Plato's unchanging Forms are contrasted with the changeable phenomena of the senses. Aristotle's Unmoved Mover moves by desire, not by physical contact; Berkeley's infinite mind, like his finite minds, is a subject, not a possible object, of perception; Leibniz's Monads are immaterial atoms, modelled on mathematical points and psychological selves rather than on the particles of physics; Bradley's Absolute, though linked in some unclear way with experience, is mainly characterised in such logical terms as rational, non-contradictory, supra-relational, harmonious and all-inclusive. These metaphysicians would all accept Kant's contention that their entities do not exist in space, though much of what they say about them makes it more doubtful whether they would agree they also do not exist in time. Nor, on the other hand, do they consider their entities to be merely models.

The question is whether the admission that metaphysical entities are in principle not experienceable by the senses is fatal either to the possibility of any knowledge about them, as Kant held, or to the possibility that statements about them are verifiable, and that the sentences which make those statements are meaningful, as the Logical Positivists held.

First, there is much which we can know and much we can say meaningfully which has nothing to do with sense experience. Into this class would fall what pertains to pure mathematics and to logic. But both Kant and the Logical Positivists would object that this is true in so far as or because these subjects do not treat of what actually occurs. The Logical Positivists would allow their intelligibility only because they do not deal with what exists at all, or with anything which goes beyond the analytic expansion of their subject matter; whereas Kant would allow the intelligibility of mathematics only because it deals with the purely formal part of our experience of space and time. But metaphysics claims that what it introduces are existing, though non-spatial and, perhaps, non-temporal entities, and hence that these statements are not purely analytic. Kant would agree with them that their statements, if they are properly metaphysical, must be synthetic. Furthermore, I don't think that the classical metaphysicians do claim that their conclusions, such that there exists a Form of Justice, an Unmoved Mover, an infinite spirit, an infinite set of Monads, an Absolute, are necessary truths. That is, such metaphysical statements are not intended, as Kant would put it, to be *a priori*. They were not intended to be put in the same class — Kant's class of synthetic *a priori* statements — as mathematical statements. What is claimed by the metaphysician is that any such statement necessarily follows from the facts of experience and his necessary conceptual principle. That is, for example, because just acts exist, it follows, by the principle of the one over many, that justice must exist; or because objects do exist unperceived by humans, it follows, by the principle of *esse est percipi*, that some other spirit perceives them. To say they exist is not a necessary truth, but a truth which necessarily follows. This is the sense in which metaphysicians insist that such and such must be so.

A second line of escape from the objection that the ontological conclusions of metaphysicians, unlike those of scientists, are not open to verification by sense experience, is to contend that experience need not be confined to the senses. Kant, it will be remembered, always allowed the possibility, though nothing more, of the suggestion that sense experience might be a mere human limitation, and that there might be something which he referred to as 'intellectual intuition', by which knowledge could be obtained of that which was not open to inspection by the senses. More recently, some have suggested that psychological experience, by which we become aware of our thoughts and feelings, our decisions, deliberations, etc. is not sense experience. Now metaphysicians generally have insisted that their entities, though not open to sense experience, could be experienced, though not at present, by some non-sensory faculty. Thus, Plato held that his Forms were visible to the eye of the mind; Aristotle suggested that by pure thought one could approach closer to his God, and that God himself attracted the world by desire for him; Berkeley seems to have allowed that there could be what he called a 'notion' of the infinite mind as there could be of finite minds; and both Leibniz's Monads and Bradley's Absolute were apprehendable by the intellect. Even Kant, though not admitting the possibility of any human knowledge of metaphysical things in themselves (noumena), did hold that they could be thought of and he had no doubt of their existence.

It must be stressed, however, first, that there is a strong suggestion in most of these metaphysicians that any such contact with their entities by the human mind or soul is only possible when the mind is freed from the bodily means by which it usually makes contact with objects. Secondly, and most importantly, no clear indication is given of what such intellectual apprehension would be like. Though such analogies as vision, eye of the soul, notion, intellectual intuition, etc. are mentioned, what would it be like to 'see' a Form, to contemplate an Aristotelian pure thought, to have a 'notion' of a mind, to fix the intellect on a Monad or the Absolute? Thirdly, there is no suggestion by metaphysicians that any such apprehension of their transcendent entities is at all akin to our experience of psychological elements. Finally, is it true that our awareness of our thoughts and feelings provides an example of a non-sensible experience of entities? An examination of what it is to be aware of a thought or feeling would, I think, suggest, first, that what we are aware of is not an entity of any kind — 'thoughts', 'feelings' are not the names of objects, but are used in various ways to indicate certain of our abilities, tendencies, reactions, etc. — and, secondly, that such awareness is based in variously different ways on sensory and kinaesthetic experiences of a variety of physiological items.

A third way of facing the objection that metaphysical statements about transcendent entities are unverifiable by sense experience is to admit it, but to contend that some generally accepted scientific statements which postulate the existence of unobservables are equally unverifiable. Such a contention, however, is doubtful. As we saw, first, though scientists often postulate what cannot in fact be observed, as in the posited existence of the planet Neptune, these are not something unobservable in principle. Secondly, some of the entities introduced by scientists, though unobservable in principle, are claimed not to be anything actually existing, but only part of a model by which to understand the phenomena under investigation. Whether such a model later comes to be accepted as an actual picture of reality seems to depend partly on whether in fact its constituents can be observed, for example, by the later more sophisticated instruments of observation. Thirdly, some of the postulated entities, such as coronium, animal spirits or the aether are in fact abandoned by scientists on the very ground that they are in principle unobservable. Fourthly, all the entities postulated by scientists, whatever their other characteristics, are expressly held to possess spatial and temporal characteristics. Fifthly, whether or not the scientific entities themselves are experienceable, they are only admitted by science if they can predict and explain what is in fact experienceable.

A fourth type of answer to the charge of unverifiability is that typical of those twentieth-century philosophers who have tried to rehabilitate metaphysics. This type of answer tries to meet the charge by accusing it of irrelevance on the ground that metaphysical assertions are not intended to be, literally at least, either true or false, and are, therefore, not genuine candidates for the test of verifiability. This, as we saw, was the answer given, in different forms, by Collingwood, Wisdom and Lazerowitz. Collingwood, it will be remembered, argued that traditional metaphysical assertions, such that every event has a cause or that God exists, are not propositions, but absolute presuppositions of a particular age or way of thinking, which as such cannot be true or false. The metaphysician's job, he argued, is to make historical, and therefore verifiably true or false, statements, about what were the absolute presuppositions of a given system. Wisdom, on the other hand, argued that the typical traditional metaphysician's assertions are not to be taken literally and, therefore, not to be assessed as verifiably true or false statements, but as paradoxes which serve to illuminate commonly overlooked similarities and differences between our concepts. Lazerowitz considered the utterances of metaphysicians as expressions, not statements, of deep psychoanalytic conditions in the metaphysician. As expressions they are no more true or false than any other way of showing our feelings.

I have tried to show, however, in the relevant chapters, not only that the arguments on which these characterisations of the assertions of metaphysicians are based are fallacious — that is, that such statements as every event has a cause or nothing moves or Forms exist are neither unverifiable presuppositions nor paradoxes nor expressions of wishful thinking — but also that such accounts of metaphysics bear no relation to what the acknowledged classical metaphysicians actually did. Though it is perfectly legitimate to uncover absolute presuppositions, to use remarks such as 'Everyone is selfish' as paradoxes, or to express one's worry about change as 'Nothing moves', there is no reason to suppose that any metaphysician did this and, therefore, no good reason for calling these practices metaphysics. Hence, none of these attempts to rehabilitate metaphysics is a legitimate way to answer the objection that the statements of metaphysicians, especially or at least those of an ontological nature which postulate the existence of unobservable entities, such as Forms, Monads, God or the Absolute, are unverifiable by the senses and, as such, unable to satisfy the Kantian criteria for possible knowledge, or the Logical Positivists' criteria for meaningfulness.

Are we then to accept the accusation that what metaphysicians say is either unknowable, as Kant argued, or meaningless, as the Logical Positivists maintained, on the ground, admitted by metaphysicians themselves, that it is unverifiable by any possible sense experience? Clearly both metaphysicians and anti-metaphysicians would agree that metaphysic entities, such as Forms or Monads, cannot exist in space and time if they are unexperienceable by the senses. They are to this extent quite unlike the extra entities introduced by science. But while metaphysicians would be quite happy to accept the existence of non-spatial and non-temporal entities, their opponents would demand that some alternative means of verifying their existence be suggested, an alternative whose possibility Kant, but not the Logical Positivists, allowed, but whose actuality even Kant would not admit and no metaphysician has as yet plausibly argued for.

Though there are, as we saw in the appropriate chapters, objections both to Kant's analysis of the notion of our knowledge of the world and to the Logical Positivists' analysis of the idea of meaning, we do not really need to take a position on this, for any assessment of either the knowability or the meaningfulness of metaphysics has, I now wish to argue, little to do with its verifiability by the senses. It is to be sought in quite a different place.

First, the charge of meaninglessness — even in the sense of not saying anything which could be true or false — and of unknowability is implausible. It is implausible to suggest that hosts of commentators on Plato's theory of Forms, on Leibniz's Monadology, or on the sayings of most metaphysicians, have been discussing what is meaningless. In fact, they have usually been offering various interpretations of what they thought Plato, Leibniz, etc. did or must mean, and either accepting it as true or rejecting it as false. Such interpretations try in the main to discover exactly what in fact the various concepts introduced by metaphysicians, that is, the concept of a Form or a Monad or an infinite spirit, play in their respective systems. To that extent at least it is assumed that the terms for metaphysical entities gain a meaning from the system somewhat as the terms in, for example, Euclid's geometry or Newton's dynamics gain a meaning from their systems.

It is equally implausible to suggest that rival metaphysicians, however much they disagreed with what their opponents said, usually supposed it to be meaningless. They did often suppose their principles to be full of contradictions and conceptually false. Aristotle seriously discussed Plato's 'one over many' as Berkeley seriously discussed Locke's material hypothesis. Rival metaphysicians considered that they were contradicting each other and commentators on them have taken the same view. Furthermore, those who have described the ontological hypotheses of metaphysicians, at least of their rivals, as romances, fairy tales or pictures of an enchanted world have thereby absolved them from the charge of meaninglessness in the way that we allow that science fiction, however fantastic and false, gives an understandable picture of a possible world. Moreover each metaphysician claimed of his own views both that they could be and also that they had been proved.

Secondly, the reason why one cannot prove the existence, for example, of Plato's Forms, Leinbiz's Monads or Berkeley's God, is not primarily their unverifiability, but that they are not something which, like a unicorn, could exist, but does not, but that they are, like a cube equal in volume to two other cubes, or like a substance with negative weight, something which does not exist because it could not. A mathematician who asserted that a cube could be equal to two other cubes would be saying something conceptually false, not something nonsensical. No mathematician really believes that Fermat's last theorem, namely that $X^n + Y^n \neq Z^n$ for any $n > 2$, or Wittgenstein's example, namely that 'There are three sevens in the expansion of π', are meaningless because no-one knowns how to verify them, any more than the sceptic who contends that 'I get the same pain you have when I eat unripe gooseberries' is unverifiable believes it is meaningless.

What is wrong with Plato's view that if there are instances of anything, there must be some thing of which these are instances, is not
that it is meaningless, but that it is conceptually false because he has
moved from 'something' to 'some thing' on the mistaken analogy
with the correct view that, for example, if there are copies of anything, then there must be some thing, namely an original, of which
these are copies. Equally when a non-metaphysical philosopher
argues, as has commonly been done, that because a man who
believes, even falsely, must believe something, then there must be
some thing, for example a proposition, which he believes, he is not
saying anything meaningless — though he is saying something
unverifiable by our senses — but something conceptually false on a
false analogy with the correct view that if a man sees something,
there must be some thing which he sees. Again, when a philosopher
argues, as has commonly been done, that because someone who
achieves a result by his action — for example who by shooting
someone kills him — has done two things, he must have committed
two acts, he is not saying anything meaningless — though again it is
something unverifiable by the senses — but something conceptually false on a false analogy with the correct view that a man
who laughs when he shoots has committed two acts. 'There are
propositions in addition to sentences' and 'There are acts of
murder in addition to shootings' say something true in the same
way as 'There is what is exemplified in addition to its exemplifications', but someone who thought, as many have done, that propositions or acts of murder are extra entities, is making the same kind of
mistake, saying something which is conceptually false, as one who
thinks that what is exemplified is an entity extra to its exemplifications. One can sensibly express the point that an Englishman who
says 'It is raining' and a Frenchman who says 'Il pleut' are saying
the same thing, by saying that each is making the same statement or
expressing the same proposition, just as one can sensibly express
the point that two hills have the same outlines and gradients by
saying that both have the same contours. But just as it would be a
mistake to suppose that contours are extra entities observable either
by the senses or by some other means, so it would be a mistake to
suppose that propositions are something observable either by the
senses or by some other means.

None of our examples is saying anything meaningless, and we
have no difficulty in seeing exactly what they are saying. The fact
that we do not, even in principle, know what a proposition or the
extra act of murder would be like, any more than we know what a

Form would be like, is not due to the unverifiability by our senses of any statement about it, but to such a statement's conceptual falsity.

There is in fact a basic similarity between metaphysical arguments and other philosophical arguments which we should naturally expect if, as I contend, both are essentially aimed at the analysis of concepts. There is no more reason to suppose that because the metaphysical conclusion is not verifiable by sense-perception, therefore it is meaningless, than to suppose this about other philosophical conclusions. For example, a typical argument for the conclusion that we never see material objects, such as trees and tables, but only their appearances — what eighteenth-century philosophers called 'ideas' and twentieth-century philosophers 'sense-data' — goes like this. The first premiss is that there admittedly exist both cases where we would ordinarily say we see an object, such as a dagger, and cases where we would ordinarily say we are having the hallucination of seeing a dagger. The second premiss is a philosophical analysis which suggests that common to both cases is something neutral about which type of case it is, namely our having a certain experience which the philosopher analyses as 'seeing what looks like (or the appearance of) a dagger'. From which it is concluded that we cannot know in supposedly seeing a dagger that we have anything else than this common neutral component of seeing the appearance of a dagger. Now the philosopher who accepts the conclusion — and it is accepted by many Logical Positivists even in the form of an existential assertion that what we directly or really see are sense-data — does not contend that it is open to verification or falsification by the senses. There is no experience which would be different if it or its rival were true or false. Nor does the philosopher who rejects it base his rejection on its unverifiability by the senses. He objects that it results from the logical fallacy of supposing that seeing what looks like a chair must be incompatible with seeing a chair, whereas the two are just as compatible as, for example, sitting on the edge of a chair and sitting on a chair. Or that it results from a fallacy of supposing that to have the experience of seeing what looks like or appears to be X is to see an entity called a look or an appearance of X.

Another example of the basic similarity between arguments in metaphysics and arguments in other areas of philosophy, and between the metaphysician's postulation of extra entities and that of other philosophers, is provided by the latter's answer to the question 'What is thinking?' Such an answer sometimes arises in this way. Since we can think without talking, and talk without thinking, and think as we talk, then clearly thinking and talking are different. It is easy then to be influenced by a certain sort of analogy. We can talk without gesturing, and gesture without talking, and gesture as we talk, because gesturing is another action additional to talking which may or may not accompany it. Philosophers have sometimes concluded that similarly thinking is another action additional to talking, which may or may not accompany it. Difficulties in saying exactly what kind of an action it is are brushed aside by calling it a hidden, non-physical, spiritual, mental, etc. action. The form of argument here is analogous to that of one of Plato's arguments for the existence of Forms. Just as a copy can be seen to be imperfect by comparison with its perfect original so, he thought, any judgement that an item in the world is imperfect must be due to comparison of the item with a remembered original, its Form. The philosopher's mistake is also the same as that of the metaphysician. Just as Plato's conclusion can be shown not to follow from his premises by drawing attention to another way in which something can be seen to be imperfect, for example by our ability to think of something better, so the philosopher's postulation of an additional non-physical action of thinking can be shown not to be necessary by drawing attention to another way in which thinking and talking can differ, for example the way in which talking and repeating oneself, standing to attention and obeying an order, playing the piano and practising, differ. Here the second thing we do is not an additional act, but just the first action in particular circumstances.

Metaphysics also shares with some parts of philosophy its use of transcendental arguments, that is, arguments designed to show that all, or even some important part, of an undoubted experience would not be possible unless certain other beliefs were accepted. For example, one of Wittgenstein's central arguments was that our ordinary use of words to talk about our sensations is only possible if we accept that there are public criteria for their applicability. Strawson in somewhat similar vein, perhaps here anticipated by Kant, held that I can sensibly ascribe experiences to myself only if I can also ascribe them to other people.

The conceptual nature of metaphysics helps us to understand the attempts, as old as Aristotle, to characterise metaphysics by at the same time comparing and contrasting it with science. Sometimes it is suggested that it is more general or more systematic than science; yet clearly this is not true in the sense that it is encyclopaedic. Sometimes it is suggested that it tackles problems which science cannot, at least at the time, solve; yet clearly this is not true in the sense that it can be more successful than science on the same problems. It is only true in the sense that the problems of metaphysics are logically different from those of science. They are conceptual, while those of science are empirical, even though the metaphysician's arguments lead him to draw ontological conclusions which make him appear to be a super-scientist offering a rival selection of those things not dreamt of in our everyday philosophy. Thus, Plato considered his Forms as a rival explanation to the water, air, etc. of the Milesians, and the scholastics suggested 'substantial forms' as solutions to the scientists' investigations of the nature of fire, heat, etc. Intertwined in the work of many metaphysicians, such as Plato, Aristotle, Descartes, Berkeley and Leibniz, are scientific and conceptual speculations. Most of the classical metaphysicians would not have drawn a clear line between metaphysics and science, nor accepted that their conclusions or the entities they postulated were generically different from those of the scientists. Wittgenstein, we saw, accused metaphysicians and philosophers generally of supposing that, for example, their belief in sense-data was analogous to the scientists' belief in electrons.[4] 'Thinking is an incorporeal process' is, he said, a typically bad way of distinguishing the concept of *thinking* from that, for example, of *talking*, because it sounds like a scientific remark which a psychologist might make. It is only if metaphysical statements and scientific statements are regarded, as they were both by their exponents and their opponents, as rivals in the same field, namely knowledge of the universe, that the same test of meaningfulness or of knowledge, namely verifiability by the senses, could be appropriate.

Though I have stressed the introduction of extra entities as typical both of the classical metaphysicians and of scientists, it is, of course, true that some metaphysicians, and certainly many non-metaphysical philosophers, as well as most scientists, also advance views which are at variance with those of the ordinary man, not merely or so much in suggesting something more than we dream of, but also in suggesting something different from it. Thus, Copernicus suggested that it is the earth, not the sun, which moves; Columbus showed that the earth is round, not flat; the microscopists convinced us that there is more in a drop of water than meets the eye. Equally, Heraclitus maintained that, contrary to our common belief, everything moves, while Zeno insisted that nothing moves. Some sceptics have argued that material objects do not exist; others that other people do not; others that time is unreal. Just as scientists have suggested that a material object, such as a tree or a table, is empirically a collection of physical atoms, so several metaphysicians have suggested that it is a collection of perceptions (Berkeley) or a collection of non-physical atoms (Leibniz). A metaphysics which suggests that the world is different from what we think, rather than that it contains more than we think, might be called, as it sometimes is, an immanent metaphysics, as contrasted with what I contend is the more common transcendent metaphysics.

In all this it would be easy to show, as is commonly accepted, that though the scientists' conclusions are based on empirical premisses, the philosophical conclusions are deduced from conceptual premisses. For example Zeno's conclusion that nothing moves was based on such arguments as this: one cannot move from A to B since any such move logically implies a prior move from A to half-way to B, which implies a prior move to half-way to half-way to B, *ad infinitum*. One could also show that both the scientist's and the metaphysician's conclusion follows a pattern of one premiss which states what is accepted or given in experience, and one premiss which states either the scientist's empirical law or the metaphysician's conceptual principle. Finally one could subject immanent metaphysics to exactly the same anti-metaphysical accusations of meaningfulness and defend it in exactly the same way as I have both accused and defended transcendent metaphysics.

The failure of any one system of metaphysics to prevail over its rivals and to convince the majority in the way that theories in the individual sciences usually succeed or indisputably fail has given rise to various explanations, especially among present-day philosophers. As early as Kant and as late as the Logical Positivists, it was suggested that the reason is that the metaphysician tries to say something which is at least unknowable and at worst meaningless. Collingwood argued that the reason was that metaphysicians uncover absolute presuppositions which cannot be true or false and, therefore, agreed or disagreed with, but only seen for what they are. Wisdom suggested that their sayings were intended only to be paradoxes and, therefore, not to taken as literally true, while Lazerowitz considered them only as rationalisations of psycho-analytic malaises. I have argued, on the other hand, that the assertions of metaphysicians can be as true or false, and for the same reasons, as those of other philosophers. Their failures are due, I have contended, to various different specific logical fallacies peculiar to each metaphysician, and not to any general misconception other than a confusion of the empirical with the conceptual. It may be that the total failure of any metaphysician to offer any principles from which there follows the need to postulate the existence of any entities additional to, or any features different from, those which we either encounter in the world, or are introduced to by scientists, suggests that any such implication is impossible. But though I think that a belief in Forms, Monads, the Absolute, an Infinite Spirit or an Unmoved Mover is a conceptual mistake for the same kinds of reasons that a belief in propositions, sense-data, thinking as an inner process or murder as an act additional to the act by which we murder is a mistake, and that a belief that nothing moves, or that everything moves, is mistaken for reasons analogous to the mistaken belief that everything one does is selfish, or that no-one can know what another thinks, I cannot see that a metaphysician's or a philosopher's belief in extra entities or in different features must necessarily be mistaken.

But as Kant contrasted a genuine metaphysics, which examines the *a priori* constituents of experience, with a pseudo-metaphysics, which claims possible knowledge of things beyond experience, so we can contrast a metaphysics, on which I have suggested all metaphysics is and historically has been based, which examines our most general concepts, such as existence, substance, identity, causality, etc. and a metaphysics which, on the basis of this examination, postulates the existence of entities undreamt of by our ordinary thinking. The former is conceptual, the latter ontological. The former is as legitimate as any part of philosophy, the latter, whether legitimate or not, has not yet proved itself.

In answer to Hume's famous rhetorical questions, metaphysics would claim, and I have tried to show could properly claim, to contain both some 'abstract reasoning', namely in such conceptual premises as the 'one over many', the 'many towards one', '*esse est percipi*', 'the future in the present', 'the unreality of the self-contradictory', etc., and also some 'reasoning of matters of fact and existence', namely in the postulation of such entities as Forms, Monads, an infinite Spirit and an Unmoved Mover, or of such different features as total motion or total rest. This is not to say that either these pieces of abstract reasoning or these pieces of reasoning of matters of fact are valid, but only that they are genuine.

Notes

1. L. Wittgenstein (1958), *Blue and Brown Books*, Basil Blackwell, Oxford, p. 182.

2. L. Wittgenstein (1974), *Philosophical Grammar*, Basil Blackwell, Oxford, sect. 10; *Blue and Brown Books*, pp. 130, 143.

3. *Blue and Brown Books*, p. 55.

4. *Blue and Brown Books*, p. 70.

Index